Natural Stone
A Guide to Selection

Natural Stone
A Guide to Selection

Studio Marmo

Text by Frederick Bradley

W. W. Norton & Company
New York • London

First American edition published by W. W. Norton & Company, Inc. 1998

First published in Italy by Studio Marmo 1997 under the title LA SCELTA DELLE ROCCE ORNAMENTALI IN ARCHITETTURA: Caratteristiche Estetiche, Tecniche e Commerciali dei Materiali Lapidei / THE CHOICE OF DIMENSION STONE IN ARCHITECTURE: Aestetic, Technical and Commercial Characteristics of Natural Stone

For information about permission to reproduce selections from this book, write to Permissions, W. W. Norton & Company, 500 Fifth Avenue, New York, NY 10110.

The text of this book is composed in Helvetica
with the display set in Futura

Natural Stone: A Guide to Selection was conceived and produced by Francesco Bellandi, Simone Bellandi, and Francesca Lofaro, Studio Marmo.

Material from ASTM C 119 is reprinted with permission from the Annual Book of ASTM Standards, copyright American Society for Testing and Materials, 100 Barr Harbor Drive, West Conshohocken, PA 19428, e-mail: service@astm.org

Library of Congress Cataloging-in-Publication Data

Scelta delle rocce ornamentali in architettura. English.
　　　Natural stone : a guide to selection / Studio Marmo ; text by Frederick Bradley.
　　　　　p.　cm.
　　　An edited version of the English text published in La scelta delle rocce ornamentali in architettura. Italy : Studio Marmo. 1997.
　　　Includes bibliographical references and index.
　　　ISBN 0-393-73028-X
　　　1. Building stones. I. Bradley, Frederick. II. Studio Marmo (Florence, Italy) III. Title
TA426.S354　1998　　　　　　　　　　　　　　　　　　98-7480
691'.2—dc21　　　　　　　　　　　　　　　　　　　　　CIP

W. W. Norton & Company, Inc., 500 Fifth Avenue, New York, NY 10110
http://www.wwnorton.com

W. W. Norton & Company Ltd., 10 Coptic Street, London WC1A 1PU

0 9 8 7 6 5 4 3 2

Contents

Foreword

When Pope Leo X commissioned Michelangelo Buonarroti to make the facade of San Lorenzo Basilica in Florence, Michelangelo left his workshop and hastily ventured off to the steep slopes of the Apuan Alps to find the best marble befitting the work at hand. The great master was well aware of the fact that using stone was no easy task and so, to avoid any unpleasant surprises, he preferred to choose the marble himself, even before it was taken from the quarry.

Hence, the choice of dimension stone for architectural purposes is an age-old problem. It is true that an artist must know the characteristics of the material he/she is using, yet since Renaissance times the choice of dimension stone has become more difficult, and even Buonarroti would probably have had problems today.

There is currently a vast range of stone varieties on the market and new varieties continue to appear with new colors and patterns to stimulate the taste of architects and designers. A stone's aesthetic characteristics alone are not enough, though, to determine their choice. In addition, it is necessary to have information as to the quality constancy, quantities available, block sizes and a series of other parameters which are often ignored until a problem arises and the selected material is seen to be unsuitable for its use.

Thus, the problem resides above all in the lack of information as regards the possible uses of the dimension stone varieties available on the market.

The purpose of this guide is to provide information in this respect, although obviously without the presumption of totally overcoming the problem. The author aims to provide a useful tool for architects and designers, whether they are already acquainted with stone materials and require extra information or they are newcomers to the world of stone and wish to have the basic information necessary prior to using stone materials.

The layout of the guide and the language used have the specific purpose of making communication easier between architects and designers on one hand and stone suppliers and operators on the other. The commercial varieties in the second part of the guide have been chosen from the most important ones available on the international market.

I should first like to thank Arch. Maria Rosa Lanzi for her advice and information when this guide was still merely an idea. I thank Paola Blasi, Silvano Galletti, Marco Galletti, Giovanni Borraccini and Marco Lombardi for the assistance provided. My sincere thanks also go to Francesco Ceccarelli, Adriano Moriconi and Marco Garancini for their revision of the chapter on granite and Giovanni Vianello for the information he provided on marble. I am grateful to Moreno Pastine for his critical review of the guide and his conviction that it will achieve its goals. Finally, my thanks to Pennie Sabel and the Marble Institute of America for their help in preparing the English-language edition.

Frederick Bradley

Part One

Introduction
to the Selection
of Natural Stone

1. Terminology and Classification

O ne of the main problems facing designers who decide to use dimension stone is what to call a certain commercial variety so that people will know exactly to what material they are referring.

This may seem obvious, yet there is a great deal of confusion in the stone industry, which often leads to incomprehension. This is not only between the designer and the supplier, but also between the latter and the producer, for example, that is, among those who actually work in the industry too.

There are basically four reasons for this chaos as regards stone terminology:

a) The need to offer a stone product with an attractive name which is supposed to strike the imagination rather than give information about the material.
Only too often is the same material sold by various companies offered on the market under totally different names and, for obvious reasons, the companies do not know (or do not want to know!) the name created by their competitors.

b) The lack of "D.O.C" names for dimension stone varieties.
Since people are free to allocate names to stone varieties as they wish, it is possible to exploit the commercial names (and thus the image) of well-known materials to place other materials on the market which do not necessarily have the same quality characteristics. This is unfair competition, which may lead to problems as regards the image and reliability of materials which have a consolidated position on the market.

c) The lack of world-recognized standard terms.
The stone industry has always been undermined by the lack of objective standards to govern production. As far as the materials are concerned, despite the current efforts to find a solution to the problem, standards are still lacking. In fact, people continue to use the terms they like best.

d) The relative lack of workers' knowledge as regards the scientific nature of stone varieties.
This is yet another problem typical of the industry since dimension stone has always been classed a poor mineral and therefore of little interest for applied geology. Consequently, raw natural stone has always been considered according to its commercial value, and its peculiar petrographic and mineral properties are practically never taken into consideration.

Thus, designers often have a difficult job on their hands to cope with the numerous names given to a stone variety, without fully understanding what type of material it is and hence without knowing its real potential uses.
What is basically required, therefore, is clarity to provide designers with guarantees as to their choice of materials.

The purpose of this guide is certainly not to clear up the problem regarding dimension stone terminology, although the author does intend to provide some basic information to guide designers in their choice of materials.

There are two types of terms: *commercial terms,* i.e., those recognized on the market and thus those generally used at work, and *scientific terms,* which are used when technical/scientific detail is required (for example, when problems arise due to an improper use of a stone material).
Despite the fact that the commercial terms do not often correspond to the scientific terms, it will be observed how groups of rocks of the same origin usually have very similar aesthetic and commerical characteristics. Again this stresses how important it is to know the origin of rocks and therefore their lithologic, petrographic and mineral properties, or rather to have a scientific understanding of rocks.

In actual fact, all designers who regularly use dimension stone should have some insight, albeit general, as to the origins and "scientific" properties of rocks. Some may not agree with this, but using dimension stone without understanding it is rather like cooking without knowing the ingredients.
It is certainly not worth giving a detailed scientific classification of rocks in this guide. A summary of the scientific groups and their general characteristics which influence the identification of the corresponding commercial groups is sufficient for our purposes.
From a scientific viewpoint, all rocks are divided into three main groups according to their origins.

Magmatic rocks. These are rocks formed by the cooling of existing magma.
The rocks belonging to this group vary significantly in pattern and color, according to the genetic characteristics and the chemical composition of the original magma.
Magmatic rocks may be defined as:
- *intrusive* when the magma has cooled deep down inside the earth's crust;
- *subvolcanic* when the magma has cooled near the earth's surface;
- *effusive* or *volcanic* when the magma which has poured out of the earth's crust has cooled in a subaerial or subaqueous environment (including all lavas).
For the purpose of this guide it is important to mention that rocks formed due to the accumulation of debris of volcanic origin belong to this group and are called *piroclastic* rocks.

Chemically, a magma may have an *acid, intermediate* or *basic* composition, but since magmatic rocks are mostly composed of minerals which contain silicon, they are also defined as silicatic.

Sedimentary rocks. These are rocks formed either due to the accumulation of preexisting debris and the consolidation thereof following a phenomenon called diagenesis (*clastic* origin) or through direct chemical precipitation of the minerals of which they are composed (*chemical* origin).

The former can be divided into groups based on their mineralogical composition, which varies according to the minerals or materials which have generated them. The composition may vary, although most sedimentary rocks of clastic origin are either:
- *carbonatic* when they are formed predominantly of minerals and/or carbonatic lithoid elements (calcite, dolomite, magnesite, etc.)
or:
- *silicatic* when they are formed of minerals and/or silicatic lithoid elements (feldspars, micas, clayey minerals, etc.)

Sedimentary rocks of chemical origin may derive either from precipitation from saturated liquids of varying chemism or from precipitation caused by living organisms (for example the madreporic formations of the coral reefs). In both cases, the mineralogical composition of the rocks used for ornamental purposes is practically always *carbonatic* (rocks derived from a similar chemical process but of a siliceous composition are, however, widely used as jewels, for example, agate).

Metamorphic rocks. These are rocks formed from variations in the texture and mineralogical composition of preexisting magmatic or sedimentary rocks in response to different pressure and temperature conditions from the original formational environment. Scientifically, these rocks are divided according to the degree and type of metamorphism which has generated them and according to their chemical-mineralogical composition. For the purpose of this guide, it is sufficient to make a division on the basis of the varying mineralogical composition of the lithotypes most frequently used for dimension purposes.

MARBLE	- Marble in the strict commercial sense (hereafter called Marble s.s.) - Limestone - Travertine - Onyx
GRANITE	- homogeneous - oriented - veined
QUARTZITE	
STONE	- Sandstone - Schist and Slate - Gneiss - Porphyry - Basalt, Trachyte, etc. (Lava Rocks) - Peperino and Tuff (Piroclastic Rocks) - Limestone and Tuff limestone - Conglomerates

Fig. 1 - Table summarizing the commercial groups of dimension stone

These may be:
- *carbonatic* when they are formed predominantly of carbonatic minerals (calcite, dolomite, magnesite, etc.);
- *silicatic* when they are formed of silicatic minerals (feldspars, micas, clayey minerals, etc.);
- *siliceous* when they contain a very high percentage of quartz crystals (SiO_2).

Commercially speaking, dimension stone can be divided into two categories (Fig. 1).

Marble. The term "marble" is quite a loose term and includes lithotypes which are different in composition and origin and have different commercial characteristics too. According to standard ASTM C119 the Marble Group includes stone which ". . . comprises a variety of compositional and texture types, ranging from pure carbonate to rocks containing very little carbonate that are classed commercially as marble (for example, serpentine marble). Most marbles possess an interlocking texture and a range of grain size from cryptocrystalline to 5mm. All marble as here defined must be capable of taking a polish."

In practice, from the commercial point of view, the term Marble includes no less than four groups of materials, in particular:

- *Marble in the strict sense of the word* (Marble s.s). This includes all carbonatic rocks of metamorphic origin and some ophiolitic rocks (serpentinites and ophicalcites). The abovementioned ASTM standard defines these materials as serpentine marble:

- *Limestone.* This includes all carbonatic rocks of sedimentary origin which take polish, except onyx and travertine (*).

- *Travertine.* This includes carbonatic rocks of sedimentary origin formed by chemical precipitation in a subaerial environment. They are highly porous (**).

- *Onyx.* This includes carbonatic rocks of sedimentary origin formed by chemical precipitation in underground cavities. They have characteristic concentric bands.

(*) Standard ASTMC 119 defines several varieties of limestone according to the mineral composition or texture.

(**) UNI Stone Products Standard 8458 treats travertines as a separate group and defines them as "chemically deposited limestone rocks with spongework; some varieties can be polished."

Granite. Standard ASTM C119 defines granite as "the visibly granular, igneous rock generally ranging in color from pink to light or dark grey and consisting mostly of quartz and feldspar . . . accompanied by one or more dark minerals. The texture is typically homogeneous but may be gneissic or porphyritic. . . . Some dark granular igneous rock, though not properly granite, are included in the definition. . . ."

From a more commercial viewpoint, there is currently no precise classification of granite. Identification is based on the prominent aesthetic characteristics which, according to the material in question, may be the color, pattern or grain. Following an initial classification usually based on color, all granite varieties on the market can be divided into smaller groups according to patterns which normally correspond to commercial differences too. The three principal groups are:

- *Homogeneous granite* or granite with a homogeneous pattern, where the minerals are evenly distributed to form a visibly isotropic crystalline groundmass.

- *Oriented granite* or granite with an oriented pattern, where the minerals are distributed according to a certain orientation which can be seen on a tile sample.

- *Veined granite* or granite with a veined pattern, where the minerals form veins of a different color to the groundmass and varying orientation, creating a flexuous movement in the rock.

(*) Some authors believe that Quarzites should be included in the Stone group. These materials, however, have physical-mechanical properties and therefore can be used in the same way as many varieties of commercial granite. In fact, Quartzite varieties have their own peculiar characteristics and hence are considered a separate group on the market.

Quartzite. There are relatively few quartzite varieties among commercial stone varieties, which is why they are still not considered as a separate group by many experts (*). These rocks have actually acquired their own commercial identity though and this, together with the fact that they also have their own technical and commercial characteristics, allows for their classification as a separate group. Commercially speaking, this group includes metamorphic rocks derived from quartz sandstone which are composed almost entirely of quartz and are hard, tough and can be polished. Quartzite varieties which are not very hard and tend to crumble cannot be polished and so are included in the Stone group.

Stone. This is the most heterogeneous commercial group of dimension stone materials. It includes numerous lithotypes which differ a great deal as far as their composition and nature are concerned and often have no scientific connections.
ASTM standards do not consider Stone as a single group of materials, and the majority of the materials that are usually called "stone" in the commercial sense are included in the Sandstone group and Slate group (ASTM C119).

It is probably because of the vast number of commercial characteristics of the lithotypes that the Stone category is not divided into well-defined commercial groups, and often scientific terms are used. The only characteristic common to all materials which can be defined as Stone is the fact that they cannot be polished, although again there are important exceptions, especially among the harder materials (porphyry, some gneiss varieties, etc.). Here below is a classification of stone, using scientific terms in most cases which, contrary to the rule, are used in commercial practice too.

- *Sandstone* - including sedimentary and metamorphic rocks which are generally silicatic with medium to coarse grains and are often easily split into even-surfaced slabs. Some varieties can be polished.

- *Schist and sandstone* - including metamorphic rocks which are generally silicatic with fine grains and can be split into even- or uneven-surfaced slabs. Some varieties can be polished.

- *Gneiss* - including metamorphic rocks which are silicatic with medium to coarse grains, generally compact and easy to split into even-surfaced slabs. Some varieties can be polished.

- *Basalt, Trachyte* (Lava Rocks) - including magmatic rocks with fine grains which are generally not very compact due to the presence of small cavities in the rocky mass. These materials cannot usually be polished.

- *Porphyry* - including magmatic rocks which are compact, hard, tough and easily cut into even-surfaced slabs. These materials can normally be polished.

- *Peperino, Tuff* (Piroclastic Rocks) - including sedimentary rocks which are predominantly silicatic, soft, not very compact and often have a granular structure.

- *Limestone and limestone tuff* - including soft sedimentary rocks which are mainly carbonatic, generally not very compact and rather crumbly.

- *Conglomerates* - including sedimentary rocks with a heterogeneous composition which are generally not very compact but are fairly hard.

This classification certainly should not be considered official, yet it corresponds to the classification generally used.

Fig. 2 gives the scientific terms corresponding to the main commercial types of natural stone used.

		Type Origin Composition	MAGMATIC ROCKS			SEDIMENTARY ROCKS			METAMORPHIC ROCKS	
			Intrusive	Sub-volcanic	Effusive	Clastic Carbonatic	Silicatic	Chemical	Carbonatic	Silicatic
	Marble					Limestone		Travertine Onyx	Marble s.s.	Marble s.s.
	Granite		Homogeneous Oriented	Homogeneous absolute black						Veined Oriented
	Quartzite									Quartzite
	Stone				Porphyry Basalt Tuff Peperino Trachyte	Limestone	Sandstone Conglom.			Slate Schist Gneiss

COMMERCIAL GROUP

Fig. 2 - Correspondence between commercial and scientific terminology used to describe dimension stone. (The scientific groups are actually much more complex; those shown in the table refer to natural stone used for ornamental purposes.)

Natural Stone in Architecture

1, **2** - BAHA'I WORLD CENTRE,
Israel
- Project: Arch. Sahba
- Supplier: Henraux S.p.A.
  Lucca (Italy)
- Materials: Bianco Piastrone

1

2

3

4

19

5 - KIARONG MOSQUE, Brunei
  - Project: Arch. Zaini
  - Supplier: Cia.Mar. s.r.l.,
    Carrara (Italy)
  - Materials: Bianco
    Acquabianca, Blue Pearl

6 - WORLD TRADE CENTRE,
    Wasta Terminal, Stockholm
    (Sweden)
  - Project: Arken, Erskine &
    Tengbom
  - Supplier: International
    Italmarmi s.r.l., Massa, Italy
  - Materials: Verde Alpi, Bianco
    Carrara, Bardiglio, Breccia
    Oniciata, Rosso Asiago,
    Botticino Classico

7

7, **8** - TRUMP TOWER,
New York (USA)
- Project: Swanke Hayden
Connell Architects
- Materials: Breccia Pernice
- (Photo Arch. Alberto Ricci
Archives)

8

21

9 - 851
- Project: Arch. Mario Bellini
- Execution: UP & UP s.r.l.
  Massa (Italy)
- Materials: Bianco
  Pennsylvania

9

10

10 - BELLINI 1
- Project: Arch. Mario Bellini
- Execution: UP & UP s.r.l.
  Massa (Italy)
- Materials: Bardiglio Fumo di
  Londra, Bardiglio, Bianco
  Pennsylvania

11

12

11, **12** - Y. S. CLUB, Taipei (Taiwan)
- Project: George C.T. Woo and Partners
- Materials: Bianco Statuario, Verde Patrizia
- (Photo courtesy of T.S.S. Europe s.r.l).

13 - GRACECHURCH, City Office, London (UK)
- Project: Sheppard Robson
- Supplier: International Italmarmi s.r.l., Massa (Italy)
- Materials: Bianco Statuario, Bianco P, Rojo Alicante, Negro Marquiña

13

15

14 - I GIGLI Commercial
Center, Florence (Italy)
- Project: Arch. Adolfo
Natalini
- Supplier: UP & UP s.r.l.
Massa (Italy)
- Materials: Rosso Carpazi,
Bardiglio Fumo di Londra,
Bianco Lago

15 - Throne room floor
- Supplier: Elle Marmi s.r.l.,
Carrara (Italy)
- Materials: Portoro, White
Thassos, Rosso Verona

16 - V.I.P. CLUB, Singapore
- Project: Steven J. Leach
- Supplier: Elle Marmi s.r.l.,
Carrara (Italy)
- Materials: Giallo Siena,
Afyon, Rouge Griotte
(Rouge du Roi), Malakite

16

18

17, 18 - SAN PANCRAZIO
CHURCH, Turin (Italy)
- Supplier for restoration:
Elle Marmi s.r.l. Carrara
(Italy)
- Materials: Travertino
Romano

17

19 - CROCKER CENTER,
     Los Angeles (USA)
   - Project: S.O.M. Architects
   - Materials: Balmoral Red
   - (Photo courtesy of T.S.S.
     Europe s.r.l)

20

20 - MORGAN STANLEY
     BUILDING, Canary Wharf,
     London (UK)
   - Project: S.O.M. Architects
   - Supplier: Henraux S.p.A.
     Lucca (Italy)

21 - U.O.B. , Singapore
   - Project: K.T.A. Architects
   - Materials: White Pearl
   - (Photo courtesy of T.S.S.
     Europe s.r.l)

21

27

22 - TRIGON CENTER, Berlin
(Germany)
- Supplier: Henraux S.p.A.
Lucca (Italy)
- Materials: Blanco Galicia

23 - KREDIET BANK, Brussels
(Belgium)
- Project: Arch. Jasper
- Supplier: Henraux S.p.A.
Lucca (Italy)
- Materials: Funil

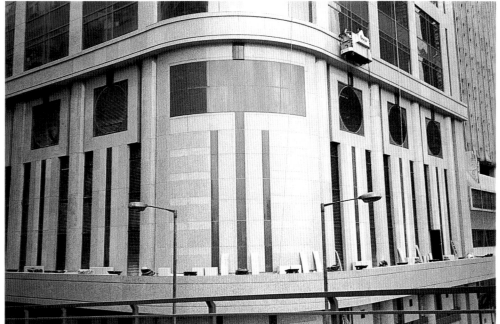

24 - PEARL ORIENTAL CENTRE,
Hong Kong
- Supplier: International
Italmarmi s.r.l., Massa (Italy)
- Materials: Rosa Ghiandone

25 - CEROIL HOTEL, Bejing
(China)
- Supplier: International
Italmarmi s.r.l., Massa (Italy)
- Materials: Giallo Veneziano

25

26, 27 - FATBUREN, Stockholm
        (Sweden)
       - Project: Bo K. Jessel
       - Supplier: International
         Italmarmi s.r.l., Massa
         (Italy)
       - Materials: Multicolor
         (flamed)

28 - ALLIED BANK PLAZA,
     Houston (USA)
   - Project: S.O.M. Architects
   - Supplier: Henraux S.p.A.
     Lucca (Italy)
   - Materials: Balmoral Red,
     Emerald Pearl
   - (Photo courtesy of T.S.S.
     Europe s.r.l.).

27

28

29 - HILTON PALACE,
  Beersheba (Israel)
  - Supplier: Henraux S.p.A.
  Lucca (Italy)
  - Materials: New Red, Rosa
  Porriño

30 - EMBANKMENT PLACE,
  London (UK)
  - Project: Terry Ferrel
  Partnership
  - Supplier: Henraux S.p.A.
  Lucca (Italy)
  - Stone Consultant: Ing.
  Sergio Sacchelli
  - Materials: Grigio Sardo,
  Aveiro

30

31

31, **32** - 885 Third Avenue, New York (USA)
- Project: Philip Johnson-Burgee
- Materials: Napoleon Red
- (Photo Arch. Alberto Ricci Archives)

32

2. Finished Products

2.1 GENERAL DETAILS

Over recent years, there has been a significant improvement in production technology which now assures performance and accuracy levels which were unthinkable in the past. Thanks above all to this progress, dimension stone now has many uses both in architecture and in the building industry in general.

Dimension stone is predominantly used for facings and floorings, that is, 60% of world production. It is also used, although to a lesser extent, for funerary art (15%) and special work (10%).

In addition to the more traditional consolidated uses, there is an increasing demand for products which are particularly versatile, both aesthetically and technically.

This wide range of uses corresponds to an equally wide range of products.

Although this guide does not intend to deal with stone processing in detail, a brief outline of the main products and possible surface treatments is provided. The description of the individual groups of natural stone in the second part of the guide will make references to this information.

2.2 TYPES OF PRODUCTS

Dimension stone materials are available on the market in five main product groups according to their most common uses.

Modular elements
These are mass-produced elements normally used for floorings and facings. They include:

Modular tiles of standard sizes and thicknesses produced away from the installation site; the four main sizes available are: 15 x 30 cm and 30 x 30 cm, from 0.7 to 1 cm thick (depending on the material), 30 x 60 cm and 60 x 60 cm from 1 to 1.5 cm thick. These elements are generally ready to be installed.

Strips produced from slab cut-offs in sizes and shapes established by the designer according to their specific use. Their thickness varies according to the type of stone material and the size of the strips but it is generally between 1.5 and 2 cm for floors and 1.5 and 3 cm for facings.

Cut sheets

Products are made according to cut sheets when they are to be used for floorings and facings with special designs, including pieces of different shapes, sizes and surface treatments. Each piece is numbered and located according to the drawings. If the design is particularly complicated, it is worthwhile carrying out a mock installation in the workshop to check the quality of the work before it is finally installed.

Panels on supports

These are decorative panels used as features in floorings and facings. They are produced by applying decorative designs onto average-quality stone panels which serve as supports. The designs are usually small and fairly complicated. When they are installed, the supports can be left or removed; in the latter case, the pieces are assembled and stuck together along their edges (*preassembled products*). The high degree of accuracy achieved using this technique would not be possible using other traditional techniques.

Lightweight laminated panels

The manufacturing process for these products, also known as *thin marble elements,* is similar to the above-mentioned process for panels on supports. The main difference is that lightweight materials are used for the supports (honeycombed aluminum, fiberglass, etc.). The final products are therefore extremely light (between 15 and 25 kg/sq.m) and are ideal wherever weight is a limiting factor in the choice of material.

Solid stone pieces

These are cubes or parallelepipeds of various sizes more than 3 cm thick. They are generally used for outside paving and kerbs (see glossary).

As far as funerary art is concerned, the products generally used are *modular strips* and *solid stone pieces*, whereas in the case of special works, the products depend on the designer's specific requirements and cannot be categorized.

2.3. SURFACE TREATMENTS

Whatever the stone product may be, when it is installed it always has one face which can be seen. This reveals the aesthetic characteristics of the stone which thereby performs its ornamental function.

The aesthetic perception of a given material is not to be considered in absolute terms, though, since it can be significantly influenced by the type of surface treatment on the finished product. Moreover, in addition to altering the main aesthetic characteristics (color, pattern), the different surface treatments alter the physical-mechanical properties of the material too and hence its performance.

Thus, surface treatments may be applied not only to enhance the material's aesthetic characteristics, but also its functional characteristics according to the designer's requirements. The various treatments commonly used to finish the surface of natural stone are the following.

Polishing

Polishing creates a reflecting surface using abrasives and then polishing substances (oxalic acid, lead monoxide, etc.). This is the typical finish given to dimension stone whenever possible. However, many commercial types (belonging to the Stone group in particular) have mechanical and mineralogical characteristics which make polishing either impossible or only possible to a certain degree, with unacceptable aesthetic results. Polishing gives a material brightness and a mirror-like effect, intensifies the colors and enhances the pattern. In terms of mechanics, it reduces the porosity of the material, thereby increasing its resistance to humidity and chemical agents. On the other hand, in view of the fact that the surface becomes totally smooth, it tends to be slippery, especially when wet.

Honing

Honing is achieved by abrasion too, but creates a smooth although not reflecting surface and varies according to the type of abrasive used. This finish can be performed on all types of materials and maintains the material's natural aesthetic characteristics more than any other treatment, even though it makes the color shades slightly opaque.

Impact treatment

This alters the surface of the rock by means of mechanical or manual percussion using different tools. The resulting surface finishes are named after the various tools used (bush-hammering, chiselling, dolly pointing, etc.). These treatments greatly alter the aesthetic perception of the stone, by subduing the colors and reducing the effect of the pattern and grain; yet they also make it possible to achieve interesting light contrasts and chiaroscuro effects. From a functional viewpoint, the rough surface obtained creates an anti-slip surface even when wet, although it is also easily soiled. Impact treatment can also reduce the mechanical resistance of the finished product, especially if it is performed deep into the material, and consequently allows pollution to penetrate the rock.

Flaming

Flaming consists of passing a nozzle emitting a high-temperature, high-speed flame over the surface to be treated. The surface thus becomes rugged and irregular but with no sharp edges. Aesthetically speaking, flaming generally reduces the intensity of colors, i.e., they are toned down (although in some cases the color is significantly changed), and the perception of vein patterns. This treatment may reduce the mechanical resistance of the finished product since the surface of the material is removed. It is particularly suitable for polymineral rocks composed of minerals with varying degrees of dilatability and fusion, which are the majority of commercial varieties belonging to the Granite group.

Sandblasting

Sandblasting consists of passing a high-pressure jet of siliceous sand, carborundum or steel shot over the surface to be treated which thereby undergoes light, even abrasion. The result is an evenly rough but not rugged surface with lighter colors than those of the untreated material and a subtler pattern than the original one. In view of the rough surface created, albeit only slightly rough, a sandblasted surface is anti-slip and easily soiled.

Fig. 3 - Surface treatments
(Pietra di Matraia):
a - Polished
b - Honed
c - Scored
d - Chiselled
e - Bush-hammered
f - Dolly-pointed
g - Pointed
h - Sandblasted

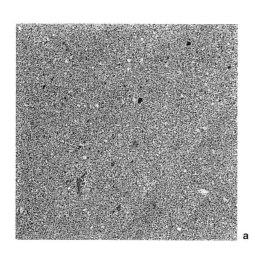
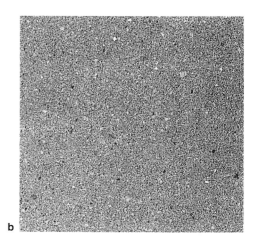
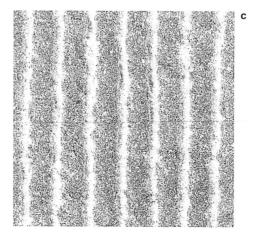
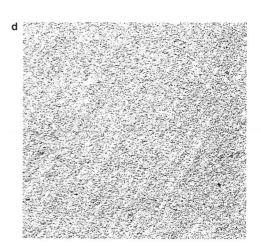

Natural splitting

This is usually performed on materials which can be readily separated along well-defined parallel planes (*parting*). Such materials generally belong to the Stone group. Splitting is carried out by percussion along the lines of potential discontinuity (normally corresponding to the bedding plane), and the irregularity of the surface varies according to the material.

Filling

Filling consists of plugging any small holes on the surface of the material. This is performed to improve the aesthetic characteristics of the finished product by eliminating the physical discontinuities and, above all, to improve some of its functional characteristics (cleaning, maintenance, etc.). The filler is generally the same color as the dominant color of the surface, although transparent resins can also be used. The latter give a certain feeling of depth in larger cavities.

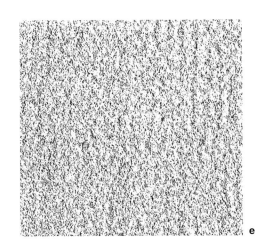 e

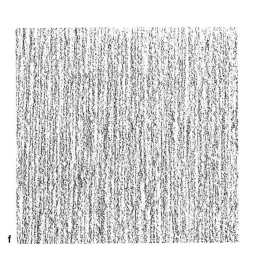 f

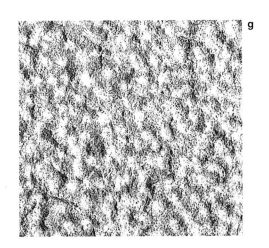 g

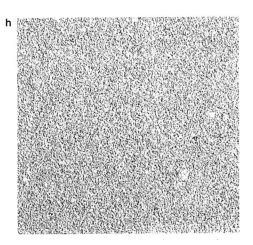 h

Plastic net to reinforce the slab

Reinforcement

The purpose of this treatment is to increase the mechanical resistance of materials with cracks or potential lines of discontinuity. It consists of applying to the back of slabs resin which is the same color as the material to completely fill the cracks. In order to reinforce the slab still further, a plastic net is normally fixed to the slab over the resin.

3. Commercial Characteristics

T he commercial value of a dimension stone material depends on a series of factors which contribute to varying degrees to its potential uses (Fig. 4).

In brief, these are:

a) *Aesthetic characteristics*

b) *Technical properties*

c) *Availability*

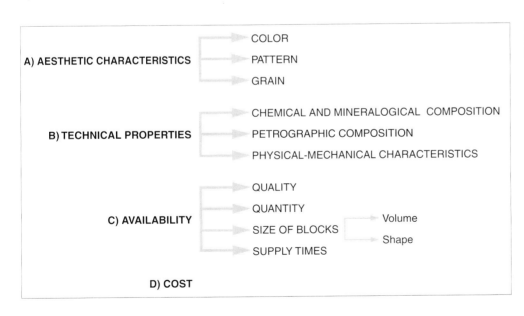

Fig. 4 - Factors determining the possible uses of a rock for ornamental purposes

3.1 AESTHETIC CHARACTERISTICS

Even though in a few cases stone is used more for its structural characteristics, it usually requires good aesthetic characteristics if it is to be used on a large scale. In actual fact, the stone industry relies on the aesthetic value of materials to the extent that it is very much dependent on man's changing tastes and fashions.

Given its essentially ornamental function, stone must meet the aesthetic requirements of designers in their capacity as end users and specifiers of aesthetic solutions to customers.

The aesthetic value of a dimension rock depends on three basic elements: *color*, *pattern* and *grain*.

COLOR   The *color* of a material is usually by far the most important element and often determines its commercial potential without taking into account other aesthetic parameters. Analysis of the international markets shows how the market characteristics of natural stone differ mainly on the basis of color. Marble and granite varieties, which together represent 90% of the international market, can be divided into three commercial groups with three different color categories.

The first group includes common materials which are available and required in large quantities. The price of these materials is relatively low, yet their market is fairly constant.

The second group includes materials of a higher commercial value than the first group. These are traditional materials which are easy to apply and mostly used for quality furnishings. The demand is often lower than the supply and the cost is fairly high.

The third and final group includes materials of a high commercial value, as in the case of the above materials. The market, though, for these materials is variable and is subject to marked ups and downs which sometimes take place in a relatively short time. The materials are not easy to use because of their colors, and they are more subject to changing tastes than the other groups. Their prices are usually high.

For each group, Fig. 5 shows the colors of the different types of materials based on the international market in 1995-1996. The information in the table may vary over

Fig. 5 - Main dimension stone materials classed according to market characteristics

MARKET	MARBLE	HOMOGENEOUS GRANITE	ORIENTED GRANITE	VEINED GRANITE	QUARTZITE	COLOR CATEGORIES
High-quality, medium/high-cost materials characterized by colors which are easy to use; often supply does not satisfy demand; availability is generally constant	White, Pink, Black, Red, Green	Red, Black, White, Brown, Blue	Red, Pink, Green, Yellow	Red, Pink		*Classic*
High-quality, medium/high-cost materials with limited uses compared to the classics; demand may vary considerably; in many cases availability is not constant	Violet, Yellow, Brown	Green, Yellow, Sky blue	Brown	Green, Violet, Yellow	Sky blue, Pink, Green	*Special*
Average-quality, relatively low-cost materials; availability is generally very good and fairly constant	Beige, Grey	Pink, Grey	Grey			*Common*

time according to changing tastes and the availaility of the various materials. Furthermore, the colors may vary from marble to granite varieties.

The commercial varieties currently available on the market cover the entire color range and one material may provide a number of color combinations.

An understanding of the reasons why a rock is a certain color is essential in order to understand and prevent any problems related to the color characteristics of the commercial varieties which may arise at the supply stage or even when the material has been installed. The reasons are many and diverse and often the overall color of one commercial variety derives from a series of colors which may have very different origins.

In practically all rocks, red is caused by a high concentration of microscopic crystals of hematite (Fe_2O) which is a very common ferrous oxide in nature. In low concentrations, it gives the rock a pink color.

Black granite varieties take their color from the large quantity of mafic minerals from basic chemism (pyroxenes), the natural color of which is dark.
In Marble s.s. varieties, black originates from bituminous substances derived from a reductive process dependent on the organic material in the original sedimentation environment. The grey color of marble varieties is due to the presence of microscopic crystals of pyrite (FeS), a ferrous sulfide which also derives from chemical transformations without oxygen. White Marble varieties do not have accessory components or traces which hide the light color of the calcite and/or dolomite crystals (the minerals which make up the highest percentage of these rocks). The same applies to white granites, which are white mainly because of the originally white crystals of the feldspars and plagioclases. These, however, do not usually account for more than 40% of the entire crystalline mass.

In all rocks, the color yellow derives from limonite (Fe_2HO_3). This is a ferrous hydroxide which can give a brown color in high concentrations.

The origins of the color green can be very diverse. In Marble s.s. varieties it is often caused by minerals from the chlorite group or other minerals such as serpentine. In granite, it is often due to the presence of amphiboles (eg. actinolite) or epidote (pistacite), although it may be caused by iron compounds inside the originally white minerals (feldspars).

The color blue also has various origins. In quartzites it is caused by a silicate (dumortierite), while in granite varieties it may derive from sodalite, which is blue, or the presence of rutile (TiO_2) inside the quartz crystals. In marble varieties the blue color may be due to the presence of kyanite crystals, although it is more often due to an optical effect caused by the light when it crosses the crystalline structure of the rock's minerals.

In granite varieties, the blue color is often due to the presence of labradorite, a plagioclase which changes color according to the angle of incidence of the light.

Among the less frequent colors, violet is generally caused by manganese oxides, while brown may derive from high concentrations of ferrous hydroxides.

Although color is an intrinsic property of each individual rock, in many cases it is possible to alter the color according to the cutting direction of the slabs. This is possible when the color or the colored elements are not evenly distributed inside the rock, i.e., when they follow what is generally the pattern of the rock itself.

PATTERN

The *pattern* of a rock is formed by the texture, i.e., the spatial orientation of the individual components in the rocky mass, be they minerals (as in the case of magmatic rocks and almost all metamorphic rocks) or lithic elements (as in many sedimentary rocks).

From a commercial viewpoint, the pattern of a rock may be *homogeneous*, *oriented*, *veined*, *nuvolato* (cloud-like), *brecciated* or *ghiandonato* (acorn-like).

A pattern is *homogeneous* when no dominant fabric can be seen on a tile or slab sample and the rocky mass looks isotropic since it does not change according to the cutting direction. Varieties with homogeneous patterns can therefore be cut in any direction without altering the aesthetic characteristics.

Typical homogeneous materials are the granite varieties commercially known as *homogeneous* which are mostly red, pink, grey and dark blue. Marble varieties are rarely homogeneous and are basically limited to white or pink materials, whereas this is a more common feature of Stone, generally grey varieties, but red and black varieties too.

Fig. 6 - Veined pattern on marble (Photo courtesy of Geol. C. Musetti)
a - Excavation front on Bianco Statuario quarry parallel to *contro* direction
b - Quality selection of Bianco Statuario according to the pattern
c - Block of Calacatta Carrara
(I) *Contro* direction
(II) *Secondo* direction

a

A pattern is *oriented* when the rock's elements are seen to follow a distinct orientation on a tile or slab sample. In commercial slang, the orientation of a rock is called its rift. In this case, the cutting direction influences the material's aesthetic characteristics which vary according to the spatial ratio between the cutting surface and the orientation of the rock. There are three conditions which correspond to three extreme cases (Fig. 6):

a) the cutting surface is at right angles to the bedding plane; the oriented pattern fades away and disappears when the bedding plane is totally unidirectional. In commercial slang this cutting direction is called the hard way (head, tough way);

b) the cutting surface is at right angles to both the bedding plane and the head surface; in this case the oriented pattern of the rock is accentuated. In commercial slang this cutting direction is called the easy way (grain);

c) the cutting surface is parallel to the bedding plane and at right angles to both the head and the grain. The pattern of the rock is always oriented but the minerals of which it is composed are often larger than those in b). In commercial slang this cutting direction is called the rift (bedding plane, grain).

Obviously, in addition to these three cases, there are the in-between cases. These are known as the false hard way, false easy way and false rift, since the angle of the cutting surface is near to one of the above three surfaces a), b) or c).

b

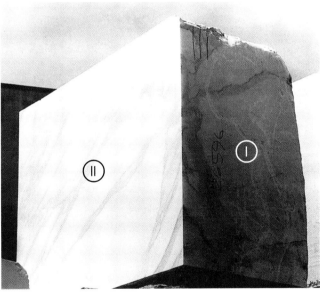

c

In general, however, oriented materials are always cut into slabs or tiles on the hard way or the easy way. In this way, the movement of the rock can either be emphasized or subdued according to the desired aesthetic results. When cut along the rift, the size of the crystals or clasts which form the rock is accentuated and this is not very attractive.

Many granite varieties have this pattern that may derive either from magmatic fluidity, which often creates delicate undulations, or from metamorphosis, which generally creates a very distinct and fairly rectilinear orientation. In both cases, the most frequent colors are red, yellow and, to a lesser extent, green. There are also numerous oriented marble varieties, although their formation is obviously different from that of granite varieties. In the case of marble, the orientation is generally due to a bedded texture typical of many sedimentary rocks, i.e., limestone and travertine. As far as Stone varieties are concerned, oriented patterns are typical of schists (often grey or grey-green), but in the other commercial subgroups they only really occur in some basalt varieties which are always grey and similar varieties of a lighter color (whitish, pink).

A *veined* pattern, as the name suggests, consists of veins which cross the groundmass of the rock. If the veins are isoriented, then the material has a well-defined bedding plane; the more varied their orientation, the more irregular the pattern. Again, slabs or tiles are usually cut along the easy way or the hard way with the longer side more or less parallel to the direction of the bedding plane. Veined materials are particularly suitable to create what are known as *quarter-match* and *book-match* patterns, where slabs cut from the same block are arranged in twos or fours so that they mirror each other.

The cutting direction greatly affects the aesthetic characteristics, especially in the case of materials with a precise bedding plane. If cut according to the easy way, the vein pattern stands out well; if cut according to the hard way, the veins may be reduced to shapeless specks, spots or irregular lines; if cut according to the rift, undulating or semicircular shapes often appear and this pattern is known in commercial slang as spadellato (flattened out).

Veined patterns are the most traditional and the most frequent among Marble varieties and Marble s.s. varieties in particular. In the latter, the veining is generally grey on a white or pink groundmass, although it may also be green or reddish-colored, still on a white or grey groundmass or white on a black groundmass. As for Limestone, in addition to the above-mentioned colors, there may also be yellow veining on a black, pink, beige or brown groundmass. The veining may be of various shapes and sizes on different-colored backgrounds. In the case of veined Granite varieties, rather than an element added to the still groundmass, the veining actually forms the groundmass, giving the rock an undulating appearance which is accentuated by the difference in the color of the various veins. Many commercial varieties have black veins together with red or pink veins (the most frequent combination), although they may also be together with green, violet, yellow and even orange veins. A fairly frequent color combination is green with pink or, less frequently, with white. Quartzite varieties have similar veining to Marble varieties. The most popular commercial variety is a white quartzite with sky-blue veinings. Finally, as far as Stone varieties are concerned, veined patterns are rare and are only seen on a few Lava Rocks and

Sandstone varieties. These have brownish-yellow-colored veinings on a yellowish- or grey-colored groundmass.

The characteristic of the pattern known as *nuvolato* is a fairly even-colored groundmass containing light-colored, egg-shaped bodies with indefinite and irregular outlines which look like cloudy formations. This pattern may either derive from the intrinsic structure of the rock (as is the case of all the other types of patterns) or it can be created artificially by cutting veined materials almost parallel to the direction of the bedding plane (false rift). The development surfaces of the veins on the cut slabs therefore have fairly irregular, faded edges which tend to curve or even form circles like clouds.

This cutting technique is not often used and is anyway not suitable for all veined materials. Among the materials which give pleasing aesthetic results are Marble s.s. and Limestone varieties and Schist and Slate varieties belonging to the Stone family.

The *brecciated* pattern is produced by a specific genetic characteristic of certain types of rocks. It is generated when a rock is formed by the accumulation of fragments of various shapes and sizes from other rocks which are completely or partially bonded by a groundmass matrix. If there is no specific orientation in the accumulation, there are no particular preferences for the cutting direction to make slabs and tiles. In some cases though, the breccias are oriented or veined and so what was said for these two patterns is applicable.
In view of the peculiar genetic characteristics, especially in Limestone varieties, the *brecciated* pattern may signify a reduction in the resistance to physical-mechanical stress. Thus, slabs in these materials often have to be reinforced. Because of its particular origin, this pattern is typical of certain Marble s.s. and Limestone varieties. In the former, the pattern is appropriately called *arabescato* and the commercial varieties may be white, yellow-ivory, pink and white and less frequently reddish-violet; in the latter, they may be pink and reddish-colored and beige and cream too. Breccia-like patterns also occur in Marble s.s. varieties such as Rosso Levanto and Verde Alpi and in Stone varieties such as Peperino.

Finally, the *ghiandonato* pattern is typical of certain Granite and Stone varieties and is due to a particular type of crystal grain size.

GRAIN

The *grain* (granulometry in scientific terminology) defines the size and, in some cases, the shape of the crystalline or lithic elements which constitute a rock. Although from a commercial viewpoint there are three types of grain, i.e. *fine*, *medium* and *coarse*, there are no precise indications as to the range of sizes which each type should include. It is common practice though to use two different scales, one for Granite varieties only and one for Marble s.s, Stone and Quartzite varieties. The former considers a fine or medium grain what the latter considers a medium or coarse grain. In fact, what is considered a fine grain for Marble, Stone and Quartzite varieties does not exist for granite varieties and what is considered a coarse grain for Granite varieties is normally of no interest commercially for Marble and Stone varieties (with only a few exceptions). Despite the numerous types of grain in nature, commercially speaking there is practically only one. This is a type of coarse grain which is normally found in homogeneous and oriented Granite varieties (although it is also found in some Stone varieties), where the crystals of one mineral, generally feldspar, are much larger than the crystals of the other components of the rock. When a rock has this kind of structure, petrographically defined as porphyroid, it is called *ghiandone* or *ghiandonato*, the large-sized crystals being like acorns. In scientific terms, medium- and coarse-grained Marble s.s varieties are commercially known as *crystalline* rocks.

Grain size is much less significant than color or pattern as far as the general aesthetic value of a material is concerned, yet the size of the rock's components can affect both the deepness of the color and the beauty of the pattern. A good example of Granite is Absolute Black, which has a deeper color in the fine-grained varieties; likewise in coarse-grained Marble varieties the veins are much less distinct than in fine-grained varieties (a positive factor in some cases, especially when the veins are strong colors).

In practice, in addition to its influence on the aesthetic characteristics of a material, the *grain size* is also important as regards the physical-mechanical properties of a material, and hence its possible uses. For example, fine-grained marble varieties often have a much greater compressive strength and hardness than coarse-grained materials. This means that they are more difficult to work but they can be made into a wider range of finished products and have a wider range of uses.

On the other hand, some coarse-grained materials and certain Marble s.s. varieties in particular are easily damaged if used for floorings and elements with sharp edges.

3.2 TECHNICAL CHARACTERISTICS

From a technical standpoint, a stone material's range of possible uses depends on the petrography, mineral and chemical composition and physical-mechanical properties of the corresponding lithotype. Together, these factors constitute the technical characteristics of the commercial variety which it is necessary to consult when selecting a material and establishing its possible uses.
Although there is a relationship between the above factors, they each contribute in their own way to the possible uses of a material. Their individual importance depends on several design variables such as the environment, installation methods, the type of finished product, the performance required, etc.

Thus, a designer should always have a complete picture of the technical characteristics of materials of possible interest so as to assess the validity of the choice.

Following is a description of the above factors together with their role in the technical behavior of a material.

Petrography
Petrography defines the characteristics and the origin of the minerals which form a rock as well as their ratio in the rock's structure. In practice, it is important to know the petrography of a rock above all to understand and avoid weathering problems (color variations, reduction of the mechanical resistance, etc.) when used in certain conditions (strong sunlight, exposure to polluting

agents, etc.). Normally, the petrographic description must be considered together with the mineral and chemical descriptions. A *petrographic analysis* involves the microcopic examination of a section of the material (*thin section*).

Mineral composition

Mineralogy describes the type and characteristics of the minerals which form a rock. The mineral composition of a commercial variety provides important information as to its workability as well as certain physical-mechanical properties. Furthermore, it is indispensable in order to understand and avoid many forms of aesthetic alteration (color variations, appearance of spots, etc.) for an assessment of the possible uses and the natural weathering of the material. A laboratory *mineralogical analysis* consists of x-ray diffractometry.

Chemical composition

This parameter defines the type and percentages of the chemical elements which form a rock. The chemical composition of a material provides important information as to its possible uses in specific environmental conditions (e.g., polluted atmosphere) and establishes if, over time, it has a tendency to show weathering or color defects. A laboratory *chemical analysis* involves a mass spectrometry.

Physical-mechanical properties

In order to be used as a dimension stone, a rock must have a series of physical-mechanical properties which, together, are responsible for specific workability and durability characteristics and hence possible uses. The main physical-mechanical properties of a rock which determine its use as dimension stone are the following:

The *unit weight per volume* is the ratio between the weight and the apparent volume of the material (i.e., including the holes inside the material too or its *porosity*) which corresponds to its actual weight. This is fundamental in the assessment of the loads that a material exerts on the fixing and support structures. It also provides information as to the compactness of the material.

The *compressive strength* defines a material's ability to withstand loads. This is indispensable for materials made into products with a structural function (solid columns, arches, etc.) but it is also important for cladding and flooring which, for many reasons, are subjected to compressive stress.

The *compressive strength after freeze-thaw cycles* defines a material's ability to withstand loads in environments with significant temperature changes above and below 0°C. A material is considered fragile in freezing conditions if, after freeze-thaw cycles (from -10°C to + 35°C), its resistance drops by over 25%. It is therefore fundamental to have this information if a material is to be used externally (paving, cladding) in climatic conditions with significant temperature changes over 24 hours.

The *porosity* denotes the volume of the holes inside the material compared to the volume of the rock and provides information as to its compactness and therefore indirectly its mechanical resistance. In addition, it provides useful information as to the rock's capacity to contain liquids within its structure.

The *absorption* defines a material's capacity to absorb liquids and therefore indirectly gives indications as to its *porosity*. It is important to know a material's absorption if the material is to be used where it is frequently in contact with liquids (bathrooms, kitchens, exterior uses, etc.).

The *modulus of rupture* establishes a material's ability to withstand bending pressure. This is extremely important for a dimension stone material, since mechanical stress which causes bending either directly or indirectly occurs in many applications (external cladding especially in areas with strong winds, stairs, roofs, shelves, funerary stones, floating floors, lintels, etc.).

The *coefficient of thermal expansion* establishes a material's ability to expand when subjected to high temperatures. This is only important when a material is used in particularly hot environments or climates and especially when used externally in a place exposed to direct sunlight. In such cases it is important to be careful in the use of light and dark materials together since they may react differently to increases in temperature, thereby creating an imbalance in the structure of the building.

The *elasticity* establishes a material's ability to withstand mechanical stress. This property is directly related to the material's ability to withstand bending pressure and is important when assessing the effects of lithostatic loads on a material, especially in cladding.

The *abrasion resistance* of a rock is its ability to withstand wear. This is fundamental in assessing a material's suitability for internal and external flooring (including roads), shelves, etc.

The *impact strength* of a rock gives indications as to the strength of a material subjected to concentrated loads. This is fairly important when a material is to be used for external and internal floorings and shelves.

The *hardness* provides indications as to the ability of the material to withstand scratches (*Mohs hardness*) and the resistance of the various crystalline components of the material to concentrated loads (*Knoop microhardness*). This property is of great importance, especially when a material is to be used for floorings, shelves, claddings near high-traffic areas, etc.

All the above physical-mechanical properties can be analyzed using specific laboratory tests following standard procedures set out by official standards bodies. Since there is not one international standards body officially recognized throughout the world, in practice it is necessary to refer to testing standards set by the various countries which may, however, vary from one country to another. Frequently, the country where the supplier has the material tested is not the country where the material is to be used. Thus, a designer does not always have the information necessary to fulfil design requirements, and it is often necessary to have the tests carried out again according to specific standards.

In most cases, the materials commonly found on the international market are tested according to ASTM procedures (American Standard Testing Method) if they are to be used mostly on the American market or UNI (Ente Nazionale Italiano di Unificazione) if they are for the Italian market.

Fig. 7 shows the importance of the various properties according to the most frequent uses in the building industry with the ASTM and UNI standard codes for the various physical-mechanical tests used on materials for ornamental use.

Often though, in practice it is necessary to understand how a certain material behaves in conditions other than those covered by the standard physical-mechanical tests with a view to preventing any deterioration. This generally occurs when a material is to be used in certain environmental conditions, such as very polluted or particularly humid and salty atmospheres, etc. It is in fact possible to subject a material to purpose-made tests although these are only conducted in a few specialized laboratories. Moreover, the interpretation of these is still rather limited, especially because of the necessity to recreate, in a short time, effects which in normal conditions would occur over years. Among the most frequent additional tests are:

- *corrosion by chemical agents* which gives indications as to a material's behavior in the presence of polluting agents, generally ones present in the atmosphere of urban areas;

- *exposure to ultraviolet rays* which provides information as to the behavior of a material exposed to strong sunlight;

- *exposure to a very salty atmosphere* which provides information as to the behavior of a material exposed to the action of salt.

Fig. 7 - Importance of the physical-mechanical properties of dimension stone according to its use and standard laboratory test codes
very important ooo
important oo
not very important o

	Weight per unit of volume	Compressive strength	Compressive strength after freezing	Imbibition	Flexural strength/ Modulus of rupture	Linear thermal expansion	Modulus of elasticity	Abrasion resistance	Impact strength	Knoop microhardness
Internal claddings	ooo	ooo	o	o	oo	o	o	o	o	o
External claddings	ooo	ooo	ooo	ooo	ooo	ooo	ooo	o	o	o
Internal floorings	oo	o	o	oo	oo	o	o	ooo	ooo	ooo
External pavings	o	oo	ooo	ooo	oo	oo	oo	ooo	ooo	ooo
Cantilevered stairs	ooo	oo	o	o	ooo	o	ooo	ooo	ooo	ooo
Shelves	ooo	oo	ooo	ooo	ooo	oo	o	ooo	ooo	ooo
Roofs	ooo	o	oo	ooo	ooo	ooo	o	o	o	o
Bathroom furnishings	oo	o	o	ooo	o	o	o	o	o	o
Funerary art	o	o	oo	ooo	ooo	oo	o	o	o	o
Structural elements	ooo	ooo	ooo	ooo	ooo	o	oo	oo	oo	oo
ASTM Standard	C 97	C170		C97	C880/C99	D2845	C580/C1352	C241		
UNI Standard	9724/2	9724/3		9724/2	9724/5		9724/8	RD.2234	32.07.248.0	9724/6

There are specific ASTM standards which define the minimum properties that materials included in the different groups of dimension stone should perform to be used in the stone industry. These standards are:

ASTM C503-96	Standard Specification for Marble Dimension Stone (Exterior)
ASTM C568-89e 1	Standard Specification for Limestone Dimension Stone
ASTM C615-96	Standard Specification for Granite Dimension Stone
ASTM C616-95	Standard Specification for Quartz-based Dimension Stone
ASTM C629-96	Standard Specification for Slate Dimension Stone

Physical-mechanical tests on natural stone are normally conducted on standard specimens which do not take into account the shape or size of the product to be installed (*). This means that the tests provide information on the stone itself but they are not necessarily to be considered in absolute terms. A material may react differently to physical and mechanical stress according to the type of finished product in question and in most cases it is the behavior of the finished product which interests a designer above all.

In some cases, the type of finished product and its surface finishing (see paragraph 2.3) may influence the physical-mechanical properties of a certain material to such an extent that tests are required to assess the physical-mechanical behavior of the finished product ready for installation or even practically already installed. In the latter case, for instance, tests are carried out on complete prefabricated panels made of thin stone elements fixed to a metal load-bearing structure which is then to be installed directly onto the building structure.

In order to meet these requirements, though, highly specialized laboratories are required, and the high costs involved are not always justified.

3.3 AVAILABILITY

When selecting a stone material, it is extremely important for designers to know how much material is actually available with the aesthetic and technical characteristics set out in the pre-design stage. There are four factors which determine the availability of natural stone, that is, the *constancy of the aesthetic characteristics of the material*, the *volumes available*, the *characteristics of the raw material production* and the *delivery times*.

Constancy of the Aesthetic Characteristics

The importance of the *constancy of the aesthetic characteristics* varies from one material to another. In the case of homogeneous colored or patterned materials, tolerance of variations is very low and even small alterations may impair the quality of the material. Tolerance is higher when it comes to certain materials, the aesthetic value of which is based on the heterogeneity of the pattern or color, especially if this can be seen on the cut slabs. Veined granite varieties are perhaps the best example. It is necessary to establish an aesthetic range corresponding to the quality of the material for the assessment of the aesthetic variations. This range often includes elements which would invariably be considered aesthetic defects in other materials.

In actual fact, when discussing natural stone, the definition of the word *defect* is anything but accurate and is sometimes even subjective. If we were to make a definition, it could be said that all physical or chemical elements in a material which may compromise its use either by altering its aesthetic characteristics recognized by the market or by lowering its physical-mechanical resistance much below the normal levels of similar materials are defects. Fig. 8 shows the most common defects to be found in natural stone and their remedies, if at all possible.

TYPE OF DEFECT	SCIENTIFIC NAME	DESCRIPTION	MATERIALS AFFECTED	MAIN EFFECTS	POSSIBLE SOLUTIONS
Catena	Dike	Straight, light-colored veining from a few centimeters to a few dozen centimeters thick	Homogeneous and oriented granite	Aesthetic impairment	---
Biscie/Fili	Schlieren	Black, straight or undulating, thread-like veining, generally in bands a few dozen centimeters thick	Homogeneous and oriented granite	Aesthetic impairment	---
Patches/ Black spots	Mafic xenolith	Ovaloid, black body generally a few centimeters across	Homogeneous and veined granite	Aesthetic impairment	---
Oil stains		Greasy-looking, irregular-shaped rings a few dozen centimeters across	All types of black, green and white granite	Aesthetic impairment	Treatment of polished surface with solvents
Magrosità		Minute abrasions of the rock which cannot be polished; visible above all in glaring light	Marble and granite	Aesthetic impairment and higher probability of deterioration	Resin-coating of surface to be polished
Rust spots	Oxidation	Rust-colored stains and rings	Marble, granite and stone	Aesthetic impairment	---
Strappi	Microfractures	Minute fractures which appear as light-colored lines from a few to a few dozen centimeters long, often occurring in series	Marble and granite	Aesthetic impairment Possible reduction in the rock's mechanical resistance	Resin-coating of the polished surface
Durea	Silica concentrations	Irregular-shaped, grey or brownish-colored areas harder than the rocky mass which may have tiny cavities	Veined marble and granite	Aesthetic impairment	---
Tarolo	Cavities	Small, irregular-shaped holes, either sporadic or in series	Marble	Aesthetic impairment	Filling before polishing
Luccica	Glints from sparry calcite crystals	Much larger crystals than those in the surrounding rocky mass	Marble	Aesthetic impairment and structural damage in places	---
Frescume		Whitish- or yellowish-colored stripes or spots on the polished surface	Marble	Aesthetic impairment	---
Peli furbi	Microfractures	Closed fractures which open up during processing or after installation	Marble, granite and stone	Structural yielding	---
Peli ciechi	Microfractures	Fractures inside the block which are not visible on the surface	Marble, granite and stone	Reduction in block yield	---
Manine/ Stelline	Glints from crystalline surfaces	Light-colored, star-shaped reflections a few centimeters across	Absolute black granite	Aesthetic impairment	---

Fig. 8 - The most common defects found in dimension stone

VOLUMES AVAILABLE
By *volumes available*, it is meant that there must be sufficient quantities of material with the established aesthetic and technical properties available either in the quarry (after production waste) or already in blocks. Information about the constancy of a material's aesthetic characteristics and the volumes extractable from the quarry are provided by detailed geological surveys conducted on site.

CHARACTERISTICS OF THE RAW MATERIAL PRODUCTION
The *characteristics of the raw material production* include the shape and size of the blocks produced in the quarry, both in absolute terms and with reference to any aesthetic orientation in the stone, which may affect its commercial value and its physical-mechanical properties. The best shape for a block is a squared parallelepiped (*squared blocks*). In many cases, though, especially as regards some Marble varieties, the quarry production may consist either partially or entirely of *shapeless pieces*. The size of squared blocks varies according to the type of material. In general, marble blocks are smaller (on average 2.4 x 1.60 x 1.60 = 6cu.m) than granite blocks (on average 2.8 x 1.8 x 1.8 = 9cu.m). However, this is certainly not a rule and there are many exceptions in both groups.

SUPPLY TIMES
Supply times refer to production of the raw material, its transportation to the sawmill and transformation into a finished product. In the quarry, the supply time is substantially based on the yield of useful material out of the total quarried and the production capacity of the quarry. The yield of the material is given in the detailed geological survey mentioned above, whereas the production capacity can be assessed according to the machinery available in the quarry and the operativeness of the quarrying workers. The supply time for the finished product depends on the production capacity of the processing plant.

4. Decay of Natural Stone

It is a common view that the use of natural stones in the building industry grants a special worth to the work, a sort of extra value hardly obtained by using other building materials. This view arises from the aesthetic features of natural stone and, of course, from its production costs, as well as from the implicit concept of natural stone's hardness, resistance, and durability, all factors that characterize the monuments of the past, the buildings of bygone civilizations.

However, all of us know that stone also undergoes the processes of natural decay, which sooner or later brings its unavoidable destruction. These processes are usually very slow compared to human history, so they may not be found in works of natural stone realized centuries or even millennia ago.

But recent history also records problems caused by the decay of stone installed only for decades, which can cause damage that is both aesthetic and structural, and which compromises the resistance of the material.

What is the link between such decay and, for example, buildings like the Colosseum and St. Peter's Church in Rome, where the deterioration of stone, if it exists, has not involved the integrity of the structure? Of course, there have been some cases where decay of stone has emerged in a rather short period, but these are limited, considering the large number of buildings. (Among them may be mentioned the flaking of a kind of sandstone used in the past centuries in some towns of Tuscany and now completely destroyed).

Though the different speeds of decay of natural stone may appear anomalous, the explanation is rather simple and can be found in several elements we must understand in order to find an answer to such problems. We cannot, within the scope of this volume, investigate this subject in detail, but at least we can give a basic knowledge of the problem, considering two very important points: the main causes of decay of natural stone and how to prevent it during stone selection.

At the moment of its use, each kind of stone is in environmental conditions highly different from those of its formation and therefore it is in a position of imbalance in the new environment. Under these conditions stone is subjected to the action of weathering, which consists of a sequence of processes caused by the new environment; these processes interfere with the structure and chemical composition of the material and can change the characteristics of the stone. Speaking in very general terms, it is possible to group these processes as follows:

- physical processes
- chemical processes
- biological processes

The main physical processes are:

Temperature variations. These involve the change of temperature over 24 hours that, in some cases, may reach 40° to 50°C. The variations cause an expansion of the individual crystals of which the stone is composed, producing variations several tenths of millimeters per meter in the material. Serious problems could also be caused by severe temperature variations of the water inside the stone which induce strong pressure variation.

Freeze/thaw action. This is a phenomenon connected to the water contained in the stone in its natural status. The change of water in ice brings an increase in

Fig. 9 - External façade of Finland Hall, Helsinki (Finland). Warping of marble slabs, about 21 years after installation. The marble shows a general decrease of physical-mechanical properties probably caused by the action of particular weather conditions (daily freeze/thaw alternation) in a polluted atmosphere (acid rain).

Fig. 10 - External façade of Finland Hall, Helsinki, showing the difference between the original marble slabs (warped and grey-colored) and a new marble slab(center).

9

10

volume of about 9% and, consequently, causes a high pressure in the internal structure of the stone, reducing the cohesive strength of the crystals and increasing the porosity of the material.

Salt action. This occurs when the water of the crystals contains some salts which can crystallize when the humidity changes. Though the crystallization is a chemical process, it generates mechanical variations which induce strains inside the crystal structure of stone, causing an effect similar to freeze/thaw action.

The main chemical processes are:

Hydration/Oxidation. This process may create problems, especially if it acts on ferrous metals contained in the rock. In the presence of water these can be transformed into limonite, changing the original color of the material (formation of rust).

Reaction with SO_2. Sulphurous anhydride is one of the main polluting agents of the atmosphere; its action unfolds on many materials rich in calcium carbonate (marble and limestone) that in presence of water, transform into calcium sulfate (gypsum), changing the mineralogical composition, the structure and therefore the physical-mechanical properties of the stone. In addition, chemical reaction increases the volume of the material.

Reaction with CO_2. Carbon dioxide is naturally present in the atmosphere in small quantities. When, due to pollution, the concentration increases, in the presence of water it can cause the dissolution of marble, transforming the

Fig. 11 - External façade of Finland Hall, Helsinki: detail of the warped slabs.

Fig. 12 - Finland Hall, Helsinki: warping does not occur in interior cladding.

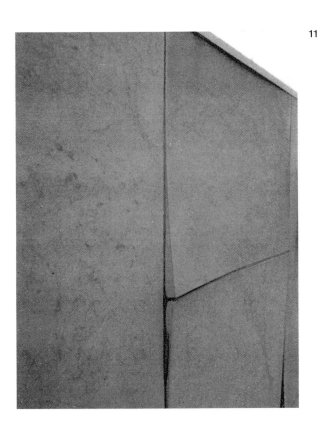

11

12

calcium carbonate into calcium bicarbonate, which, being soluble, can be easily removed, reducing the volume of the stone.

Moisture action. Normally stone contains a certain quantity of water. In conditions of high humidity (fog, ground moisture, etc.), stone can absorb more water by capillarity. The capillary travel of moisture can cause dissolution phenomena in many kinds of stone (sandstone, marble, etc.). Nevertheless, the main problems occur in dry and wet cycles, which can led to the formation of surface crusts (hardening phenomena, honeycomb formation, etc.).

Hydrolysis. This is a process which involves rocks rich in silicates, containing feldspars (such as granites); these minerals react with OH ions generating clay minerals. Though this phenomenon is one of the main causes of the natural decay of granites, it is very slow and therefore rather difficult to find in stone used for building. Its action may be faster in the presence of polluting agents.

The main biological processes are:

Growth of algae, fungi and lichens. Presence of these microorganisms on the superficial parts of stone gives rise to aesthetic damages, modifying the original color. Most of these organism produce also acids which cause a chemical desegregation of stone surface.

Bird droppings. The presence of a high quantity of bird droppings can generate a chemical reaction which causes a partial desegregation of stone.

Of course, all the decay processes described above do not act in the same way on every kind of stone. Their effect can be very different from one case to

Fig. 13 - Dissolution phenomenon affecting a white marble statue, Massa (Italy). As a result of the low CaCO$_3$ content the veins are affected by dissolution and appear in relief on the white groundmass.

another, and is related to a number of features which can influence type and speed of decay. These features are:

- physical-mechanical characteristics of the stone
- type of finishing of the stone product
- physical-mechanical characteristics of stone product
- installation technique
- environmental characteristics of the installation site

It is well known how each of these features includes several other elements that, acting together in different ways, may affect the speed of decay of the stone. Moreover, the causes of decay do not act separately, but they contribute in various measures to the deterioration of the material installed following certain methods and in a specific environment.

What are the possible measures to adopt in case of decay? Actually, in most cases, when the effects of decay become evident, it is late to intervene in such a way as to obtain a satisfactory result. In these cases we often have to replace the stone. Both the causes and the predisposing elements of damage may be manifold, and it is hard to find a solution for each of them.

In the last thirty to forty years, the choice of stone has aimed mainly to satisfy the aesthetic requirements, to fulfil the ornamental function of the material. Those who select the material have looked more to the visual features, without considering whether the chosen material, installed under certain conditions, might deteriorate. Such choices probably have been influenced, as already noted, by the concept that because of the hardness and durability of natural stone, the material does not need any special check. But if this may have been

Fig. 14 - Black marble in exterior, Massa (Italy). The original polished surface was damaged when exposed to direct sunlight and rain (lower part).

Fig. 15 - Black marble in exterior, Massa (Italy). Detail of damage to the original polished surface from exposure to direct sunlight and rain (lower part).

14

15

justified in the past, nowadays this association has lost its general validity, for these three reasons:

- stone no longer serves the structural function it had in the past, when it was used mainly for massive elements; moreover, stone processed according to the present size, shape and type of finish shows physical-mechanical characteristics very different to those of the massive stone in its natural status
- modern finishes (like high-grade polishing, for example) are more easily damaged than finishes used in the past, which were more similar to the natural surface of stone
- the causes of decay have increased, especially because of pollution

Thus, the designer has to consider the risk that material chosen on an aesthetic basis only may be subjected to more or less noticeable decay. It is therefore necessary to select material after carrying out a set of controls, previously judged needless, in order to prevent problems.

The real solution is to understand if the decay may be foreseen and, if possible, to identify the techniques to avoid it. The experience of the last few years has really contributed to our understanding of how and when stone can be installed without any risk, as well as of the tendency to decay of some rocks installed in particular environmental conditions. Now, for example, it is known worldwide that most of the green marble included in the lithological group of the ophiolites, if installed in exteriors exposed to atmospheric agents, tend to lose their polish very quickly. It is also known that a marble with medium to coarse grain used for floors subjected to frequent trampling will be exposed to scratches and breakage of single crystals.

If we wish precautionary action to be really effective, experience is not sufficient. It is essential to examine all the features that determine the tendency of stone to decay. The task is hard, since there are a lot of variants; it is difficult to establish fixed rules that can give an absolute guarantee that the selected material will not be subject to short-term decay. The best approach is to study case by case, at least when the characteristics of a project suggest such a control.

The present technical knowledge allows us to investigate many factors that determine stone decay. In addition to the physical-mechanical tests described in chapter 3, which give a basic knowledge of the material, other analyses are very important to have a complete picture of the situation. Some tests for the physical-mechanical characteristics of the finished product have been defined recently; moreover, experts have begun to investigate the possible alterations induced in stone by different installation techniques, and the influence on stone decay of particular finishing techniques.

The information obtained with these tests is just partly sufficient to the aim; it may be useless if not compared to the possible causes of decay through studies covering the various aspects of the problem, and this is particularly true for projects located in certain environmental conditions. For example, a detailed analysis of the atmosphere of a metropolitan area is essential to prevent problems caused by pollution, in association, or not, with particular humidity conditions.

Once the possible causes of decay have been established, specific laboratory techniques allow us to check the behavior of the stone under environmental conditions compared to the actual ones (see section 3.2) and consequently to find precautionary actions.

5. Selection Procedures and Quality Control

The selection of a dimension stone to be used in a project is a very delicate operation since it greatly determines the success of a project. Its selection involves the examination of all the parameters which indicate the possible uses of a certain stone (which basically correspond to those which define the stone's commercial characteristics described in the previous chapter) with reference to the design specifications.

Generally, when selecting a stone material for ornamental use, the designer gives priority to the aesthetic characteristics and in particular its color and then its pattern. The choice of the color often becomes an actual clause in the contract, which must be strictly respected.

Despite their obvious importance, in many cases parameters such as availability of the necessary volumes, delivery times and technical characteristics are only checked after the final selection of the material, which is based exclusively on the color and cost established at the design stage. If such parameters are underestimated, though, this may lead to serious problems in course of execution. It is not unusual to hear of cases where, faced with not only technical but also legal problems, it is necessary to replace a material. This occurs either during the execution stage because the material is not available in the quantity and quality initially set out or upon completion of the project because the material has turned out to be unsuitable for the use in question.

The importance of each individual parameter in the global evaluation of the suitability of a certain material may vary significantly from one project to the next, consequently affecting the priority of the tests. In general, though, it is a good idea to follow a well-defined time schedule in order to create a complete picture and thereby reduce the possibility of mistakes to the minimum.

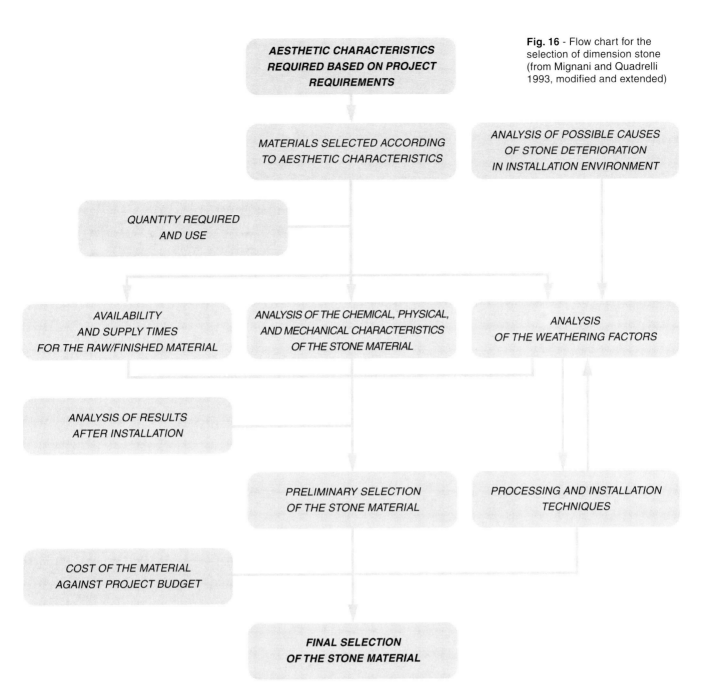

Fig. 16 - Flow chart for the selection of dimension stone (from Mignani and Quadrelli 1993, modified and extended)

Fig. 16 shows a flow chart of the steps required for the rational selection of a stone material. Here again, according to the designer's requirements, the aesthetic characteristics mark the point of departure according to which a certain number of materials potentially suitable for the project are identified.

Once selected, the potential materials must be examined in terms of their *availability*, *technical characteristics* and the *weathering factor* on the basis of the environmental conditions of the site where the material is to be installed. (The environmental data should be collected beforehand at the design stages.)

As mentioned, availability may be taken for granted, yet often designers cannot control production (or more simply it is not their job to do so). Hence, especially in the case of large orders, suppliers may find it difficult to honor their commitments and this may be detrimental to the outcome of the project. Although there may be

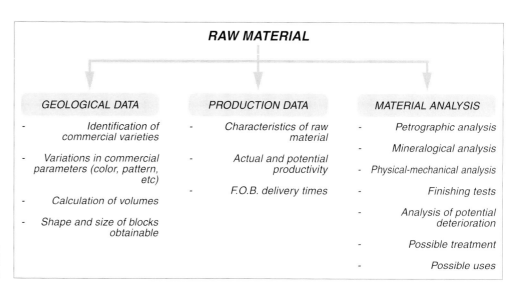

Fig. 17 - Parameters regarding the raw material to be analyzed prior to selection

many reasons, this situation essentially stems from the actual suppliers' difficulties in keeping the entire production cycle under control: from the production of the raw material in blocks to the transformation of the blocks into finished products.

Generally, as far as transformation is concerned, the problem can be avoided by checking the production capacity of the processing plant. The problem is not so easy to resolve when it comes to calculating the production capacity of a quarry though. This is because the processing firm (which normally supplies the material) obtains the material either from dealers or from the quarry owner with whom there may be an exclusive contract. Relatively few processing firms own their own quarries of the materials they process. Obviously, if the entire quantity of material necessary for the project is already stored as blocks, the problem of availability does not exist. In this case, all that is required is a quality control of the blocks and an analysis of the physical-mechanical properties of the lot of material selected. In many cases, however, especially when large quantities are required, when a new commercial variety is selected (which is consequently not used much) or when a material is extracted from one quarry only, it is hard to find the desired quantities of blocks available in a storage yard. In such cases, selection should include an *analysis of the factors which determine availability actually in the quarry*, perhaps even before the material is extracted (Fig. 17).

First and foremost, the *constancy of the aesthetic characteristics* should be checked as well as the *volumes available* of the material in question. This must be carried out by highly qualified experts to define the extractive potential of a deposit before it is exploited. The information collected will finalize the preliminary selection and give useful indications to guide excavation in order to reach the production targets required by the project.

The analysis should examine the *characteristics of the raw material extracted*, in particular the shape and size of the blocks and their quality (that is the aesthetic characteristics) and, if necessary, the shape of the blocks, taking into account any orientation.

Finally, it must be established whether or not there are the necessary conditions to meet the *supply times* set out in the project. Supply times obviously have to be assessed throughout the entire production cycle, from the production of the raw material to its transportation to the sawmill, processing and the delivery of the finished product.

In order to verify the *technical characteristics* of a material, it is necessary to conduct the complete series of laboratory tests (petrographical, chemical, mineralogical and physical-mechanical) required to classify dimension stone on the raw material and the finished product, obviously taking into account the planned installation techniques.

To assess the extent to which a material is prone to *weathering*, specific tests other than the standard ones are required. Initially, this aspect may be examined by comparing the environmental data with the material's specific characteristics. Should this comparison show that there is a theoretical possibility that the material will deteriorate, specific tests must be conducted (maybe at a later stage of the selection process) both on the raw material and on the finished product, taking into account the installation techniques.

The results of these tests enable the designer to select the stone material according to whether it is likely to achieve the performance required by the project once it is installed. Its performance obviously refers to how it behaves according to its use (e.g., resistance to atmospheric agents, anti-slip characteristics, etc.). Hence, it is not the actual stone which is directly responsible for the installed product's performance but, thanks to its technical characteristics together with other factors such as the type of finished product, the surface treatment, etc., it certainly helps to achieve the performance levels required. Fig. 18 shows the importance of the performance most commonly required of a building for the main uses of dimension stone.

Following this last analysis, the selection is finalized by the assessment of the cost of the materials which have passed the aesthetic and technical tests according to the budget in question.

To summarize, the entire selection process covers the three most important aspects of a stone supply for a project, that is, availability of the raw material, its transformation into the finished product and the installation of the finished product. Hence, the selection requires a complete analysis of the various aspects carried out by highly qualified persons and not just a simple color/cost combination.

Again, the aim of the selection procedure is to reduce the possibility of error to the minimum when selecting a material to use in a project. However, even after the tests have been carried out, the commercial characteristics of the

QUALITY CONTROL

Condensation control	Sound-proofing	Heat insulation	Water-proofing	Air permeability	Anti-slip capacity	Cleanable surface	Maintenance	Resistance to atmospheric agents	Resistance to temperature changes	Resistance to chemical substances	Resistance to seismic phenomena	Fire-resistance	
ooo	oo	oo	oo	o	o	ooo	oo	o	ooo	ooo	oo	oo	Internal claddings
o	oo	oo	ooo	ooo	o	o	ooo	ooo	ooo	ooo	ooo	oo	External claddings
oo	o	oo	oo	o	ooo	ooo	oo	o	oo	ooo	oo	oo	Internal floorings
o	oo	o	ooo	o	ooo	o	ooo	ooo	ooo	ooo	oo	oo	External pavings
o	oo	o	o	o	ooo	ooo	oo	o	oo	ooo	oo	oo	Cantilevered stairs
oo	o	oo	ooo	oo	ooo	ooo	oo	ooo	ooo	ooo	ooo	oo	Shelves
oo	oo	oo	ooo	oo	o	o	oo	ooo	ooo	oo	oo	o	Roofs

Fig. 18 - Importance of the various factors required of dimension stone according to its use
very important   ooo
important   oo
not very important   o

63

material may undergo variations during the supply. Although this is unlikely if the preliminary analysis has been conducted appropriately, this may occur at an advanced stage of the supply and it is more likely to occur in the case of large quantities of material, new materials or ones which are not widely used and/or materials which have a natural tendency to vary from one part of the quarry to another.

In order to avoid this problem, a strict *quality control* may be conducted during the execution of the project. Again, this may take place at the three production stages, that is, the raw material production, its transformation into the finished product and the installation of the finished product (*). Fig. 19 summarizes the controls to carry out during the execution of the project in addition to those carried out during selection.

Obviously, this kind of problem is most frequently incurred with the supply of the raw material. Being a natural product, the latter may be subject to variations which are not easily controlled. These are mainly aesthetic variations, although significant variations do sometimes occur as regards the physical-mechanical properties and the actual production capacity of the quarry due to changes in the characteristics of the deposit being exploited. With regard to the physical-mechanical properties, it is worthwhile conducting periodic tests to make sure there are no variations in the material quarried (e.g., every 50 cu.m of raw material or every 200 sq.m of finished products). Should variations in the productivity of the quarry arise, it is necessary to conduct a more in-depth geological survey in order to plan exploitation, bearing in mind the project aims. The quality control of the finished product and the installed finished product essentially involves checking that the products comply with the quality and

(*) No mention is made here of quality control regarding technical aspects of installation since these do not fall within the scope of this guide. For information on this subject, appropriate texts should be consulted.

Fig. 19 - Parameters to be analysed when selecting the material and during quality control procedures

RAW MATERIAL	*before project execution* technical and commercial characteristics of the material available volumes of each commercial variety actual and potential productivity characteristics of the raw material f.o.b. delivery times possible uses of the material *during project execution* technical and commercial characteristics of the raw material
FINISHED PRODUCT	*before project execution* characteristics of the finished product type of surface finish possible actual and potential productivity of processing plant supply times *during project execution* technical and commercial characteristics of the raw material before processing technical and commercial characteristics of the finished product
INSTALLED PRODUCT	*before project execution* installation techniques technical and commercial characteristics of material before installation environmental characteristics of installation site possible deterioration phenomena project completion time *during project execution* technical and commercial characteristics of material before installation technical and commercial characteristics of the finished product

technical standards set out in the project. In the case of the finished product, in addition to its intrinsic qualities (surface finishing, gauging, etc.), it is important to see that any cutting directions match the orientation of the material (*). Likewise, in the case of the installed finished product, it is necessary to see that design specifications are followed as regards the spatial orientation of the elements of the stone or at least the combinations of the various elements are correctly made so as not to create color or pattern variations which could impair the final aesthetic impact.

In order to avoid this kind of problem, with certain architectural designs and/or the use of materials subject to significant aesthetic variations, it is a good idea to prepare a full-scale model of the project (*mock-up*). As well as helping to identify any problems which may occur during execution, this provides an unequivocal reference model for all those involved in the execution of the project.

(*) In some cases it may be necessary to repeat the physical-mechanical tests on the finished product.

Part Two

Commercial Groups

Marble

Marble varieties are available on the international market in the following colors:

White Marble

White Marble varieties belong mostly to the Marble s.s. group, although there are some sedimentary Limestone and just a few Travertine and Onyx varieties.

Yellow Marble

There are not many yellow Marble varieties available on the international market, but the existing varieties belong to each of the four commercial groups.

Beige Marble

Beige-colored Marble varieties mostly belong to the Limestone and Travertine groups. Marble s.s. and Onyx varieties are quite rare.

Brown Marble

The majority of brown Marble varieties belong to the Limestone and Travertine groups. Brown Marble s.s. and Onyx varieties are few and far between on the international market.

Red Marble

The majority of red Marble varieties belong to the Limestone group. Varieties belonging to the Marble s.s. and Travertine groups are less frequent, although they are regularly available on the international market. Red onyx varieties are fairly rare.

Pink Marble

The pink Marble varieties available on the international market belong to the Marble s.s. and Limestone groups.

Sky Blue Marble

The sky blue Marble varieties available on the international market all belong to the Marble s.s. group.

Green Marble

Almost all green-colored Marble varieties belong to the Marble s.s. group, although there are a few which belong to the Onyx group.

Grey Marble

The majority of grey Marble varieties belong to the Marble s.s. and Limestone groups. There are only a few Travertine varieties.

Black Marble

Almost all black Marble varieties available on the international market belong to the Limestone group.

Note: The values given for the physical-mechanical tests are only indicative, since they are taken from existing literature or material furnished by various stone producer/suppliers. Where values are not reported, information was not available or could not be confirmed. The author takes no responsibility for any mistakes or omissions regarding the values given.

WHITE MARBLE S.S.

MAIN AESTHETIC CHARACTERISTICS

There is a wide range of white Marble s.s. varieties, with an extensive aesthetic range in terms of color and texture. This guide divides the varieties according to their pattern since it is this more than the color which often determines their possible uses. There are three main aesthetic types. Type (i) are marble varieties with a white crystalline groundmass which may be homogeneous or, more frequently, crossed by small, discontinuous veins and/or greyish- or yellowish-colored shadings. The color of the crystalline mass may range from pure white to ivory white (considered the best quality materials) to off-white (average quality) and white with grey shades (low quality) according to the different varieties. The grain ranges from medium to fine in most cases, although it is coarse in a few cases. Type (ii) have a white crystalline groundmass which is normally crossed by grey or yellowish-colored veins (the latter being considered better quality) or even pink veins in some cases. The veins may have a preferential direction depending on the cutting direction and thereby give the rock a definite orientation (rift). Type (ii) may also range from pure white to ivory white (considered the best quality materials) to off-white (average quality) to white with grey shades (low quality) according to the different varieties. The grain is generally fine or medium. Aesthetic type (iii) has a breccia pattern (*arabescato*). This means that the individual marble elements are elongated, isoriented and bound by a greyish-colored groundmass which varies in quantity. The shape and arrangement of the marble elements give the material a well-defined orientation (rift). They are usually a fairly pure white and the grain is fine to medium.

AESTHETIC VARIATIONS AND DEFECTS

The most significant variation in all three aesthetic types concerns the color which in many cases has grey shades if the materials are defined pure white and is greyer in the varieties which verge on grey. This variation reduces the commercial value of the materials. In actual fact, owing to the great variation in color, white marble varieties are often divided into many sub-varieties, the commercial value of which varies considerably. Unfortunately, though, there are no official standards as regards the color characteristics of the various sub-varieties. The most frequent commercial defects are small holes a few millimeters in diameter (*taroli*) and *peli chiusi* which may open up once the material is installed. In some cases, ferrous elements occur (sometimes as traces) and these may cause rust marks to appear over time.

PRODUCER COUNTRIES

The main producer country of white Marble s.s. varieties is Italy, followed by Greece and then Turkey and the United States. Limited quantities are also quarried in Spain, Rumania and Bulgaria. A white marble fairly similar to some varieties produced in Italy is produced in Russia too. Other white marble quarrying areas are in Mexico, Namibia, Brazil, India, the Philippines and Malaysia.

PHYSICAL-MECHANICAL CHARACTERISTICS
(average reference values)

		(i)	(ii)	(iii)		
absorption	(C97)	0.11	0.15	0.09	weight%	ASTM
density	(C97)	2.716	2.718	2.722	kg/cu.m	STANDARD
compressive strength	(C170)	74.8	104	93	MPa	
modulus of rupture	(C99)				MPa	
flexural strength	(C880)	17	11.4	14.5	MPa	
abrasion resistance	(C241)	12.7	16.4	16.1	hardness	

AVAILABILITY

White marble varieties of all three types extracted from the most important production centers are very readily available. The better quality materials, that is the whiter materials or those with yellow veins/shades, may only be available in limited quantities. The blocks are generally medium- and large-sized, although shapeless blocks of average and good quality materials are easily sold too, with the exception of arabescato varieties which are more frequently sold in squared blocks. In many less important production centers, availability seems uncertain owing to a lower production capacity and/or the characteristics of the deposits. In such cases, the blocks are often shapeless and/or medium to small.

USES

White Marble s.s. varieties are commonly used for interior facings and floorings and exterior facings. They are also used, although to a lesser extent, for pavings. Some medium and coarse-grained varieties are not recommended for floorings and pavings though. The surface is generally polished, although fine honing is often preferred. Another possible surface treatment which is often used is impact treatment, but this should be avoided on medium- and coarse-grained varieties. Interesting results can also be achieved with practically all aesthetic type (iii) varieties and some type (ii) varieties with quarter-match and book-match work.
Given their chemical and mineralogical composition, most varieties are sensitive to atmospheric pollution, especially in humid climates or climates with considerable temperature changes over 24 hours.

MAIN COMMERCIAL VARIETIES

Aesthetic type (i): Bianco Acquabianca, Bianco Arni, Bianco Carrara Ordinario C, Bianco Carrara Ordinario C/D, Bianco Carrara Ordinario D , Bianco Lasa, Bianco Neve Thassos, Bianco P, Bianco Royal, Bianco Sivec, Bianco Statuario, Bianco Thassos, Cremo Delicato, Crevola d'Ossola, Lasa Vena Oro, Palissandro Bluette, Pentelikon, White Cherokee, White Georgia, White Savana.
Aesthetic type (ii): Bianco Pennsylvania, Bianco Venato Carrara, Calacatta Arni, Calacatta Carrara, Calacatta Luccicoso, Calacatta Oro, Calacata Campocecina, Calacatta Vagli, Calacatta Vagli Extra, Venatino Gioia, Statuario Venato, Uliano Venato, Zebrino.
Aesthetic type (iii): Arabescato Arni, Arabescato Cervaiole, Arabescato Corchia, Arabescato Corchia Classico, Arabescato Faniello, Arabescato La Mossa, Arabescato S.E.A., Arabescato Vagli, Brouillé.

PHYSICAL-MECHANICAL CHARACTERISTICS
(average reference values)

ITALIAN STANDARD

	(i)	(ii)	(iii)	
compression breaking load	1.563	1.389	1.257	kg/cm²
compression breaking load after freezing	1.478	1321	1.131	kg/cm²
imbibition coefficient (by weight)	0.23	0.35	0.27	%
ultimate tensile strength	181	162	153	kg/cm²
impact test	48	52	44	cm
thermal linear expansion coefficient	0.0045	0.0046	0.0059	mm/m°C
frictional wear test				mm
weight per unit of volume	2.667	2.704	2.709	kg/m³
elasticity module	625.000	572.000	627.000	kg/cm²
knoop microhardness	130		165	kg/mm²

71

WHITE LIMESTONE

MAIN AESTHETIC CHARACTERISTICS

There are two aesthetic types of white limestone. Type (i) has a very compact, fine-grained groundmass which is a fairly homogeneous off-white color. The pattern is often uniform too, although there are varieties with light grey, pinkish- or yellowish-colored veins. Type (ii) is composed of an accumulation of loosely bound sea shells. The groundmass looks like a mass of curved lamellas a few centimeters across which are generally isoriented. The mass is not very compact and there is a large quantity of holes from a few millimeters to a few centimeters across.

AESTHETIC VARIATIONS AND DEFECTS

The color of aesthetic type (i) may verge on pink, grey or beige. The main defect is the occurrence of coarse elements of various colors.
There are no real aesthetic variations in type (ii). Essentially, the only defect is an excessive increase in the size of the holes.

PRODUCER COUNTRIES

White limestone varieties are extracted in many countries. The most well-known varieties of aesthetic type (i) are from Italy, although Turkey and Jordan are also important producers. Type (ii) varieties are quarried in many countries (Italy, Spain, etc.) but their production is often sporadic.

AVAILABILITY

Availability of these materials is generally limited, but this is partly due to the fact that large quantities are not normally required by the market. There are significant exceptions on local and regional markets though (e.g. Ma'an and Ajilun limestone used in the building of Amman in Jordan). The blocks are usualy small since they often have a *falda bassa* and so are not very thick.

USES

Aesthetic type (i) varieties are normally used both in the form of polished or honed tiles for facings and floorings and rough-finished solid blocks (bush-hammered or riven finish) for external facings or actual structural pieces.
The use of type (ii) varieties is limited to interiors (even though in some cases they are used for exteriors) and the surface often has a sawn or honed finish.

MAIN COMMERCIAL VARIETIES

Aesthetic type (i): Biancone, Perlino Bianco, Cremo Bello. Aesthetic type (ii) varieties are not regularly available on the international market.

PHYSICAL-MECHANICAL CHARACTERISTICS
(average reference values)

		(i)	(ii)		
compression breaking load		2.060		kg/cm²	ITALIAN
compression breaking load after freezing		1.879		kg/cm²	STANDARD
imbibition coefficient (by weight)		0.06		%	
ultimate tensile strength		155		kg/cm²	
impact test		26		cm	
thermal linear expansion coefficient		0.0040		mm/m°C	
frictional wear test				mm	
weight per unit of volume		2.670		kg/m³	
elasticity module				kg/cm²	
knoop microhardness				kg/mm²	

PHYSICAL-MECHANICAL CHARACTERISTICS
(average reference values)

absorption	(C97)	weight%		ASTM
density	(C97)	kg/cu.m		STANDARD
compressive strength	(C170)	MPa		
modulus of rupture	(C99)	MPa		
flexural strength	(C880)	MPa		
abrasion resistance	(C241)	hardness		

WHITE TRAVERTINE

These materials are formed by the overlapping of subhorizontal layers a few centimeters thick, which gives the rock a stratified appearance. The rocky mass is not usually compact and has a number of small holes more or less parallel to the direction of the layers. The layers are often fairly straight although in some varieties they are undulating. The white color is not generally evenly distributed and ranges from off-white to grey from one layer to the next. The stratified arrangement of the layers gives the rock a prominent rift which is often accentuated by the arrangement of the holes. There are varieties with few holes and/or stratification which is not very prominent. In such cases, the materials are fairly compact and the off-white color is evenly distributed.

MAIN AESTHETIC CHARACTERISTICS

The main aesthetic variations in white Travertine varieties concerns the color, which may be subject to sudden changes from off-white to grey, especially at right angles to the direction of the rift. Other variations concern the holes. If these are too concentrated or too large, they constitute a structural defect as well as an aesthetic defect since they may reduce the physical-mechanical resistance of the rock. Finally, there may be variations as to the distribution and conformation of the layers. Some varieties are appreciated for the peculiar undulating pattern of the layers, and it should be borne in mind that this may vary considerably in just a small area.

AESTHETIC VARIATIONS AND DEFECTS

The most well-known varieties of white Travertine are quarried in Italy.

PRODUCER COUNTRIES

Availability of white Travertine varieties is fairly limited due to the small number of quarrying areas and the low productivity of the quarries. The blocks are generally medium-sized.

AVAILABILITY

White Travertine varieties are suitable for all the normal uses of dimension stone, both in interiors and exteriors. Owing to the fact that they are not affected by freezing temperatures, they are also appropriate for climates with significant temperature changes. The surface is usually polished or honed. In view of their high porosity, they are easily soiled. Thus, when they are to be used for floorings and bathrooms, etc., they must be filled or reinforced with resin. They can also be used in solid blocks to fulfil structural functions. They are not recommended, however, for damp areas. They are normally cut along the hard way or easy way; when cut along the rift, the holes increase in size.

USES

Travertino Bianco.

MAIN COMMERCIAL VARIETIES

ITALIAN STANDARD				**PHYSICAL-MECHANICAL CHARACTERISTICS** (average reference values)
compression breaking load	940	kg/cm²		
compression breaking load after freezing	935	kg/cm²		
imbibition coefficient (by weight)	1.3	%		
ultimate tensile strength	125	kg/cm²		
impact test	30	cm		
thermal linear expansion coefficient	0.0050	mm/m°C		
frictional wear test		mm		
weight per unit of volume	2.430	kg/m³		
elasticity module	555.000	kg/cm²		
knoop microhardness		kg/mm²		

ASTM STANDARD				**PHYSICAL-MECHANICAL CHARACTERISTICS** (average reference values)
absorption	(C97)	1.2	weight%	
density	(C97)	2.496	kg/cu.m	
compressive strength	(C170)	61	MPa	
modulus of rupture	(C99)		MPa	
flexural strength	(C880)	9.6	MPa	
abrasion resistance	(C241)	19.1	hardness	

WHITE ONYX

MAIN AESTHETIC CHARACTERISTICS
These materials are composed of continuous overlapping bands, from a few centimeters to a few dozen centimeters thick, which form slightly undulating to highly curved patterns. The bands range from off-white to milk white and they sometimes become hyaline. These materials are generally very transparent when held to the light.

AESTHETIC VARIATIONS AND DEFECTS
As in all Onyx varieties, the main aesthetic variation concerns the color, which may have yellow, pink or green shades.

PRODUCER COUNTRIES
White Onyx varieties available on the international market are quarried in Pakistan.

AVAILABILITY
The quantities available are limited.

USES
In view of their aesthetic characteristics and availability, these materials are normally used in interiors for special pieces, including solid pieces, and small facings. They are frequently used for ornaments too. Thanks to their transparency they can be used to create special light effects.

MAIN COMMERCIAL VARIETIES
White Onyx.

PHYSICAL-MECHANICAL CHARACTERISTICS
(average reference values)

			ITALIAN STANDARD
compression breaking load	kg/cm²		
compression breaking load after freezing	kg/cm²		
imbibition coefficient (by weight)	%		
ultimate tensile strength	kg/cm²		
impact test	cm		
thermal linear expansion coefficient	mm/m°C		
frictional wear test	mm		
weight per unit of volume	kg/m³		
elasticity module	kg/cm²		
knoop microhardness	kg/mm²		

PHYSICAL-MECHANICAL CHARACTERISTICS
(average reference values)

				ASTM STANDARD
absorption	(C97)	weight%		
density	(C97)	kg/cu.m		
compressive strength	(C170)	MPa		
modulus of rupture	(C99)	MPa		
flexural strength	(C880)	MPa		
abrasion resistance	(C241)	hardness		

74

YELLOW MARBLE S.S.

These materials have a medium- to fine-grained groundmass, ranging from ivory white to light shades of yellow, crossed by deeper yellow veins, the thickness of which varies from a few millimeters to one centimeter thick. Most of the veins are isoriented subparallel to the rift of the rock.

MAIN AESTHETIC CHARACTERISTICS

The most significant variation is a variation in the color of the groundmass and the veins, which may change radically in just a small area or in some cases verge on a greyish color. The veins may correspond to lines of mechanical weakness and as such may easily give rise to fractures.

AESTHETIC VARIATIONS AND DEFECTS

The most well-known yellow Marble s.s. varieties are produced in Italy and Turkey.

PRODUCER COUNTRIES

Availability of yellow Marble s.s. varieties is fairly limited due to the small number of quarrying areas and the low productivity of the quarries. The blocks are often small- and medium-sized, shapeless blocks.

AVAILABILITY

Yellow Marble s.s. varieties are commonly used for interior facings and low traffic floorings, usually combined with other-colored materials. They are also frequently used for special solid pieces and bathroom furnishings. In view of their limited availability and cost though, they are mostly used for high-quality furnishings. The surface is generally polished so as to enhance the color. These materials often need to be reinforced with a resin backing.

USES

Afyon Yellow, Calacatta Siena, Giallo Siena.

MAIN COMMERCIAL VARIETIES

ITALIAN STANDARD			
compression breaking load	1.803	kg/cm²	
compression breaking load after freezing	1.738	kg/cm²	
imbibition coefficient (by weight)	0.35	%	
ultimate tensile strength	180	kg/cm²	
impact test	29	cm	
thermal linear expansion coefficient	0.0045	mm/m°C	
frictional wear test		mm	
weight per unit of volume	2.800	kg/m³	
elasticity module	840.000	kg/cm²	
knoop microhardness		kg/mm²	

PHYSICAL-MECHANICAL CHARACTERISTICS
(average reference values)

ASTM STANDARD			
absorption	(C97)	0.16	weight%
density	(C97)	2.674	kg/cu.m
compressive strength	(C170)	80.3	MPa
modulus of rupture	(C99)		MPa
flexural strength	(C880)	156	MPa
abrasion resistance	(C241)	12.7	hardness

PHYSICAL-MECHANICAL CHARACTERISTICS
(average reference values)

YELLOW LIMESTONE

MAIN AESTHETIC CHARACTERISTICS

These materials have a yellow groundmass with varying shades of cream and/or pink. The groundmass is sometimes crossed by a close-knit, irregular pattern of thin, pink or reddish-colored veins, only some of which correspond to *stylolites*.

AESTHETIC VARIATIONS AND DEFECTS

The most significant aesthetic variations concern the color. In particular, the yellow color of the groundmass may vary in just a short area and the pink or cream shadings may be larger and more numerous than can be seen on the samples.

PRODUCER COUNTRIES

The most well-known varieties of yellow Limestone are extracted in Italy, Spain and Israel.

AVAILABILITY

Availability of these materials is fairly limited due to the small number of quarrying areas and the low productivity of the quarries. The blocks are usually large.

USES

Yellow Limestone varieties are normally used in interiors for facings and floorings, sometimes combined with other colors.
The surface is generally polished so as to enhance the color.

MAIN COMMERCIAL VARIETIES

Crema Valencia, Giallo Reale, Giallo Tafouk.

PHYSICAL-MECHANICAL CHARACTERISTICS
(average reference values)

compression breaking load	1.975	kg/cm²	ITALIAN STANDARD
compression breaking load after freezing	1.876	kg/cm²	
imbibition coefficient (by weight)	0.30	%	
ultimate tensile strength	120	kg/cm²	
impact test	30	cm	
thermal linear expansion coefficient	0.0071	mm/m°C	
frictional wear test		mm	
weight per unit of volume	2.675	kg/m³	
elasticity module		kg/cm²	
knoop microhardness		kg/mm²	

PHYSICAL-MECHANICAL CHARACTERISTICS
(average reference values)

absorption	(C97)	0.13	weight%	ASTM STANDARD
density	(C97)	2.700	kg/cu.m	
compressive strength	(C170)	140	MPa	
modulus of rupture	(C99)		MPa	
flexural strength	(C880)	9.0	MPa	
abrasion resistance	(C241)	43	hardness	

YELLOW TRAVERTINE

These materials are formed by the overlapping of subhorizontal layers a few centimeters thick which give the rock a stratified appearance. The rocky mass is not usually compact and has a number of small holes more or less parallel to the direction of the layers. The layers are often fairly straight although in some varieties they are undulating. The yellow color is not generally evenly distributed and occurs in different shades from one layer to the next. The stratified arrangement of the layers gives the rock a prominent rift which is often accentuated by the arrangement of the holes. There are varieties with few holes and/or stratification which is not very prominent. In such cases, the materials are fairly compact and the color is evenly distributed.

The main aesthetic variations in yellow Travertine is a variation in the color which may undergo sudden changes, especially at right angles to the direction of the rift. Other variations concern the holes. If these are too concentrated or too large, they constitute a structural defect as well as an aesthetic defect since they may reduce the physical-mechanical resistance of the rock. Finally, there may be variations as to the distribution and conformation of the layers. Some varieties are appreciated for the peculiar undulating pattern of the layers and it should be borne in mind that this may vary considerably in just a small area.

AESTHETIC VARIATIONS AND DEFECTS

Traditionally, yellow Travertine is quarried in Iran; other varieties come from the United States.

PRODUCER COUNTRIES

Yellow Travertine is not readily available owing to the few quarrying areas in existence and the low productivity of the quarries. The blocks are generally small- and medium-sized.

AVAILABILITY

Yellow Travertine varieties are suitable for all the normal uses of dimension stone, both in interiors and exteriors. Owing to the fact that they are not affected by freezing temperatures, they are also appropriate for climates with significant temperature changes. However, in view of their limited availability and color characteristics, they are mostly used for luxury interiors and special solid pieces. The surface is usually polished or honed. In view of their high porosity, they are easily soiled. Thus, when they are to be used for floorings and bathrooms, etc., they must be filled or reinforced with resin. Yellow travertine varieties are not recommended, however, for damp areas. They are normally cut along the hard way or easy way; when cut along the rift, the holes increase in size.

USES

Golden Travertine, Golden Travertine Vein Cut.

MAIN COMMERCIAL VARIETIES

ITALIAN STANDARD			
compression breaking load	kg/cm²		
compression breaking load after freezing	kg/cm²		
imbibition coefficient (by weight)	%		
ultimate tensile strength	kg/cm²		
impact test	cm		
thermal linear expansion coefficient	mm/m°C		
frictional wear test	mm		
weight per unit of volume	kg/m³		
elasticity module	kg/cm²		
knoop microhardness	kg/mm²		

PHYSICAL-MECHANICAL CHARACTERISTICS
(average reference values)

ASTM STANDARD				
absorption	(C97)	0.20	weight%
density	(C97)	2.480	kg/cu.m
compressive strength	(C170)	70.1	MPa
modulus of rupture	(C99)		MPa
flexural strength	(C880)	7.5	MPa
abrasion resistance	(C241)		hardness

PHYSICAL-MECHANICAL CHARACTERISTICS
(average reference values)

77

YELLOW ONYX

MAIN AESTHETIC CHARACTERISTICS

These materials are composed of continuous overlapping bands on average a few centimeters thick which form slightly undulating to highly curved patterns. The bands are light yellow in color, sometimes with honey-colored shades which gradually turn into ivory and then white. These materials are generally very transparent when held to the light.

AESTHETIC VARIATIONS AND DEFECTS

As in all Onyx varieties, the main aesthetic variation concerns the color, which may vary considerably.

PRODUCER COUNTRIES

The most well-known yellow Onyx varieties available on the international market are quarried in Egypt.

AVAILABILITY

The quantities available are rather limited. The blocks are medium and large.

USES

In view of their aesthetic characteristics and availability, these materials are usually used in interiors for special pieces, including solid pieces, and small facings. They are frequently used for ornaments too. Thanks to their transparency, they can be used to create special light effects.

MAIN COMMERCIAL VARIETIES

Alabastro Egiziano.

PHYSICAL-MECHANICAL CHARACTERISTICS
(average reference values)

compression breaking load	kg/cm^2	ITALIAN
compression breaking load after freezing	kg/cm^2	STANDARD
imbibition coefficient (by weight)	%	
ultimate tensile strength	kg/cm^2	
impact test	cm	
thermal linear expansion coefficient	mm/m°C	
frictional wear test	mm	
weight per unit of volume	kg/m^3	
elasticity module	kg/cm^2	
knoop microhardness	kg/mm^2	

PHYSICAL-MECHANICAL CHARACTERISTICS
(average reference values)

absorption	(C97)	weight%	ASTM
density	(C97)	kg/cu.m	STANDARD
compressive strength	(C170)	MPa	
modulus of rupture	(C99)	MPa	
flexural strength	(C880)	MPa	
abrasion resistance	(C241)	hardness	

BEIGE MARBLE S.S.

These materials have a whitish-colored groundmass with frequent beige-colored speckles. The latter are elongated and narrow with blurred edges and often create a wavy pattern which gives the rock a definite orientation (rift).

The main aesthetic variation is a variation in the deepness of the beige color of the veins.

The most well-known beige Marble s.s. variety is produced in Namibia.

Availability of these materials is limited owing to the small number of quarrying areas and the low productivity of the quarries. The blocks vary in size from small to large.

In view of their aesthetic characteristics and availability, beige Marble s.s. varieties are mostly used in interiors for small floorings and facings. The surface is polished.

Karibib.

ITALIAN STANDARD			
compression breaking load	2.680	kg/cm^2	
compression breaking load after freezing	2.540	kg/cm^2	
imbibition coefficient (by weight)	0.30	%	
ultimate tensile strength	165	kg/cm^2	
impact test	35	cm	
thermal linear expansion coefficient	0.0060	mm/m°C	
frictional wear test		mm	
weight per unit of volume	2.715	kg/m^3	
elasticity module		kg/cm^2	
knoop microhardness		kg/mm^2	

PHYSICAL-MECHANICAL CHARACTERISTICS
(average reference values)

ASTM STANDARD				
absorption	(C97)		weight%	
density	(C97)	2.850	kg/cu.m	
compressive strength	(C170)	250	MPa	
modulus of rupture	(C99)	22.4	MPa	
flexural strength	(C880)		MPa	
abrasion resistance	(C241)		hardness	

PHYSICAL-MECHANICAL CHARACTERISTICS
(average reference values)

BEIGE LIMESTONE

MAIN AESTHETIC CHARACTERISTICS

There are three different aesthetic types of beige-colored limestone. Aesthetic type (i) includes materials with a fine- to very fine-grained groundmass, the color and pattern of which are essentially uniform. The color is generally light beige, although it sometimes occurs in dark shades. In some varieties the groundmass may have whitish-colored shadings a few centimeters across due to the presence of fossils. These are unevenly distributed over the groundmass. Another almost constant feature of these materials is the occurrence of thin veins, varying from a yellowish color to a reddish color or with a hyaline appearance, which cross the groundmass fairly frequently. These veins (stylolites) always form a zigzag pattern subparallel to the rift of the rock.

In aesthetic type (ii), the groundmass is composed of alternating light beige and dark beige bands, from a few millimeters to a few centimeters thick, which lie over one another. In some varieties these bands are slightly red in color. The bands are generally fairly straight and in a few cases create bland waves which are still subparallel to the rift of the rock.

Aesthetic type (iii) varieties have a scanty medium- to coarse-grained groundmass due to the small number of lithoid clasts and a larger number of fossils, the size of which varies from a few millimeters to a few centimeters. These materials are normally light or dark beige with occasional yellowish- or greyish-colored shades. In some varieties the overall color may be determined by the color of the more frequent or larger clasts. The clasts and fossils often form a regular pattern subparallel to the rift of the rock. Stylotites may also occur in varieties belonging to this third aesthetic type, although in smaller quantities than in aesthetic type (i). The color of the latter varies from yellow to red.

AESTHETIC VARIATIONS AND DEFECTS

The main variations in aesthetic type (i) concern the color. The lighter shades are generally the most popular and hence the ones with a higher commercial value. Another variation is the occurrence of fossils or clasts which are either too numerous or too prominent and therefore adversely affect the color and pattern typical of these varieties. In addition, the veins fairly frequently correspond to areas with low mechanical resistance.

In aesthetic type (ii), the bands which form the groundmass of the rock are subject to variations in shape and thickness. Since these are the main aesthetic characteristics, a certain constancy is usually required for each individual supply.

Aesthetic type (iii) is more subject to color and pattern variations than the other two types. The pattern variations, however, are generally fairly well tolerated since the pattern is not very uniform anyway. As far as color variations are concerned though, these are considered defects since they may reduce the overall quality of the project. There may be grey spots of varying shapes and sizes in aesthetic type (i) and (iii) materials in particular.

PHYSICAL-MECHANICAL CHARACTERISTICS
(average reference values)

absorption	(C97)	0.25	weight%	ASTM STANDARD
density	(C97)	2.692	kg/cu.m	
compressive strength	(C170)	129.5	MPa	
modulus of rupture	(C99)		MPa	
flexural strength	(C880)	8.2	MPa	
abrasion resistance	(C241)	37.9	hardness	

Beige-colored limestone varieties are fairly common, even though there are not many commercial productions on the international market. The main producer countries are Italy and Spain and, on a smaller scale, Greece, Egypt and Turkey. Interesting materials, but ones which are normally limited to local or regional markets, are produced in Mexico, Indonesia, Malaysia, the Philippines and some Caribbean countries.

Beige limestone varieties are generally readily available in good quantities. Of the three types described, type (iii) is the most common and is available in medium- and large-sized blocks. Availability of types (i) and (ii) may be limited, especially in the case of good-quality materials. The blocks are often medium and small and the side parallel to the hard way is much shorter than the side corresponding to the rift (blocks with a *falda bassa*, i.e., blocks which are not very thick).

AVAILABILITY

BEIGE MARBLE

Beige limestone varieties generally have the right physical-mechanical properties for all the normal uses of dimension stone, in interiors and exteriors alike. As for the surface treatment, polishing is generally preferred for interiors, while impact treatment (which lightens the material) or honing are preferred for exteriors. Aesthetic type (ii) materials in particular, with their well-defined orientation, are particularly suitable for decorative geometric patterns. Some varieties, mostly type (i) varieties, require a net backing. In view of the aesthetic characteristics and the medium-sized blocks available, beige limestone varieties are generally used in the form of tiles up to 60 x 60 cm and are frequently used for skirting boards and stairs. They are usually cut along the hard way or easy way. Some varieties are also fairly frequently used as solid dimension blocks for structural functions.

USES

Aesthetic type (i): Ambrato, Botticino Classico, Botticino Fiorito, Botticino Royal, Botticino Semiclassico, Crema Marfil, Filettato America, Filetto Rosso Trani, Fiorito Dalia, Galala, Rosa San Marco, Trani Chiaro, Trani Classico, Trani Cocciolato, Trani Fiorito.
Aesthetic type (ii): Serpeggiante Italia, Silvabella Classico.
Aesthetic type (iii): Botticino Sicilia, Breccia Sarda Chiara, Breccia Sarda Scura, Chiampo Perlato, Cremo Supremo, Crema Nuova, Mezza Perla, Napoleon Mouchete, Nocciolato Chiaro, Perla Sicilia, Perlatino, Perlato Sicilia, Perlato Royal, Perlato Svevo, Spuma di Mare.

MAIN COMMERCIAL VARIETIES

		(i)	(ii)	(iii)	
ITALIAN STANDARD	compression breaking load	1.854	2.275	1.610	kg/cm²
	compression breaking load after freezing	1.775	2.224	1.454	kg/cm²
	imbibition coefficient (by weight)	0.20	0.20	0.40	%
	ultimate tensile strength	171	224	165	kg/cm²
	impact test	31	23	34	cm
	thermal linear expansion coefficient	0.0043	0.0043	0.0039	mm/m°C
	frictional wear test				mm
	weight per unit of volume	2.669	2.665	2.669	kg/m³
	elasticity module	839.400	810.000	763.300	kg/cm²
	knoop microhardness	250		140	kg/mm²

PHYSICAL-MECHANICAL CHARACTERISTICS
(average reference values)

81

BEIGE TRAVERTINE

MAIN AESTHETIC CHARACTERISTICS

These fine-grained materials are formed by the overlapping of subhorizontal layers a few centimeters thick which give the rock a stratified appearance. The rocky mass is not usually compact and has a number of small holes more or less parallel to the direction of the layers. The layers are often fairly straight, although in some varieties they are undulating. The beige color is not generally evenly distributed and varies from one layer to the next. The stratified arrangement of the layers gives the rock a prominent rift which is often accentuated by the arrangement of the holes. There are varieties with few holes and/or stratification which is not very prominent. In such cases, the materials are fairly compact and the beige color is evenly distributed.

AESTHETIC VARIATIONS AND DEFECTS

The main aesthetic variation in beige travertine concerns the color, which may be subject to sudden changes, especially at right angles to the direction of the rift. Other variations concern the holes. If these are too concentrated or too large, they constitute a structural defect as well as an aesthetic defect, since they may reduce the physical-mechanical resistance of the rock. Finally, there may be variations as to the distribution and conformation of the layers. Some varieties are appreciated for the peculiar undulating pattern of the layers, and it should be borne in mind that this may vary considerably in just a small area.

PRODUCER COUNTRIES

The main producer country of beige travertine is Italy. Smaller quantities are also produced in Spain, Turkey and Mexico.

AVAILABILITY

The main varieties of Italian travertine are available in large quantities of medium- and large-sized blocks. Supply times may be longer for certain varieties. The travertine varieties produced in the other countries are mainly placed on the local and regional markets.

USES

Beige travertine varieties are suitable for all the normal uses of dimension stone, both in interiors and exteriors. Owing to the fact that they are not affected by freezing temperatures, they are also appropriate for climates with significant temperature changes. The surface is usually polished or honed. In view of their high porosity, they are easily soiled. Thus, when they are to be used for floorings and bathrooms, etc., they must be filled or reinforced with resin. They can also be used in solid blocks to fulfil structural functions. They are not recommended, however, for damp areas. They are normally cut along the hard way or easy way; when cut along the rift, the holes increase in size.

MAIN COMMERCIAL VARIETIES

Travertino Iberico, Travertino Romano Chiaro; Travertino Romano Classico; Travertino Romano Classico in Falda, Travertino Scabas, Travertino Striato.

PHYSICAL-MECHANICAL CHARACTERISTICS
(average reference values)

compression breaking load	957	kg/cm²	ITALIAN
compression breaking load after freezing	880	kg/cm²	STANDARD
imbibition coefficient (by weight)	1.0	%	
ultimate tensile strength	127	kg/cm²	
impact test	29	cm	
thermal linear expansion coefficient	0.0045	mm/m°C	
frictional wear test		mm	
weight per unit of volume	2.410	kg/m³	
elasticity module	525.000	kg/cm²	
knoop microhardness		kg/mm²	

PHYSICAL-MECHANICAL CHARACTERISTICS
(average reference values)

absorption	(C97)	1.2	weight%	ASTM
density	(C97)	2.496	kg/cu.m	STANDARD
compressive strength	(C170)	61	MPa	
modulus of rupture	(C99)		MPa	
flexural strength	(C880)	9.6	MPa	
abrasion resistance	(C241)	19.1	hardness	

BEIGE ONYX

These materials are composed of continuous overlapping bands on average a few centimeters thick, which form slightly undulating to highly curved patterns. The bands are alternately beige and off-white in color and in places there are thinner pinkish-colored bands. These materials are generally very transparent when held to the light.

As in all Onyx varieties, the main aesthetic variation concerns the color, which may vary considerably.

Beige Onyx varieties available on the international market are quarried in Pakistan.

The quantities available are limited.

In view of their aesthetic characteristics and availability, these materials are usually used in interiors for special pieces, including solid pieces, and small facings. They are frequently used for ornaments, too. Thanks to their transparency, they can be used to create special light effects.

Brown Onyx.

MAIN AESTHETIC CHARACTERISTICS

AESTHETIC VARIATIONS AND DEFECTS

PRODUCER COUNTRIES

BEIGE MARBLE

AVAILABILITY

USES

MAIN COMMERCIAL VARIETIES

ITALIAN STANDARD			**PHYSICAL-MECHANICAL CHARACTERISTICS** (average reference values)
compression breaking load	kg/cm^2		
compression breaking load after freezing	kg/cm^2		
imbibition coefficient (by weight)	%		
ultimate tensile strength	kg/cm^2		
impact test	cm		
thermal linear expansion coefficient	mm/m°C		
frictional wear test	mm		
weight per unit of volume	kg/m^3		
elasticity module	kg/cm^2		
knoop microhardness	kg/mm^2		

ASTM STANDARD				**PHYSICAL-MECHANICAL CHARACTERISTICS** (average reference values)
absorption	(C97)	weight%		
density	(C97)	kg/cu.m		
compressive strength	(C170)	MPa		
modulus of rupture	(C99)	MPa		
flexural strength	(C880)	MPa		
abrasion resistance	(C241)	hardness		

83

BROWN MARBLE S.S.

MAIN AESTHETIC CHARACTERISTICS

These materials have a medium- to coarse-grained crystalline beige or light brown groundmass. This is crossed by generally straight or vaguely undulating bands of varying shades of brown, the thickness and length of which varies considerably.

AESTHETIC VARIATIONS AND DEFECTS

The color and pattern of these materials may vary in just a small area, thereby having a considerable effect on their aesthetic characteristics.

PRODUCER COUNTRIES

The most well-known brown Marble s.s. varieties are produced in Brazil.

AVAILABILITY

Availability of brown Marble s.s. varieties is fairly limited due to the small number of quarrying areas and the significant aesthetic variations. The blocks are medium and large.

USES

Brown Marble s.s. varieties are mostly used in interiors for facings, special solid pieces and bathroom furnishings (in the form of tiles or, preferably, slabs). Strict quality control procedures are recommended. The surface is polished.

MAIN COMMERCIAL VARIETIES

Chocolate.

BROWN MARBLE

PHYSICAL-MECHANICAL CHARACTERISTICS

(average reference values)

compression breaking load	2.440	kg/cm²	ITALIAN
compression breaking load after freezing	2.300	kg/cm²	STANDARD
imbibition coefficient (by weight)	0.30	%	
ultimate tensile strength	120	kg/cm²	
impact test	35	cm	
thermal linear expansion coefficient	0.050	mm/m°C	
frictional wear test		mm	
weight per unit of volume	2.760	kg/m³	
elasticity module		kg/cm²	
knoop microhardness		kg/mm²	

PHYSICAL-MECHANICAL CHARACTERISTICS

(average reference values)

absorption	(C97)	weight%	ASTM
density	(C97)	kg/cu.m	STANDARD
compressive strength	(C170)	MPa	
modulus of rupture	(C99)	MPa	
flexural strength	(C880)	MPa	
abrasion resistance	(C241)	hardness	

BROWN LIMESTONE

There are two aesthetic types of brown Limestone. Type (i) varieties are composed of more or less subovoidal, pinky-beige nodules, on average a few centimeters across, embedded in a brown groundmass, which varies in quantity. The nodules are isoriented and give the materials a well-defined orientation (rift). Aesthetic type (ii) varieties are breccias composed of irregular-shaped, dark brown lithoid clasts, the size of which varies from a few millimeters to a few centimeters across, imbedded in a light brown groundmass which varies in quantity. In places, the groundmass is replaced by a calcite cement which creates white flakes a few centimeters across. Both the clasts and the groundmass are crossed by a close-knit pattern of irregular, thread-like, beige-colored veins.

The color may vary considerably, especially in aesthetic type (ii) varieties. The latter also have structural defects such as areas of mechanical weakness coinciding with the veins and holes a few centimeters across.

AESTHETIC VARIATIONS AND DEFECTS

Aesthetic type (i) varieties are mainly produced in Italy, while type (ii) varieties are quarried in Spain and Italy.

PRODUCER COUNTRIES

BROWN MARBLE

Aesthetic type (i) materials are available in limited quantities, generally in medium-sized blocks. Type (ii) materials, on the other hand, are available in good quantities, in line with market requirements, and in large-sized blocks.

AVAILABILITY

Brown Limestone varieties are normally used in interiors for floorings and, to a lesser extent, facings. Aesthetic type (i) materials are frequently used for solid pieces and aesthetic type (ii) materials for bathroom furnishings. The materials often have to be reinforced with netting. Quality-control procedures are always recommended.

USES

Aesthetic type (i) Porfirico Ramello Bruno.
Aesthetic type (ii): Breccia Paradiso, Marron Emperador, Marron Imperial.

MAIN COMMERCIAL VARIETIES

ITALIAN STANDARD					**PHYSICAL-MECHANICAL CHARACTERISTICS** (average reference values)
compression breaking load	1.760	1.580	kg/cm²		
compression breaking load after freezing	1.620	1.580	kg/cm²		
imbibition coefficient (by weight)	0.08	0.40	%		
ultimate tensile strength	175	210	kg/cm²		
impact test	35	35	cm		
thermal linear expansion coefficient	0.0050		mm/m°C		
frictional wear test		1.9	mm		
weight per unit of volume	2.650	2.650	kg/m³		
elasticity module	680.000		kg/cm²		
knoop microhardness			kg/mm²		

ASTM STANDARD				**PHYSICAL-MECHANICAL CHARACTERISTICS** (average reference values)
absorption	(C97)	0.20	weight%	
density	(C97)	2.620	kg/cu.m	
compressive strength	(C170)	87	MPa	
modulus of rupture	(C99)		MPa	
flexural strength	(C880)	57	MPa	
abrasion resistance	(C241)		hardness	

BROWN TRAVERTINE

BROWN
MARBLE

MAIN AESTHETIC CHARACTERISTICS

These materials are formed by the overlapping of subhorizontal layers a few centimeters thick, which give the rock a stratified appearance. The rocky mass is not usually compact and has a number of small holes more or less parallel to the direction of the layers. The layers are often fairly straight although in some varieties they are undulating. The brown color is not generally evenly distributed and occurs in different shades from one layer to the next. The stratified arrangement of the layers gives the rock a prominent rift, which is often accentuated by the arrangement of the holes. There are varieties with few holes and/or stratification which is not very prominent. In such cases, the materials are fairly compact and the color is evenly distributed.

AESTHETIC VARIATIONS AND DEFECTS

The main aesthetic variation in brown Travertine concerns the color, which may undergo sudden changes, especially at right angles to the direction of the rift. Other variations concern the holes. If these are too concentrated or too large, they constitute a structural defect as well as an aesthetic defect, since they may reduce the physical-mechanical resistance of the rock. Finally, there may be variations as to the distribution and conformation of the layers. Some varieties are appreciated for the peculiar undulating pattern of the layers, and it should be borne in mind that this may vary considerably in just a small area.

PRODUCER COUNTRIES

The main producer country of brown Travertine is Italy.

AVAILABILITY

The main varieties of brown Travertine are available in fairly good quantities in medium- and large-sized blocks. Supply times may be longer for certain varieties. The brown Travertine varieties produced in other countries are mainly consumed by the national and regional markets.

USES

Brown Travertine varieties are suitable for all the normal uses of dimension stone, both in interiors and exteriors. Owing to the fact that they are not affected by freezing temperatures, they are also appropriate for climates with significant temperature changes. The surface is usually polished or honed. In view of their high porosity, brown Travertine varieties are easily soiled, although not as easily as lighter-colored Travertine. Thus, when they are to be used for floorings and bathrooms, etc., they must be filled or reinforced with resin. They can also be used in solid blocks to fulfil structural functions. Brown Travertine varieties are not recommended, however, for damp areas. They are normally cut along the hard way or easy way; when cut along the rift, the holes increase in size.

MAIN COMMERCIAL VARIETIES

Travertino Noce, Travertino Noce in falda.

PHYSICAL-MECHANICAL CHARACTERISTICS
(average reference values)

			ITALIAN STANDARD
compression breaking load	1.160	kg/cm²	
compression breaking load after freezing	1.150	kg/cm²	
imbibition coefficient (by weight)	1.6	%	
ultimate tensile strength	160	kg/cm²	
impact test	35	cm	
thermal linear expansion coefficient	0.0060	mm/m°C	
frictional wear test		mm	
weight per unit of volume	2.415	kg/m³	
elasticity module	555.000	kg/cm²	
knoop microhardness		kg/mm²	

PHYSICAL-MECHANICAL CHARACTERISTICS
(average reference values)

			ASTM STANDARD
absorption	(C97)	weight%	
density	(C97)	kg/cu.m	
compressive strength	(C170)	MPa	
modulus of rupture	(C99)	MPa	
flexural strength	(C880)	MPa	
abrasion resistance	(C241)	hardness	

BROWN ONYX

These materials are composed of continuous overlapping bands, on average a few centimeters thick, which form slightly undulating to highly curved patterns. The bands are alternately brown-red and beige. In some varieties, the color variation between the different bands is a variation in the deepness of the brown-red color.

As in all Onyx varieties, the main aesthetic variation concerns the color, which may vary considerably.

The brown Onyx varieties available on the international market are quarried in Tanzania.

The quantities available are rather limited.

In view of their aesthetic characteristics and availability, these materials are normally used in interiors for special pieces, including solid pieces, and small facings.

Tanzania Brown Onyx.

MAIN AESTHETIC CHARACTERISTICS

AESTHETIC VARIATIONS AND DEFECTS

PRODUCER COUNTRIES

AVAILABILITY

USES

MAIN COMMERCIAL VARIETIES

BROWN MARBLE

ITALIAN STANDARD		
compression breaking load	kg/cm^2	
compression breaking load after freezing	kg/cm^2	
imbibition coefficient (by weight)	%	
ultimate tensile strength	kg/cm^2	
impact test	cm	
thermal linear expansion coefficient	mm/m°C	
frictional wear test	mm	
weight per unit of volume	kg/m^3	
elasticity module	kg/cm^2	
knoop microhardness	kg/mm^2	

PHYSICAL-MECHANICAL CHARACTERISTICS
(average reference values)

ASTM STANDARD			
absorption	(C97)	weight%	
density	(C97)	kg/cu.m	
compressive strength	(C170)	MPa	
modulus of rupture	(C99)	MPa	
flexural strength	(C880)	MPa	
abrasion resistance	(C241)	hardness	

PHYSICAL-MECHANICAL CHARACTERISTICS
(average reference values)

RED MARBLE S.S.

MAIN AESTHETIC CHARACTERISTICS
Red Marble s.s. varieties can be classed according to two different aesthetic types. Type (i) includes breccia materials composed of various shades of red and green clasts (varying in shape and size) imbedded in a reddish-colored groundmass which sometimes has misshapen whitish-colored spots. Both the clasts and the groundmass may be crossed by white veins, the thickness and orientation of which are variable. The second type (ii) varieties have a fine-grained, dark red groundmass intermingled with numerous, light grey lenticular elements a few millimeters long. The grey elements are usually fairly evenly distributed and their size is constant.

AESTHETIC VARIATIONS AND DEFECTS
As regards type (i) materials, there may be considerable variations in terms of both structure and color. The color is influenced by the frequency of the white veins as well as the varying shades of the clasts. The most common variations as regards type (ii) are the uneven distribution of the grey elements and the occurrence of white veins. If the latter are frequent, they may constitute a defect and thereby reduce the commercial value of the materials.

PRODUCER COUNTRIES
The main producer country of aesthetic type (i) varieties is Turkey, although there is sporadic production in Italy too. Aesthetic type (ii) varieties are from Turkey.

AVAILABILITY
Availability of aesthetic type (i) varieties is fairly limited due to the small number of quarrying areas and the low productivity of the quarries. The blocks are medium and large and usually require a *seasoning* period. Aesthetic type (ii) varieties come from one quarrying area only which does, however, guarantee a certain continuity in production. The blocks are generally medium and small.

USES
Aesthetic type (i) varieties can be used for interior facings and floorings and special pieces (e.g., table tops). The surface is always polished. These materials fairly frequently need to be reinforced with resin and netting, especially in the case of large slabs. Their use is not recommended for exteriors, since the polished surface does not last long. Aesthetic type (ii) varieties can be used for facings, floorings and pavings, both in interiors and exteriors, although in view of their aesthetic characteristics they are preferred for interiors. These materials are fairly frequently used for special pieces.

MAIN COMMERCIAL VARIETIES
Aesthetic type (i): Rosso Antico d'Italia, Rosso Lepanto.
Aesthetic type (ii): Rosso Laguna.

PHYSICAL-MECHANICAL CHARACTERISTICS
(average reference values)

	(i)	(ii)		
compression breaking load	1.377	1.630	kg/cm²	ITALIAN
compression breaking load after freezing	1.208	1.159	kg/cm²	STANDARD
imbibition coefficient (by weight)	0.57	0.20	%	
ultimate tensile strength	98	130	kg/cm²	
impact test	31	33	cm	
thermal linear expansion coefficient	0.0053		mm/m°C	
frictional wear test			mm	
weight per unit of volume	2.629	2.695	kg/m³	
elasticity module	460.000		kg/cm²	
knoop microhardness			kg/mm²	

PHYSICAL-MECHANICAL CHARACTERISTICS
(average reference values)

absorption	(C97)	weight%		ASTM
density	(C97)	kg/cu.m		STANDARD
compressive strength	(C170)	MPa		
modulus of rupture	(C99)	MPa		
flexural strength	(C880)	MPa		
abrasion resistance	(C241)	hardness		

RED MARBLE

RED LIMESTONE

There are three aesthetic types of red Limestone. Type (i) materials are composed of roundish, light red nodules embedded in a dark red groundmass which varies in quantity. The nodules are generally a few centimeters across but sometimes they merge into one another to form little, subbovoidal masses several centimeters across. They are oriented parallel to the rift of the rock.
Aesthetic type (ii) varieties are composed of a medium- to fine-grained, red groundmass which varies from brick red to blood red according to the different commercial varieties. The groundmass is crossed by more or less straight, white veins varying in direction and/or has white nodules and speckles, again varying in size and shape. Aesthetic type (iii) materials are breccias composed of a medium- to fine-grained, dark red groundmass intermingled with varying quantities of red or whitish-colored clasts and/or fossils.

The main aesthetic variation in type (i) varieties concerns the color which may vary considerably from one block to the next. Other variations include white veins which may adversely affect the chromatic and textural uniformity of the materials, thereby reducing their commercial value, and in some cases they may constitute real defects. *Magrosità* is also a common feature of some varieties. As regards type (ii) varieties, the red color may vary considerably too. In addition, though, the white elements (veins, but above all clasts and fossils) may reduce the deepness of the overall red color of the materials, thereby reducing their commercial value. In just a few cases, especially in the darker varieties, the materials have a high percentage of impurities, which makes them excessively fragile and/or quite difficult to polish. Holes quite often occur in the blocks of these materials which measure from a few centimeters to a few dozen centimeters across.
The variations in aesthetic type (iii) concern both the color, which may verge on pink, and the breccia pattern, which may have different conformations. The color variations generally reduce the value of the material, while the pattern variations are often tolerated by the market as long as they are considered normal variations typical of breccia materials.

MAIN AESTHETIC CHARACTERISTICS

AESTHETIC VARIATIONS AND DEFECTS

RED MARBLE

			(i)	(ii)	(iii)	
absorption	(C97)		0.17	0.11	0.21	weight%
density	(C97)		2.681	2.470	2.730	kg/cu.m
compressive strength	(C170)		109	110	93	MPa
modulus of rupture	(C99)					MPa
flexural strength	(C880)		10.7	10.0	8.9	MPa
abrasion resistance	(C241)				22.6	hardness

ASTM STANDARD

PHYSICAL-MECHANICAL CHARACTERISTICS
(average reference values)

89

PRODUCER COUNTRIES   The large majority of aesthetic type (i) varieties are produced in Italy, although they are also produced on a smaller scale in France and Hungary. Aesthetic type (ii) varieties are quarried in France, Spain and Albania and, on a smaller scale, in Italy, Morocco and Georgia. Aesthetic type (iii) varieties are quarried in Italy, Spain and Albania.

AVAILABILITY   All three aesthetic types of these materials are generally available in medium to small quantities, especially in the case of high-quality materials. Thus, when large quantities are required, checks on supply times and careful quality control procedures are recommended, especially for types (ii) and (iii). Most blocks are medium-sized.

USES   Red Limestone varieties are normally used in interiors for facings and, less frequently, floorings where they are often combined with other-colored materials. In many cases, they are also suitable for exteriors, but their aesthetic characteristics limit this use. The surface treatment usually applied is polishing, although in some cases impact treatment is preferred. Some varieties have to be reinforced with netting.

MAIN COMMERCIAL VARIETIES   Aesthetic type (i): Porfirico Ramello Rosso, Rosso Asiago, Rosso Mangiaboschi, Rosso Verona, Rouge Griotte.
Aesthetic type (ii): Duquesa Rosada, Pelo Red, Portasanta, Rojo Alicante, Rojo Coralito, Rojo Daniel, Rosso Agadir, Rosso Collemandina, Rouge France Isabelle, Rosso di Russia, Rosso S. Agata, Rouge France Languedoc.
Aesthetic type (iii): Arabescato Orobico Rosso, Breccia Pernice, Rosso Carpazi.

RED MARBLE

PHYSICAL-MECHANICAL CHARACTERISTICS
(average reference values)

	(i)	(ii)	(iii)		
compression breaking load	1.703	1.562	1.611	kg/cm^2	ITALIAN STANDARD
compression breaking load after freezing	1.579	1.261	1.602	kg/cm^2	
imbibition coefficient (by weight)	0.13	0.13	0.13	%	
ultimate tensile strength	137	139	126	kg/cm^2	
impact test	37	32	37	cm	
thermal linear expansion coefficient	0.0071		0.0052	mm/m°C	
frictional wear test		2.6		mm	
weight per unit of volume	2.692	2.688	2.702	kg/m^3	
elasticity module	680.000			kg/cm^2	
knoop microhardness				kg/mm^2	

RED TRAVERTINE

These materials are formed by the overlapping of subhorizontal layers a few centimeters thick, which give the rock a stratified appearance. The rocky mass is not usually compact and has a number of small holes more or less parallel to the direction of the layers. The layers are often fairly straight although in some varieties they are undulating. The red color is not generally evenly distributed and varies from one layer to the next. The stratified arrangement of the layers gives the rock a prominent rift, which is often accentuated by the arrangement of the holes. There are varieties with few holes and/ or stratification which is not very prominent. In such cases, the materials are fairly compact and the color is fairly evenly distributed.

MAIN AESTHETIC CHARACTERISTICS

The main aesthetic variation concerns the color, which may be subject to sudden changes, especially at right angles to the direction of the rift. Other variations concern the holes. If these are too concentrated or too large, they constitute a structural defect as well as an aesthetic defect, since they may reduce the physical-mechanical resistance of the rock. Finally, there may be variations as to the distribution and conformation of the layers. Some varieties are appreciated for the peculiar undulating pattern of the layers, and it should be borne in mind that this may vary considerably in just a small area.

AESTHETIC VARIATIONS AND DEFECTS

The traditional producer country of red Travertine is Iran, although very small quantities are also quarried in Ecuador.

PRODUCER COUNTRIES

RED MARBLE

Availability of red Travertine is fairly limited due to the small number of quarrying areas and the low productivity of the quarries. The blocks are generally medium-sized.

AVAILABILITY

Red Travertine varieties are suitable for all the normal uses of dimension stone, both in interiors and exteriors. Owing to the fact that they are not affected by freezing temperatures, they are also appropriate for climates with significant temperature changes. However, in view of their limited availability and peculiar color characteristics, they are mostly used for luxury interiors and special solid pieces. The surface is usually polished or honed. In view of their high porosity, they are easily soiled. Thus, when they are to be used for floorings and bathrooms, etc., they must be filled or reinforced with resin. They can also be used in solid blocks to fulfil structural functions. Red Travertine varieties are not recommended, however, for damp areas. They are normally cut along the hard way or easy way; when cut along the rift, the holes increase in size.

USES

Travertino Rosso Persiano.

MAIN COMMERCIAL VARIETIES

ITALIAN STANDARD			
compression breaking load	1.220	kg/cm²
compression breaking load after freezing	1.210	kg/cm²
imbibition coefficient (by weight)	0.11	%
ultimate tensile strength	150	kg/cm²
impact test	55	cm
thermal linear expansion coefficient	0.0035	mm/m°C
frictional wear test		mm
weight per unit of volume	2.430	kg/m³
elasticity module	520.000	kg/cm²
knoop microhardness		kg/mm²

PHYSICAL-MECHANICAL CHARACTERISTICS
(average reference values)

ASTM STANDARD		
absorption	(C97)	weight%
density	(C97)	kg/cu.m
compressive strength	(C170)	MPa
modulus of rupture	(C99)	MPa
flexural strength	(C880)	MPa
abrasion resistance	(C241)	hardness

PHYSICAL-MECHANICAL CHARACTERISTICS
(average reference values)

PINK MARBLE S.S.

MAIN AESTHETIC CHARACTERISTICS

Pink Marble s.s. varieties can be classed according to three different aesthetic types. Type (i) materials are composed of a varying pink groundmass, generally crossed by dark, mostly green veins parallel to the rift of the rock. In most varieties, the grain ranges from medium-coarse to medium-fine and the rock often has a clearly crystalline structure. Type (ii) varieties have a breccia structure composed of clasts several centimeters to several dozen centimeters across, which are alternately pink and white. The clasts are elongated and arranged parallel to the rift of the rock. Despite the fact that they are breccias, these materials normally have a very constant color and pattern. Aesthetic type (iii) varieties have a light pink groundmass crossed by numerous white speckles, the edges of which are fairly blurred, isoriented parallel to the rift of the rock.

AESTHETIC VARIATIONS AND DEFECTS

As regards type (i) materials, the main aesthetic variation is a variation in the color which often verges on white. Significant variations sometimes occur as regards the frequency and size of the veins too. *Peli ciechi* may also occur in the blocks and *peli furbi* in the slabs. The latter may affect the physical-mechanical properties which characterize the uncut material. The most common variation as regards type (ii) is the occurrence of dark spots which verge on a greenish color. These alter the basic chromatic characteristics of the material and, if they occur frequently or they are large, they may reduce the commercial value of the material too. In aesthetic type (iii) varieties, the pink color is not very constant and the rock often looks a whitish color which reduces its value considerably.

PRODUCER COUNTRIES

The majority of aesthetic type (i) materials are quarried in Portugal, although they are also quarried on a smaller scale in the United States, Zambia, Brazil and Turkey. Only one variety of aesthetic type (ii) is available on the international market and this is produced in Norway. The most well-known commercial varieties of aesthetic type (iii) are quarried in Greece.

AVAILABILITY

Aesthetic type (i) varieties are available in good quantities and almost always with short supply times. The blocks are normally medium and small. Aesthetic type (ii) varieties come from one quarrying area only which does, however, guarantee a fairly good supply, both in terms of quality and quantity. The blocks are medium and large. Availability of aesthetic type (iii) varieties is limited due to the fact that they come from one quarrying area only and the productivity is low. The blocks are generally medium and large.

PINK MARBLE

PHYSICAL-MECHANICAL CHARACTERISTICS
(average reference values)

		(i)	(ii)	(iii)		
absorption	(C97)	0.07		0.6	weight%	ASTM
density	(C97)	2.715		2.710	kg/cu.m	STANDARD
compressive strength	(C170)	72		110	MPa	
modulus of rupture	(C99)				MPa	
flexural strength	(C880)	11.5		24	MPa	
abrasion resistance	(C241)				hardness	

All three aesthetic types are best used in interiors for facings and, in some cases only, for floorings. They are frequently used for special solid pieces and bathroom furnishings. The surface is normally polished or, to a lesser extent, honed. Although some varieties have the necessary physical-mechanical properties to be used in exteriors too, their aesthetic characteristics would not be fully exploited and anyway they are only available in limited quantities of small tiles. Given the variation in color in some commercial varieties, careful quality control procedures are recommended, especially for aesthetic type (iii) varieties.

USES

Aesthetic type (i): Etowah, Rosa Aurora, Rosa Bellissimo, Rosa Estremoz, Rosa Portogallo, Rosa West. Aesthetic type (ii): Norwegian Rose. Aesthetic type (iii) Rosa Egeo.

MAIN COMMERCIAL VARIETIES

PINK MARBLE

		(i)	(ii)	(iii)	
ITALIAN STANDARD	compression breaking load	97.4	1.960		kg/cm²
	compression breaking load after freezing				kg/cm²
	imbibition coefficient (by weight)	0.05	0.10		%
	ultimate tensile strength	134	75		kg/cm²
	impact test	50			cm
	thermal linear expansion coefficient		0.0030		mm/m°C
	frictional wear test	8			mm
	weight per unit of volume	2.730	2.600		kg/m³
	elasticity module				kg/cm²
	knoop microhardness				kg/mm²

PHYSICAL-MECHANICAL CHARACTERISTICS
(average reference values)

PINK LIMESTONE

MAIN AESTHETIC CHARACTERISTICS

Pink Limestone varieties frequently have very different aesthetic characteristics which are often peculiar to each individual variety. For the sake of clarity, here materials will be classed as breccia varieties and other. Type (i) includes materials with a fine-grained groundmass, the pattern of which may be: (ia) essentially homogeneous, with occasional fossils a few centimeters across, crossed by fine veins (*stylolites*), in which case, the pink color is evenly distributed over the groundmass; (ib) slightly stratified in layers hardly visible which are subparallel to one another, in which case the color may vary from one layer to the next; (ic) with a varying pink groundmass with pink-yellowy globule-like elements a few centimeters across, in which case the grain of the groundmass and the globule-like elements is fine. Aesthetic type (ii) varieties have a breccia-like pattern with clasts varying in size from a few centimeters to several dozen centimeters across, often imbedded in a chaotic manner in the small quantity of groundmass. The color of the different varieties ranges from light pink, sometimes verging on light beige, to dark pink, almost red.

AESTHETIC VARIATIONS AND DEFECTS

The main aesthetic variation in both type (i) and type (ii) varieties concerns the color which may be lighter than the color shown on the samples. In addition, considerable pattern variations generally occur in type (ii) materials, in particular as regards the size of the clasts and their distribution in the groundmass. Some varieties, mainly type (ii) varieties, often have surface areas with low mechanical resistance too.

PRODUCER COUNTRIES

The most well-known commercial varieties of aesthetic type (i) varieties are produced in Italy and Spain, although they are also produced on a smaller scale in Greece, Turkey and Portugal. Aesthetic type (ii) varieties are quarried in Italy, France, Turkey, Iran and Portugal.

AVAILABILITY

Apart from a few exceptions, aesthetic type (i) materials are generally available in limited quantities of small- and medium-sized blocks. Aesthetic type (ii) varieties are available in limited quantities of generally medium-sized blocks.

USES

In view of their aesthetic characteristics and availability, pink Limestone varieties are mostly used in interiors for facings and floorings. They are also used for special solid pieces, especially type (ii) varieties and for bathroom furnishings. The surface is normally polished.

MAIN COMMERCIAL VARIETIES

Aesthetic type (ia): Alpenina, Perlino Rosato, Rosalia, Vagellis Pink.
Aesthetic type (ib): Chiampo Rosato, Rosa Cengi.
Aesthetic type (ic): Nembro Rosato.
Aesthetic type (ii): Arabescato Orobico Rosa, Breccia Aurora, Breccia Damascata, Breccia Oniciata, Fior di Rosa, Rosa Tea, Saint Flourian.

PHYSICAL-MECHANICAL CHARACTERISTICS
(average reference values)

	(i)	(ii)		
compression breaking load	1.805	832	kg/cm²	ITALIAN
compression breaking load after freezing	1.727	289	kg/cm²	STANDARD
imbibition coefficient (by weight)	0.12	0.29	%	
ultimate tensile strength	139	107	kg/cm²	
impact test	29	31	cm	
thermal linear expansion coefficient	0.0045	0.0038	mm/m°C	
frictional wear test			mm	
weight per unit of volume	2.686	2.715	kg/m³	
elasticity module	730.000	793.400	kg/cm²	
knoop microhardness			kg/mm²	

PHYSICAL-MECHANICAL CHARACTERISTICS
(average reference values)

		(i)	(ii)		
absorption	(C97)	0.28	0.22	weight%	ASTM
density	(C97)	2.689	2.690	kg/cu.m	STANDARD
compressive strength	(C170)	101.4	110	MPa	
modulus of rupture	(C99)			MPa	
flexural strength	(C880)	10.2	4.2	MPa	
abrasion resistance	(C241)	32.4		hardness	

PINK MARBLE

SKY BLUE MARBLE S.S.

These materials have a medium- to coarse-grained, whitish-colored crystalline groundmass crossed by frequent sky blue veins. The latter, which are on average a few centimeters thick, are either flexuous or slightly wavy and give the rock a definite orientation (rift).

MAIN AESTHETIC CHARACTERISTICS

Significant variations may occur as regards the concentration and thickness of the sky blue veins which can affect the overall color of the material and hence its commercial value. The sky blue veins often have whitish-colored dots which reduce the uniformity of the color too.

AESTHETIC VARIATIONS AND DEFECTS

The most well-known sky blue Marble s.s. varieties are quarried in Argentina, although they are also produced in Kenya and Tanzania.

PRODUCER COUNTRIES

Availability of these materials is limited, mostly due to the small number of quarrying areas. Nevertheless, supplies of the most well-known varieties are fairly continuous, in line with the quantities required by the market. The blocks are medium and large.

AVAILABILITY

Sky blue Marble s.s. varieties are essentially used in interiors for facings and special solid pieces, including bathroom furnishings. The surface is always polished.

USES

Azul Cielo.

MAIN COMMERCIAL VARIETIES

SKY BLUE MARBLE

ITALIAN STANDARD		
compression breaking load	kg/cm²	
compression breaking load after freezing	kg/cm²	
imbibition coefficient (by weight)	%	
ultimate tensile strength	kg/cm²	
impact test	cm	
thermal linear expansion coefficient	mm/m°C	
frictional wear test	mm	
weight per unit of volume	kg/m³	
elasticity module	kg/cm²	
knoop microhardness	kg/mm²	

PHYSICAL-MECHANICAL CHARACTERISTICS
(average reference values)

ASTM STANDARD			
absorption	(C97)	weight%	
density	(C97)	kg/cu.m	
compressive strength	(C170)	MPa	
modulus of rupture	(C99)	MPa	
flexural strength	(C880)	MPa	
abrasion resistance	(C241)	hardness	

PHYSICAL-MECHANICAL CHARACTERISTICS
(average reference values)

GREEN MARBLE S.S.

MAIN AESTHETIC CHARACTERISTICS

Green Marble s.s. varieties can be classed according to three different aesthetic types. Type (i) varieties are mainly carbonatic, metamorphic marble composed of a marble groundmass which varies in color from off-white to ivory white. The fine- to medium-grained groundmass is crossed by flexuous green veins which are subparallel to one another and vary in thickness and length according to the different commercial varieties. Aesthetic type (ii) is characteristic of rocks with a mostly silicatic composition known as ophiolites. The groundmass of the different varieties occurs in various shades of green and is crossed by whitish-colored veins which vary in distribution and conformation. They may create a real veining pattern or appear as irregular speckles which blend into the green groundmass. In some cases, the groundmass has a breccia-like appearance and the veins may circumscribe the individual clasts of which it is composed. Aesthetic type (iii) varieties are ophiolitic rocks composed of a dark green groundmass with faint, lighter-colored shadows which often have a definite orientation, but no veins. Finally, aesthetic type (iv) varieties are breccias with clasts varying in size from a few centimeters to a few dozen centimeters. They are mostly different shades of green, yellow and, to a lesser extent, grey. The dark-colored groundmass constitutes a small percentage of the materials. Overall, these materials are dark green, enhanced by light yellow and grey spots. The clasts are oriented, thereby giving the materials a well-defined rift.

AESTHETIC VARIATIONS AND DEFECTS

The most frequent variations in aesthetic type (i) materials are variations in the frequency and distribution of the green veins, which may be considerable, even in a short area. When the green color is not very clear and verges on grey, the quality of the material is reduced. As regards aesthetic type (ii), the frequency and distribution of the veins may vary significantly, even in the same variety. In some varieties there is also a considerable variation in the color of the green groundmass. The groundmass sometimes contains ferrous minerals a few millimeters across which are subject to oxidization and therefore may cause rust spots. These materials require a good seasoning period and often have structural defects, i.e., areas with low mechanical resistance. In aesthetic type (iii) and (iv) varieties, the green color may occur in different shades. Some varieties cannot be perfectly polished.

PRODUCER COUNTRIES

The main producer country of aesthetic type (i) varieties is Italy. Traditional producers of aesthetic type (ii) varieties are Italy first and foremost, which has the largest range of materials, followed by India, the United States and Greece. Taiwan and Guatemala also produce these materials, on a smaller scale though.
Aesthetic type (iii) varieties available on the international market are quarried in Italy and aesthetic type (iv) varieties in Egypt.

PHYSICAL-MECHANICAL CHARACTERISTICS
(average reference values)

absorption	(C97)	0.19	weight%	ASTM STANDARD
density	(C97)	2.732	kg/cu.m	
compressive strength	(C170)	147.6	MPa	
modulus of rupture	(C99)		MPa	
flexural strength	(C880)	19.6	MPa	
abrasion resistance	(C241)		hardness	

Availability of aesthetic type (i) varieties is fairly limited, especially as regards good quality materials. The blocks are generally medium-sized. Supply times, in particular, need to be checked.

In general, aesthetic type (ii) varieties are quite readily available, although the quantities produced of individual varieties are generally limited, especially as regards good quality materials. The blocks are generally medium and large. Prior to sawing, these materials require a *seasoning* period (in the form of blocks) more than the other types. There are only a few aesthetic type (iii) varieties and they are not available in large quantities. Aesthetic type (iv) materials are fairly rare. There are only limited quantities of those available on the market in generally medium-sized blocks.

In view of their good physical-mechanical properties, aesthetic type (i) varieties can be used in interiors and exteriors for facings, floorings and pavings. However, they are mainly used in interiors for facings (large polished or honed slabs) or special solid pieces. Thanks to the veined pattern, good results can be obtained with quarter-match and book-match work.

Aesthetic type (ii) and (iii) varieties are best used in interiors for facings and special pieces in quality projects. The surface is generally polished. In the case of floorings, these materials should only be used for low-traffic areas, since the polish could quickly disappear. In exteriors, their use should be limited to areas protected from atmospheric agents and direct sunlight. Slabs, in particular, of materials with many white veins and materials with a breccia pattern might need reinforcement before installation. Some aesthetic type (iii) varieties are often used in the form of riven finish tiles for external facings and pavings. Type (iv) varieties are essentially used for special solid pieces such as kitchen and vanity tops and, to a lesser extent, bathroom furnishings.

USES

Aesthetic type (i): Cipollino Apuano, Cremo Tirreno, Fantastico.
Aesthetic type (ii): Verde Acceglio, Verde Alpi, Verde Aver, Verde Giada, Verde Gressoney, Verde Guatemala, Verde Issogne, Verde Issoire, Larissa Green, Verde Patrizia, Rajastan Green, Verde Rameggiato, Verde S. Denis, Taiwan Green, Tinos Green, Vermont Green.
Aesthetic type (iii): Serpentino Classico.
Aesthetic type (iv): Breccia Fawakir.

MAIN COMMERCIAL VARIETIES

GREEN MARBLE

		(i)	(ii)	(iii)	(iv)	
ITALIAN STANDARD	compression breaking load	1.260	1.427	2.470		kg/cm²
	compression breaking load after freezing	1.150	1.215	2.270		kg/cm²
	imbibition coefficient (by weight)	0.30	0.44	0.03		%
	ultimate tensile strength	89	141	625		kg/cm²
	impact test	38	49	50		cm
	thermal linear expansion coefficient	0.0080	0.0058	0.0070		mm/m°C
	frictional wear test					mm
	weight per unit of volume	2.740	2.680	2.800		kg/m³
	elasticity module	558.500	571.000	1.330.000		kg/cm²
	knoop microhardness		243			kg/mm²

PHYSICAL-MECHANICAL CHARACTERISTICS
(average reference values)

97

GREEN ONYX

MAIN AESTHETIC CHARACTERISTICS

These materials are composed of continuous overlapping bands, on average from a few centimeters to a few dozen centimeters thick, which form slightly undulating to highly curved patterns. The bands are various shades of green, which often turns into beige. These materials are generally very transparent when held to the light.

AESTHETIC VARIATIONS AND DEFECTS

As in all Onyx varieties, the main aesthetic variation concerns the color, which may vary considerably. In addition, holes and structural defects (*peli furbi*) occur fairly frequently in these materials and may greatly reduce the yield in slabs.

PRODUCER COUNTRIES

Green onyx varieties available on the international market are produced in Pakistan.

AVAILABILITY

The quantities of green onyx available are relatively high compared with other colors. The blocks are normally small- and medium-sized.

USES

In view of their aesthetic characteristics and availability, these materials are usually used in interiors for special pieces, including solid pieces, and small facings. They are frequently used for ornaments too. Thanks to their transparency, they can be used to create special light effects.

MAIN COMMERCIAL VARIETIES

Green Onyx.

GREEN MARBLE

PHYSICAL-MECHANICAL CHARACTERISTICS
(average reference values)

compression breaking load	1.760	kg/cm²	ITALIAN STANDARD
compression breaking load after freezing	1.640	kg/cm²	
imbibition coefficient (by weight)	0.15	%	
ultimate tensile strength		kg/cm²	
impact test		cm	
thermal linear expansion coefficient		mm/m°C	
frictional wear test		mm	
weight per unit of volume	2.550	kg/m³	
elasticity module		kg/cm²	
knoop microhardness		kg/mm²	

PHYSICAL-MECHANICAL CHARACTERISTICS
(average reference values)

absorption	(C97)	0.01	weight%	ASTM STANDARD
density	(C97)	2.730	kg/cu.m	
compressive strength	(C170)	142	MPa	
modulus of rupture	(C99)		MPa	
flexural strength	(C880)	9	MPa	
abrasion resistance	(C241)		hardness	

GREY MARBLE S.S.

Grey marble s.s. varieties can be classed according to two different aesthetic types. The first type includes materials composed of a fine-grained (ia) or coarse-grained (ib) crystalline groundmass, varying in color from light grey to dark grey. In many commercial varieties the rocky mass is crossed by grey veins which are a darker color than the groundmass or by veins of different shades of white. Sometimes these veins become so large that they replace most of the grey groundmass. The veins and shadings are subparallel to one another and coincide with the rift of the rock. The second aesthetic type (ii) has an uneven grey groundmass crossed by a close-knit series of speckles which are white and, according to the different commercial varieties, pink, yellow or darker grey than the groundmass. The speckles often increase in size to form a more or less close-knit pattern.

In the first aesthetic type (ia, ib) and even in varieties without veins, the groundmass may vary in color from light grey to dark grey. The most significant variations as regards type (ii) concern the frequency and distribution of the white, pink or yellow speckles or veins, which may vary considerably even in a small area, thereby influencing the quality of the material and consequently its commercial value.

Grey marble s.s. varieties (ia) and (ib), be they with or without grey and white veins, are fairly common. The largest quantities of fine- and medium-fine-grained varieties are from Italy, while the coarse-grained varieties are mostly from the United States, Portugal, Greece, Indonesia and Mexico. Varieties with red, pink, yellow or dark grey speckles or veins (ii) are quite rare. The most well-known varieties on the international market are produced in Turkey and Italy.

MAIN AESTHETIC CHARACTERISTICS

AESTHETIC VARIATIONS AND DEFECTS

PRODUCER COUNTRIES

GREY MARBLE

			(ia)	(ib)	(ii)	
ASTM STANDARD	absorption	(C97)	0.17	0.09	0.06	weight%
	density	(C97)	2.710	2.707	2.690	kg/cu.m
	compressive strength	(C170)	130	65.5	79	MPa
	modulus of rupture	(C99)				MPa
	flexural strength	(C880)	10.5	8.2	9.8	MPa
	abrasion resistance	(C241)				hardness

PHYSICAL-MECHANICAL CHARACTERISTICS
(average reference values)

99

AVAILABILITY Potentially, as far as the deposits are concerned, availability of aesthetic types (ia) and (ib) is fairly good, yet the quantities available on the market are often limited due to the low market requirements. The blocks are generally large and well-squared (at least European materials). Aesthetic type (ii) varieties are available in limited quantities. In view of the aesthetic variations in these materials, it is advisable to carefully control the quality and check on the supply times, especially for high-quality supplies.

USES In view of their good physical-mechanical properties, the fine- to medium-fine-grained varieties (ia) are suitable for all the normal uses in the building industry, for interiors and exteriors alike. They are generally more hard-wearing and withstand mechanical stress better than other-colored Marble s.s. varieties. The most frequent surface treatments are honing or impact treatment for exteriors and polishing for interiors. The coarse-grained varieties (ib) are suitable above all for interiors and are often used for bathrooms. The surface of these materials is always polished. Type (ii) aesthetic varieties are generally used in interiors, especially for facings or where the colored veining is enhanced. For the same reason it is advisable to use medium- to large-sized slabs always with a polished surface.

MAIN COMMERCIAL VARIETIES Aesthetic type (ia): Bardiglio Carrara, Bardiglio Fumo di Londra, Bardiglio Imperiale, Blu Venato d'Italia, Nuvolato Apuano.
Aesthetic type (ib): Antique Silver, Pearl Grey, Solar Grey, Trigaches.
Aesthetic type (ii): Fior di Pesco Carnico, Grigio Carnico, Salomè, Supren, Tekmar Dove.

PHYSICAL-MECHANICAL CHARACTERISTICS
(average reference values)

	(ia)	(ib)	(ii)		
compression breaking load	1.439		1.315	kg/cm²	ITALIAN
compression breaking load after freezing	1.322		1.215	kg/cm²	STANDARD
imbibition coefficient (by weight)	0.21		0.09	%	
ultimate tensile strength	163		141	kg/cm²	
impact test	57		43	cm	
thermal linear expansion coefficient	0.0048		0.0049	mm/m°C	
frictional wear test				mm	
weight per unit of volume	2.682		2.687	kg/m³	
elasticity module				kg/cm²	
knoop microhardness				kg/mm²	

100

GREY LIMESTONE

There are two aesthetic types of grey limestone. Type (i) includes breccia materials composed of clasts (lithoids or fossils), varying in shape and on average a few centimeters across, embedded in a fine-grained groundmass, which varies in quantity. Both the clasts and the groundmass are varying shades of grey, depending on the commercial variety. Varieties belonging to type (ii) are composed of lithoids a few millimeters across, ranging in color from off-white to light grey. These elements are in close contact with one another, thereby forming a substantially homogeneous mass which looks light grey overall.

MAIN AESTHETIC CHARACTERISTICS

The chief aesthetic variations concern both the pattern and the grey color. Such variations are, however, generally quite well tolerated on the market. In some varieties the veins have planes of mechanical weakness.

AESTHETIC VARIATIONS AND DEFECTS

The most well-known varieties of grey Limestone are extracted in Italy.

PRODUCER COUNTRIES

These materials are generally readily available, in line with market requirements, normally in large-sized blocks.

AVAILABILITY

In view of their usually good physical-mechanical properties, grey Limestone varieties are suitable for all the normal uses in the building industry. The surface may be polished, although often, especially in exteriors, impact treatment is preferred. Some varieties require reinforcement with netting.

USES

Aesthetic type (i): Arabescato Orobico Grigio, Aurisina Fiorita, Repen Zolla.
Aesthetic type (ii) Aurisinia Granitello.

MAIN COMMERCIAL VARIETIES

GREY MARBLE

ITALIAN STANDARD				
compression breaking load	1.853	1.540	kg/cm²
compression breaking load after freezing	1.792	1.500	kg/cm²
imbibition coefficient (by weight)	0.40	0.12	%
ultimate tensile strength	155	140	kg/cm²
impact test	35	35	cm
thermal linear expansion coefficient	0.0042	0.0038	mm/m°C
frictional wear test			mm
weight per unit of volume	2.659	2.573	kg/m³
elasticity module	650.000		kg/cm²
knoop microhardness	160		kg/mm²

PHYSICAL-MECHANICAL CHARACTERISTICS (average reference values)

ASTM STANDARD			
absorption	(C97)	1.1	weight%
density	(C97)	2.600	kg/cu.m
compressive strength	(C170)	108	MPa
modulus of rupture	(C99)		MPa
flexural strength	(C880)	14	MPa
abrasion resistance	(C241)		hardness

PHYSICAL-MECHANICAL CHARACTERISTICS (average reference values)

101

GREY TRAVERTINE

MAIN AESTHETIC CHARACTERISTICS

These materials are formed by the overlapping of subhorizontal layers a few centimeters thick which give the rock a stratified appearance. The rocky mass is not usually compact and has a number of small holes more or less parallel to the direction of the layers. The layers are often fairly straight, although in some varieties they are undulating. The grey color is not generally evenly distributed and occurs in alternate beige and grey layers. The stratified arrangement of the layers gives the rock a prominent rift which is often accentuated by the arrangement of the holes.

AESTHETIC VARIATIONS AND DEFECTS

The main aesthetic variation in grey Travertine concerns the color, which may undergo sudden changes, especially at right angles to the direction of the rift. Other variations concern the holes. If these are too concentrated or too large, they constitute a structural defect as well as an aesthetic defect since they may reduce the physical-mechanical resistance of the rock. Finally, there may be variations as to the distribution and conformation of the layers. Some varieties are appreciated for the peculiar undulating pattern of the layers, and it should be borne in mind that this may vary considerably in just a small area.

PRODUCER COUNTRIES

The main producer country of grey Travertine is Italy.

AVAILABILITY

The main varieties of grey Travertine are available in fairly limited quantities of medium- and large-sized blocks. Supply times may be longer for certain varieties.

USES

Grey Travertine varieties are suitable for all the normal uses of dimension stone, both in interiors and exteriors. Owing to the fact that they are not affected by freezing temperatures, they are also appropriate for climates with significant temperature changes. The surface is usually polished or honed. In view of their high porosity, grey Travertine varieties are easily soiled. Thus, when they are to be used for floorings and bathrooms, etc., they must be filled or reinforced with resin. They can also be used in solid blocks to fulfil structural functions. Grey Travertine varieties are not recommended, however, for damp areas.

They are normally cut along the hard way or easy way; when cut along the rift, the holes increase in size.

MAIN COMMERCIAL VARIETIES

Silver Travertino.

GREY MARBLE

PHYSICAL-MECHANICAL CHARACTERISTICS
(average reference values)

			ITALIAN STANDARD
compression breaking load	0.40	kg/cm²	
compression breaking load after freezing	0.35	kg/cm²	
imbibition coefficient (by weight)	1.3	%	
ultimate tensile strength	125	kg/cm²	
impact test	30	cm	
thermal linear expansion coefficient	0.0050	mm/m°C	
frictional wear test		mm	
weight per unit of volume	2.430	kg/m³	
elasticity module	555.000	kg/cm²	
knoop microhardness		kg/mm²	

PHYSICAL-MECHANICAL CHARACTERISTICS
(average reference values)

				ASTM STANDARD
absorption	(C97)	1.2	weight%	
density	(C97)	2.540	kg/cu.m	
compressive strength	(C170)	40	MPa	
modulus of rupture	(C99)		MPa	
flexural strength	(C880)	16.0	MPa	
abrasion resistance	(C241)	21.2	hardness	

BLACK LIMESTONE

There are two aesthetic types of black limestone currently available. Type (i), commercially known as absolute black, is composed of a very fine-grained, homogeneous, deep black crystalline mass with no other aesthetic features. Type (ii) varieties, on the other hand, are composed of a black crystalline mass crossed by veins which are most commonly white or off-white but can also be different shades of golden yellow. The white veins may be haphazardly distributed, creating an irregular pattern on the black background. The yellow veins are almost always parallel to the rift of the rock and may occur in thin lines or flares and waves, thereby giving the rock a *nuvolato* pattern.

Aesthetic type (i) may have areas of various shapes and sizes where the black appears lighter, verging slightly on a grey color. Infrequent, thin, whitish-colored veins may also occur in places, thereby reducing the quality of the material. The most popular type (ii) varieties are those with golden yellow veins, which are generally found together with whitish-colored veins. The quality of the materials with white veins only is normally indirectly proportionate to the frequency of the veins. If there are too many white veins, the overall color of the rock is lighter. Moreover, their occurrence in large quantities may reduce the physical-mechanical properties of the material. Type (ii) materials may have areas verging on a greyish color too. In both types there may be areas which are difficult to polish.

AESTHETIC VARIATIONS AND DEFECTS

Aesthetic type (i) varieties are quarried in Belgium. Aesthetic type (ii) with white veins only is quarried mostly in Spain and, on a smaller scale, in Mexico and Greece. Varieties with yellow veins are mainly quarried in Italy.

PRODUCER COUNTRIES

Aesthetic type (i) materials are available in limited quantities, generally in small blocks. Aesthetic type (ii) with white veins only are available on the international market in fairly good quantities of large-sized blocks. Availability of varieties with yellow veins is limited, even though they are produced in medium- and large-sized blocks.

AVAILABILITY

Black Limestone varieties are customarily used in interiors for special elements (table tops, small columns, random-length solid pieces, etc.), but they are also used for facings, albeit generally small ones. Aesthetic type (ii) varieties with white veins only can be used in external facings too, in areas protected from rain and, above all, direct sunlight which could make the groundmass turn grey. The latter type may need reinforcement with netting.

USES

Aesthetic type (i): Nero Belgio.
Aesthetic type (ii): Nero Creta, Negro Marquiña, Negro Mexico, Noir Saint Laurent, Portoro.

MAIN COMMERCIAL VARIETIES

ITALIAN STANDARD		(i)	(ii)		PHYSICAL-MECHANICAL CHARACTERISTICS (average reference values)
	compression breaking load	988		kg/cm²	
	compression breaking load after freezing			kg/cm²	
	imbibition coefficient (by weight)	0.13		%	
	ultimate tensile strength	122		kg/cm²	
	impact test	27		cm	
	thermal linear expansion coefficient	0.0041		mm/m°C	
	frictional wear test			mm	
	weight per unit of volume	2.689		kg/m³	
	elasticity module			kg/cm²	
	knoop microhardness			kg/mm²	

ASTM STANDARD			(ii)		PHYSICAL-MECHANICAL CHARACTERISTICS (average reference values)
	absorption	(C97)	0.15	weight%	
	density	(C97)	2.710	kg/cu.m	
	compressive strength	(C170)	125	MPa	
	modulus of rupture	(C99)		MPa	
	flexural strength	(C880)	10.1	MPa	
	abrasion resistance	(C241)		hardness	

BLACK MARBLE

Granite

Granite varieties are available on the international market in the following colors:

WHITE GRANITE Homogeneous, oriented and veined varieties of white granite are available on the international market.

YELLOW GRANITE The majority of yellow granite currently on the market is oriented, although there are also veined varieties and a few homogeneous varieties.

BROWN GRANITE There are homogeneous and oriented brown granites on the market. In both cases the aesthetic characteristics of the different varieties may vary significantly. There follows a description of the most well-known varieties on the international market.

RED GRANITE Red granite is available in homogeneous, oriented and veined commercial varieties.

PINK GRANITE The majority of commercial varieties of pink granite have homogeneous or veined patterns, yet there are also a good number of oriented varieties.

POLYCHROMATIC GRANITE Polychromatic granite varieties are materials with two or more dominant colors other than the black color of mafic minerals and/or the white color of feldspars. Almost all the commercial varieties available on the international market are veined; only a few belong to the homogeneous and oriented groups.

VIOLET GRANITE Homogeneous and veined varieties of violet granite are available on the international market.

SKY BLUE GRANITE The only varieties of sky blue granite available on the international market are homogeneous.

BLUE GRANITE The most well-known varieties of blue granite available on the international market have a homogeneous pattern, although there are also veined varieties.

GREEN GRANITE There are homogeneous, oriented and veined green granites regularly available on the international market. Each group includes two or three aesthetic types which are sometimes very different from one another and therefore need to be described separately.

GREY GRANITE The majority of grey granite varieties available on the international market are homogeneous or oriented. Veined varieties do exist but are only found in local markets and not on the international market.

BLACK GRANITE Black granite varieties exist only as homogeneous materials and are classed as *black granite* or *absolute black granite*. These two groups have very different characteristics and therefore have to be dealt with separately.

Note: The values given for the physical-mechanical tests are only indicative, since they are taken from existing literature or material furnished by various stone producer/suppliers. Where values are not reported, information was not available or could not be confirmed. The author takes no responsibility for any mistakes or omissions regarding the values given.

HOMOGENEOUS WHITE GRANITE

MAIN AESTHETIC CHARACTERISTICS

Homogeneous white granite varieties have a white or off-white groundmass with black and grey dotting caused by the black and grey minerals which form an integral part of the rock. The uniform pattern makes the overall color look homogeneous though, and in the best quality materials the black dots (normally only millimeters across) are practically "absorbed" by the white background. The grain size of the different varieties ranges from fine to large.

AESTHETIC VARIATIONS AND DEFECTS

The only significant aesthetic variation concerns the groundmass, which tends to look greyish in color due to a high concentration of grey crystals. In this case, however, the material should be considered a grey granite, even though grey granite varieties have different commercial characteristics to white ones. The main defects include uniform white veins *(catene)* which cross the rocky mass and concentrations of dark minerals forming black spots, bands or lines *(bisce)* which adversely affect the uniformity of the color.

PRODUCER COUNTRIES

The most well-known varieties on the international market are produced in Italy and Spain, although some varieties are also produced in Portugal, Norway, Canada, etc.

AVAILABILITY

The availability of the high-quality materials is limited since they are often taken from areas next to grey granite production areas, but average-quality materials are readily available. Blocks are medium to large.

USES

Homogeneous white granite varieties are suitable for all uses, in interiors and exteriors alike. The finished products are normally slabs or tiles of various sizes. The surface can be polished, flamed or bush-hammered. Bush-hammering enhances the overall white color of the rock. Given the light color of the materials, flamed and bush-hammered surfaces on floorings and pavings tend to be easily soiled.

MAIN COMMERCIAL VARIETIES

Blanco Berrocal, Blanco Cristal, Blanco Galizia, Blanco Real, Bianco Baveno, Bianco Sardo, Caesar White, Tolga White.

PHYSICAL-MECHANICAL CHARACTERISTICS
(average reference values)

compression breaking load	1.425	kg/cm²	ITALIAN
compression breaking load after freezing		kg/cm²	STANDARD
imbibition coefficient (by weight)	0.27	%	
ultimate tensile strength	139	kg/cm²	
impact test	61	cm	
thermal linear expansion coefficient	0.0069	mm/m°C	
frictional wear test	3.5	mm	
weight per unit of volume	2.603	kg/m³	
elasticity module	365.000	kg/cm²	
knoop microhardness		kg/mm²	

PHYSICAL-MECHANICAL CHARACTERISTICS
(average reference values)

absorption	(C97)	0.18	weight%	ASTM
density	(C97)	2.660	kg/cu.m	STANDARD
compressive strength	(C170)	155	MPa	
modulus of rupture	(C99)		MPa	
flexural strength	(C880)	12.5	MPa	
abrasion resistance	(C241)		hardness	

ORIENTED WHITE GRANITE

The groundmass of oriented white granite varieties is a whitish color which often verges on off-white and even a greyish color. It is composed of crystals that are often medium- to fine-grained with a definite orientation which does not usually vary significantly as seen on a cut slab. The overall color may alter due to the presence of accessory minerals (in limited quantities). These are normally black and/or red and may be a few millimeters to a few centimeters across. If there is a high concentration of black accessory minerals (often in the shape of lamellas), the orientation may be more prominent, but the overall color of the rock is darker.

MAIN AESTHETIC CHARACTERISTICS

The aesthetic variations include an excessively grey groundmass or an excessively grey overall appearance of the rock due to a high percentage of quartz and high concentrations of black accessory minerals respectively. In some cases the red accessory minerals are too big and/or unevenly distributed over the groundmass. The most prominent defects are tears *(strappi)* which may become open fractures, an uneven distribution of the color and small white veins *(catene)* which adversely affect the oriented movement of the rock. In some cases, the occurrence of ferrous minerals may give rise to rust spots over time.

AESTHETIC VARIATIONS AND DEFECTS

The main producer countries are India and Brazil, although some varieties are also produced in the United States and Canada.

PRODUCER COUNTRIES

In general, oriented white granite varieties are fairly readily available thanks to the relatively high number of varieties. It is, however, quite difficult to produce large quantities of high-quality material. The blocks are medium and large.

AVAILABILITY

These materials may be used for floorings, pavings and facings, in interiors and exteriors alike. The use of large slabs highlights the movement of the pattern. Care should be taken when using materials with highly oxidizing elements for exteriors. The surface is generally polished, although in some cases flaming can create interesting effects. Should large quantities be required, careful quality-control procedures are recommended.

USES

Bethel White, Cardinal White, Galaxy White, Imperial White, Panafragola, Samba White, Solar White.

MAIN COMMERCIAL VARIETIES

ITALIAN STANDARD

compression breaking load	2.051	kg/cm²
compression breaking load after freezing	1.761	kg/cm²
imbibition coefficient (by weight)	0.35	%
ultimate tensile strength	116	kg/cm²
impact test		cm
thermal linear expansion coefficient	0.0062	mm/m°C
frictional wear test		mm
weight per unit of volume	2.471	kg/m³
elasticity module	422.600	kg/cm²
knoop microhardness		kg/mm²

PHYSICAL-MECHANICAL CHARACTERISTICS
(average reference values)

ASTM STANDARD

absorption	(C97)	0.21	weight%
density	(C97)	2.694	kg/cu.m
compressive strength	(C170)	144	MPa
modulus of rupture	(C99)		MPa
flexural strength	(C880)	16.2	MPa
abrasion resistance	(C241)		hardness

PHYSICAL-MECHANICAL CHARACTERISTICS
(average reference values)

107

VEINED WHITE GRANITE

MAIN AESTHETIC CHARACTERISTICS

The groundmass of veined white granite varieties is a whitish color which often verges on off-white and even a greyish color. It is composed of crystals that are often medium- to fine-grained with a dominant orientation which does not usually vary significantly as seen on a cut slab. There are frequent concentrations of dark minerals which appear as winding bands of varying shapes and sizes, thereby giving the material a definite orientation. If there are a lot of these bands, the material becomes light grey in color. In places there are red minerals a few millimeters to a few centimeters across which are unevenly distributed along lines subparallel to the orientation of the material.

AESTHETIC VARIATIONS AND DEFECTS

The aesthetic variations include an excessively grey groundmass or an excessively grey overall appearance of the rock due to a high percentage of quartz and high concentrations of black accessory minerals respectively. In some cases, the red minerals are too big and/or unevenly distributed over the groundmass. The most prominent defects are tears *(strappi)* which may become open fractures and small white veins *(catene)* which adversely affect the oriented movement of the rock. In some cases the occurrence of ferrous minerals may give rise to rust spots over time.

PRODUCER COUNTRIES

The main producer countries are India and Brazil, although some varieties are also produced in the United States.

AVAILABILITY

In general, veined white granite varieties are readily available for small and medium orders. It is, however, quite difficult to produce large quantities of high-quality material. The blocks are medium and large.

USES

These materials may be used for floorings, pavings and facings, in interiors and exteriors alike. The use of large slabs highlights the movement of the pattern. Care should be taken when using materials with highly oxidizing elements for exteriors. The surface is generally polished, although in some cases flaming can create interesting effects, despite the fact that it almost completely eliminates the veined pattern.
Should large quantities be required, careful quality-control procedures are recommended.

MAIN COMMERCIAL VARIETIES

Eidelweiss, Kashmir White, Silver Cloud, Viscount White.

PHYSICAL-MECHANICAL CHARACTERISTICS
(average reference values)

			ITALIAN STANDARD
compression breaking load	2.080	kg/cm^2	
compression breaking load after freezing	1990	kg/cm^2	
imbibition coefficient (by weight)	0.40	%	
ultimate tensile strength	132	kg/cm^2	
impact test		cm	
thermal linear expansion coefficient	0.0065	mm/m°C	
frictional wear test		mm	
weight per unit of volume	2.620	kg/m^3	
elasticity module	365.000	kg/cm^2	
knoop microhardness		kg/mm^2	

PHYSICAL-MECHANICAL CHARACTERISTICS
(average reference values)

			ASTM STANDARD
absorption	(C97)	weight%	
density	(C97)	kg/cu.m	
compressive strength	(C170)	MPa	
modulus of rupture	(C99)	MPa	
flexural strength	(C880)	MPa	
abrasion resistance	(C241)	hardness	

HOMOGENEOUS YELLOW GRANITE

Homogeneous yellow granite varieties are composed of a crystalline mass, ranging in color from a soft, light yellow to a deep yellow which is almost brown. The color is never usually totally homogeneous and color variations can be seen even on slabs in the form of deep yellow rings or spots scattered over the light yellow crystalline mass. The grain may be coarse or fine.

The color may vary signficantly from one block to the next, even to the extent that it is impossible to achieve acceptable aesthetic results. In particular, if the yellow color is too light, it sometimes verges on grey and this greatly reduces the value. Variations as regards grain size and pattern are fairly well tolerated by the market, as long as they are not too prominent. In some cases, if the material is exposed to atmospheric agents, rust spots may appear.

Homogeneous yellow granite varieties are extracted in Brazil and Namibia.

There are few commercial varieties of homogeneous yellow granite. Availability is generally limited, since there are only a few active quarries and it is difficult to maintain precise quality standards, especially as regards large orders.

Despite the fact that they do not withstand mechanical stress as well as granite varieties of other colors, from a technical viewpoint their characteristics are good enough for the traditional uses, that is, facings and floorings. However, it is advisable to limit their use to interiors. Their color makes them particularly suitable for special pieces in luxury furnishings. In this case though, it should be borne in mind that they generally have a high absorption coefficient. The surface is normally polished; flaming creates an interesting effect, especially on medium- and coarse-grained varieties, although in some cases it tends to give the material a pinkish color.

Amarelo Real, Giallo Antico.

MAIN AESTHETIC CHARACTERISTICS

AESTHETIC VARIATIONS AND DEFECTS

PRODUCER COUNTRIES

AVAILABILITY

USES

MAIN COMMERCIAL VARIETIES

ITALIAN STANDARD			
compression breaking load	1.136	kg/cm²	
compression breaking load after freezing	1.078	kg/cm²	
imbibition coefficient (by weight)	0.35	%	
ultimate tensile strength	96	kg/cm²	
impact test		cm	
thermal linear expansion coefficient	0.0085	mm/m°C	
frictional wear test		mm	
weight per unit of volume	2.621	kg/m³	
elasticity module		kg/cm²	
knoop microhardness		kg/mm²	

PHYSICAL-MECHANICAL CHARACTERISTICS
(average reference values)

ASTM STANDARD			
absorption	(C97)	weight%	
density	(C97)	kg/cu.m	
compressive strength	(C170)	MPa	
modulus of rupture	(C99)	MPa	
flexural strength	(C880)	MPa	
abrasion resistance	(C241)	hardness	

PHYSICAL-MECHANICAL CHARACTERISTICS
(average reference values)

ORIENTED YELLOW GRANITE

MAIN AESTHETIC CHARACTERISTICS

The varieties of oriented yellow granite vary in color from a soft, light yellow to a deep yellow which is almost brown. The color is never usually totally homogeneous and color variations can be seen even on slabs. Often it is concentrated in deep yellow rings round the dark minerals or diluted inside the larger, light yellow crystals. These materials are generally coarse-grained with subovoidal feldspar crystals a few centimeters across but there are also medium-grained varieties. All varieties have isoriented crystals which give the rock a definite orientation. Many varieties sometimes have thin blackish veins in places which are oriented parallel to the rift of the rock.

AESTHETIC VARIATIONS AND DEFECTS

The color may vary signficantly from one block to the next, even to the extent that it is impossible to achieve acceptable aesthetic results. In particular, if the yellow color is too light, it sometimes verges on grey and this greatly reduces the value. Variations as regards grain size and pattern are fairly well tolerated by the market if they are not too prominent. In some cases, if the material is exposed to atmospheric agents, rust spots may appear.

PRODUCER COUNTRIES

Homogeneous yellow granite varieties are extracted in Brazil.

AVAILABILITY

Availability of oriented yellow granite varieties is limited since there are only a few active quarries. In many cases, it is quite hard to maintain the same color characteristics for large orders. Nevertheless, there are fairly continuous supplies of the most well-known varieties. The blocks are always large.

USES

Despite the fact that they do not withstand mechanical stress as well as granites of other colors, from a technical viewpoint their characteristics are good enough for the traditional uses, that is, facings and floorings. However, it is advisable to limit their use to interiors. Their color makes them particularly suitable for special pieces in luxury furnishings. In this case though, it should be borne in mind that they generally have a high absorption coefficient. The surface is normally polished; flaming, if possible, in some cases tends to give the material a pinkish color. With large supplies, it is advisable to carry out strict quality-control procedures.

MAIN COMMERCIAL VARIETIES

Giallo Fiorito, Giallo Veneziano, Santa Cecilia.

PHYSICAL-MECHANICAL CHARACTERISTICS
(average reference values)

			ITALIAN STANDARD
compression breaking load	1.578	kg/cm²	
compression breaking load after freezing	1.599	kg/cm²	
imbibition coefficient (by weight)	0.38	%	
ultimate tensile strength	104	kg/cm²	
impact test	41	cm	
thermal linear expansion coefficient	0.0013	mm/m°C	
frictional wear test		mm	
weight per unit of volume	2.682	kg/m³	
elasticity module		kg/cm²	
knoop microhardness	625	kg/mm²	

PHYSICAL-MECHANICAL CHARACTERISTICS
(average reference values)

				ASTM STANDARD
absorption	(C97)		weight%	
density	(C97)	2.680	kg/cu.m	
compressive strength	(C170)	106	MPa	
modulus of rupture	(C99)		MPa	
flexural strength	(C880)		MPa	
abrasion resistance	(C241)		hardness	

110

VEINED YELLOW GRANITE

These materials have a crystalline groundmass composed of alternate bands of crystals (varying in color from light yellow to yellow verging on brown) and in size (from fine to medium-coarse) and veins of fine-grained, black crystals. Both the bands and the veins may vary significantly in terms of shape and thickness even on a cut slab. In some materials the black veins are replaced by reddish-colored speckling. Some varieties are enhanced by dark red crystals which are generally distributed along the rock's main orientation.

MAIN AESTHETIC CHARACTERISTICS

There are frequent variations both as regards the color and the pattern. Such variations are normally well tolerated by the market, although if they are particularly noticeable they may be considered defects, or the materials may be considered different commercial varieties. However, variations which are invariably taken as pattern or color defects in other-colored materials increase the quality of these materials.

AESTHETIC VARIATIONS AND DEFECTS

Veined yellow granite varieties traded on the international market are extracted in Brazil and India.

PRODUCER COUNTRIES

The production of veined yellow granites is generally rather limited and may be subject to considerable variations in quality, even from one block to the next. Thus, the supply of large quantities may take time and definitely requires careful quality-control procedures. On the other hand, the use of small selected lots may achieve results which are difficult to repeat and hence unique. Blocks are generally large.

AVAILABILITY

Owing to their aesthetic characteristics and availability, veined yellow granite varieties are particularly suited to quality interiors, both facings and floorings. The best results are achieved with slabs or large tiles. Often, quarter-match and book-match patterns give attractive results. Polishing is always preferable for the surface.

USES

Juparanà Classico, Juparanà Champagne, Juparanà Colombo, Juparanà Delicado, Shivakashi, Viara.

MAIN COMMERCIAL VARIETIES

ITALIAN STANDARD			
compression breaking load	1.514	kg/cm^2	
compression breaking load after freezing	1.450	kg/cm^2	
imbibition coefficient (by weight)	0.18	%	
ultimate tensile strength	93	kg/cm^2	
impact test		cm	
thermal linear expansion coefficient	0.0076	mm/m°C	
frictional wear test		mm	
weight per unit of volume	2.566	kg/m^3	
elasticity module	549.600	kg/cm^2	
knoop microhardness		kg/mm^2	

PHYSICAL-MECHANICAL CHARACTERISTICS
(average reference values)

ASTM STANDARD				
absorption	(C97)	0.13	weight%	
density	(C97)	2.440	kg/cu.m	
compressive strength	(C170)	155	MPa	
modulus of rupture	(C99)		MPa	
flexural strength	(C880)	9.0	MPa	
abrasion resistance	(C241)		hardness	

PHYSICAL-MECHANICAL CHARACTERISTICS
(average reference values)

HOMOGENEOUS BROWN GRANITE

MAIN AESTHETIC CHARACTERISTICS

The classic aesthetic type (i) is composed of light brown, mostly subcircular crystals a few centimeters across, embedded in a medium-grained, blackish-colored groundmass. The size of the brown crystals is normally varied and their distribution is irregular, yet overall the material is quite homogeneous. Another type (ii) has medium-sized, brown crystals, which are darker than those in the previous variety. The crystals are often coalescent and form a fairly homogeneous mass intermingled with relatively few, small black crystals. A third type (iii) is composed of medium- and large-sized, dark and/or light brown crystals which are often bordered by a thin, lighter-colored line. This type has black minerals too, but they are much smaller crystals and less concentrated than in the other two types.

AESTHETIC VARIATIONS AND DEFECTS

In all three types, the main aesthetic variation is a variation in the color of the brown crystals. Type (ii) often has concentrations of black minerals which form subovoidal spots several centimeters long and these are invariably considered defects. Some type (i) varieties may look *magrose*.

PRODUCER COUNTRIES

Type (i) materials are mainly produced in Finland, while the majority of type (ii) and (iii) varieties are from Brazil, although some are from Canada, and Saudi Arabia.

AVAILABILITY

Type (i) is the most common of the three types described, and it is generally the one available in the largest blocks. Type (iii) includes several varieties which are on the whole fairly readily available both in terms of quantity and quality. Type (ii) is the least readily available and problems may arise with large orders required in short times.

USES

In view of their good technical characteristics, homogeneous brown granite varieties are suitable for all the normal uses of dimension stone in both interiors and exteriors. Owing to the fact that they are readily available, types (i) and (iii) are particularly suited to even large facings and floorings, although they also have the right aesthetic characteristics to be used for special pieces in quality furnishings. Type (ii) is also used above all for the latter. If they are to be used for larger projects, strict quality-control procedures are recommended. The surface of all three types is generally polished, although good results can be achieved with flaming too, especially on type (i).

MAIN COMMERCIAL VARIETIES

Aesthetic type (i): Baltic Brown, Monola Brown.
Aesthetic type (ii): Marron Guaiba.
Aesthetic type (iii): Caledonia, Caffè Bahia, Crystal Brown, Labrador Antique.

PHYSICAL-MECHANICAL CHARACTERISTICS
(average reference values)

	(i)	(ii)	(iii)		
compression breaking load	1.986	1.570	1.640	kg/cm²	ITALIAN STANDARD
compression breaking load after freezing	1.777	1.465		kg/cm²	
imbibition coefficient (by weight)	0.20	0.12	0.22	%	
ultimate tensile strength	118	53	118	kg/cm²	
impact test	62	58	50	cm	
thermal linear expansion coefficient	0.0070	0.0040	0.0090	mm/m°C	
frictional wear test		0.7	0.7	mm	
weight per unit of volume	2.640	2.540	2.732	kg/m³	
elasticity module	548.000	215.000		kg/cm²	
knoop microhardness				kg/mm²	

PHYSICAL-MECHANICAL CHARACTERISTICS
(average reference values)

		(i)	(ii)	(iii)		
absorption	(C97)	0.14		0.36	weight%	ASTM STANDARD
density	(C97)	2.678		2.693	kg/cu.m	
compressive strength	(C170)	148		170	MPa	
modulus of rupture	(C99)				MPa	
flexural strength	(C880)	4.9		14.6	MPa	
abrasion resistance	(C241)				hardness	

ORIENTED BROWN GRANITE

The most common varieties have large, ovoidal, dark brown crystals (*ghiande*), sometimes verging on a reddish color, embedded in a grey-black groundmass. The brown crystals are isoriented parallel to the bedding plane (rift), thereby giving the stone a definite polarity. There are varieties which have the same aesthetic characteristics as homogeneous brown granite type (iii) but their crystals are isoriented so the rock has an oriented pattern.

MAIN AESTHETIC CHARACTERISTICS

The main aesthetic variations are a variation in the brown color of the crystals and a variation in their distribution, which means that they are sometimes concentrated and sometimes less frequent, thereby affecting the uniformity of the pattern.

AESTHETIC VARIATIONS AND DEFECTS

The most well-known varieties are quarried in Canada and Brazil.

PRODUCER COUNTRIES

AVAILABILITY

There are not many quarrying areas for oriented brown granite varieties. Nevertheless, the most well-known varieties are readily available both in terms of quantity and quality and block sizes.

In view of their good technical characteristics, homogeneous brown granite varieties are generally suitable for all the normal uses in both interiors and exteriors. They are suitable for facings, floorings, pavings and special solid pieces alike.

USES

Autumn Brown, Marron Cafè, Polichrome.

MAIN COMMERCIAL VARIETIES

ITALIAN STANDARD			
compression breaking load	2.326	kg/cm^2	
compression breaking load after freezing	2.181	kg/cm^2	
imbibition coefficient (by weight)	0.13	%	
ultimate tensile strength	143	kg/cm^2	
impact test	72	cm	
thermal linear expansion coefficient	0.0050	mm/m°C	
frictional wear test	1.8	mm	
weight per unit of volume	2.706	kg/m^3	
elasticity module		kg/cm^2	
knoop microhardness		kg/mm^2	

PHYSICAL-MECHANICAL CHARACTERISTICS
(average reference values)

ASTM STANDARD				
absorption	(C97)	0.16	weight%
density	(C97)	2.689	kg/cu.m
compressive strength	(C170)	156	MPa
modulus of rupture	(C99)		MPa
flexural strength	(C880)	7.9	MPa
abrasion resistance	(C241)		hardness

PHYSICAL-MECHANICAL CHARACTERISTICS
(average reference values)

HOMOGENEOUS RED GRANITE

MAIN AESTHETIC CHARACTERISTICS

The best-quality materials have a deep red crystalline groundmass, homogeneously intermingled with misshapen black and/or grey crystals ranging from a few millimeters to a few centimeters across. The red groundmass is usually irregular but in some cases it is composed of subcircular or rectangular crystals up to 1-2 centimeters across. Some varieties also have a whitish-colored dotting which reduces the deepness of the red when observed from a distance.

AESTHETIC VARIATIONS AND DEFECTS

The principal aesthetic variations concern the color and can be so strong as to represent a real commercial defect. In many cases the red is not so deep as in the first quality material and may even verge on pink. White dotting may occur in all varieties, yet in varieties where it is a normal feature it may be quite widespread. The final result is a negative effect on the color characteristics of the material. Another type of variation consists of concentrations of red or black/grey minerals which may appear as spots of color once the material is installed, thereby adversely affecting the general chromatic uniformity of the material.

PRODUCER COUNTRIES

The main countries producing homogeneous red granite are Finland and India. Smaller quantities of this kind of material are also excavated in Sweden, South Africa and, to a lesser extent, in Brazil.

AVAILABILITY

In view of the numerous varieties available, there are no problems as regards average-sized orders but difficulties may arise for larger quantities. Normal supply is for medium-sized blocks.

USES

Homogeneous red granite varieties are normally used in interiors and exteriors for facings, floorings and pavings. Owing to their value, these materials are often selected for prestigious buildings and quality furnishings. They are quite frequently used locally for monumental stones too. The finished products are normally tiles or slabs, and the surface is generally polished. Good results can also be achieved with flaming, but in some cases it gives the color a tinge of orange. For large projects it is advisable to check on the quantities available prior to orders.

MAIN COMMERCIAL VARIETIES

African Red, Balmoral Red FG, Balmoral Red CG, Capaõ Bonito, Carmen Red, Eagle Red, Imperial Red, New Imperial, New Rubin, Rosso Braganza, Rosso Toledo, Tranas Red.

PHYSICAL-MECHANICAL CHARACTERISTICS
(average reference values)

			ITALIAN STANDARD
compression breaking load	1.928	kg/cm^2	
compression breaking load after freezing	1.784	kg/cm^2	
imbibition coefficient (by weight)	0.18	%	
ultimate tensile strength	158	kg/cm^2	
impact test	50	cm	
thermal linear expansion coefficient	0.0084	mm/m°C	
frictional wear test		mm	
weight per unit of volume	2.625	kg/m^3	
elasticity module	594.300	kg/cm^2	
knoop microhardness		kg/mm^2	

PHYSICAL-MECHANICAL CHARACTERISTICS
(average reference values)

				ASTM STANDARD
absorption	(C97)	0.17	weight%	
density	(C97)	2.636	kg/cu.m	
compressive strength	(C170)	165	MPa	
modulus of rupture	(C99)		MPa	
flexural strength	(C880)	12.2	MPa	
abrasion resistance	(C241)		hardness	

ORIENTED RED GRANITE

Unlike the previous type of materials, the groundmass of oriented red granite varieties is generally, although not always, composed of regular-shaped crystals which are usually ovoidal. The crystals are often evenly oriented, thereby giving the material a definite polarity (rift). Again, the best-quality varieties have a deep red groundmass, although the range of shades is fairly limited. The orientation of the pattern is generally constant as seen on the cut slab. Varieties are available both with and without white crystals.

MAIN AESTHETIC CHARACTERISTICS

The principal aesthetic variations concern the color and can be so strong as to represent a real commercial defect. In many cases the red is not so deep as in the first quality material and may even verge on pink. White dotting may occur in all varieties, yet in varieties where it is a normal feature it may be quite widespread. The final result is a negative effect on the color characteristics of the material. Another type of variation consists of concentrations of red or black/grey minerals which may appear as spots of color once the material is installed, thereby adversely affecting the general chromatic uniformity of the material.

AESTHETIC VARIATIONS AND DEFECTS

Oriented red granite varieties are mainly quarried in Argentina, Sweden, Russia, India, Egypt and, to a lesser extent, in Brazil.

PRODUCER COUNTRIES

In general, the availability of these materials is limited due to the lack of commercial varieties and the low production capacity of the quarrying areas.

AVAILABILITY

Oriented red granite varieties can be used in interiors and exteriors for facings, floorings and pavings. They are frequently used for special solid pieces too, especially when an oriented pattern is preferable to the static pattern of homogeneous granites. Large tiles or slabs are advisable to enhance the movement of the material. The surface is normally polished, although excellent results can often be achieved with flaming, especially in the case of varieties with large crystals. Flaming does, however, considerably decrease the movement of the pattern.

USES

Aswan Red, Rosso Perla India, Rosso Santiago, Sierra Chica, Vanga Red.

MAIN COMMERCIAL VARIETIES

RED GRANITE

ITALIAN STANDARD			
compression breaking load	1.978	kg/cm²
compression breaking load after freezing	1.904	kg/cm²
imbibition coefficient (by weight)	0.17	%
ultimate tensile strength	137	kg/cm²
impact test	53	cm
thermal linear expansion coefficient	0.0060	mm/m°C
frictional wear test		mm
weight per unit of volume	2.645	kg/m³
elasticity module	575.000	kg/cm²
knoop microhardness		kg/mm²

PHYSICAL-MECHANICAL CHARACTERISTICS (average reference values)

ASTM STANDARD			
absorption	(C97)	0.70	weight%
density	(C97)	2.670	kg/cu.m
compressive strength	(C170)	150	MPa
modulus of rupture	(C99)		MPa
flexural strength	(C880)	10.5	MPa
abrasion resistance	(C241)		hardness

PHYSICAL-MECHANICAL CHARACTERISTICS (average reference values)

115

VEINED RED GRANITE

MAIN AESTHETIC CHARACTERISTICS

These materials have a crystalline groundmass with a distinct flowing pattern created by the uneven overlapping of alternate, undulating, red and black-grey veins. The red veins may vary from brick red to red with a slight orange tone and there may also be white dotting which reduces the deepness of the overall red color. Significant variations may also occur as regards the shape, thickness and concentration of the veins of both colors. Consequently, the general color/pattern of the different materials may vary considerably. In particular, the color of the materials may range from bright red or slightly orange-red to brick red and even grey-red. The grain size is almost never constant and varies from medium to large as seen on a cut slab.

AESTHETIC VARIATIONS AND DEFECTS

As is true of all veined granite varieties, there may be significant variations in the aesthetic characteristics of the commercial varieties belonging to the group in question. The most frequent variations concern the shape and size of the black-grey veins. If there are many of these or they are large, they darken the color of the stone; if there are few or they are small, they reduce the flowing pattern of the material, which is obviously one of its qualities. In both cases, the stone loses its "personality" and looks like a bad copy of the original or even a completely different material. Another possible defect is the occurrence of *catene* or straight veins almost at right angles to the rift. If these are frequent or large, they may affect the flowing pattern.

PRODUCER COUNTRIES

Classical producer countries of veined red granite are India and Brazil. Some varieties are also produced in South Africa and, to a lesser extent, Madagascar.

AVAILABILITY

Availability varies considerably according to the different varieties. The predominantly red varieties are available in limited quantities of medium-sized blocks, whereas the red-grey varieties are more readily available. In view of the natural variations in the aesthetic characteristics, suppliers may well include similar varieties to the ones selected in large orders. In this case, it is advisable to conduct strict quality-control procedures on the raw material.

USES

Veined red granite varieties usually have the right characteristics to be used in interiors and exteriors for facings, floorings and pavings. However, owing to their aesthetic characteristics and limited availability, they are best used for luxurious interiors, (medium- to large-sized slabs) or for special solid pieces such as table tops. The flowing veined pattern makes these materials particularly suitable for quarter-match and book-match work. In order to highlight the movement of the pattern, it is always preferable to polish the surface.

MAIN COMMERCIAL VARIETIES

Cobra, Funil, Jacaranda, Juparanà Africa, Multicolor Red, Rainbow, Tiger Red, Tupim.

PHYSICAL-MECHANICAL CHARACTERISTICS
(average reference values)

compression breaking load	1.790	kg/cm²	ITALIAN STANDARD
compression breaking load after freezing	1.668	kg/cm²	
imbibition coefficient (by weight)	0.31	%	
ultimate tensile strength	133	kg/cm²	
impact test		cm	
thermal linear expansion coefficient	0.0086	mm/m°C	
frictional wear test		mm	
weight per unit of volume	2.660	kg/m³	
elasticity module	566.650	kg/cm²	
knoop microhardness		kg/mm²	

PHYSICAL-MECHANICAL CHARACTERISTICS
(average reference values)

absorption	(C97)	weight%	ASTM STANDARD
density	(C97)	kg/cu.m	
compressive strength	(C170)	MPa	
modulus of rupture	(C99)	MPa	
flexural strength	(C880)	MPa	
abrasion resistance	(C241)	hardness	

HOMOGENEOUS PINK GRANITE

Homogeneous pink granite varieties have a homogeneous groundmass of pink, white, grey and, to a lesser extent, black crystals. They are medium- to coarse-grained materials and some varieties have a *ghiandonato* pattern with pink crystals some centimeters across. Their color ranges from a very soft pink to a deep pink which verges on red.

MAIN AESTHETIC CHARACTERISTICS

The principal aesthetic variations include a lighter pink color or fewer pink crystals. In both cases, the rock tends to look greyish in color because of its other components. Common defects are veins (*bisce*) or black spots (*toppe*) and light-colored veins (*catene*) which cross the crystalline mass. Such defects reduce the value of the material.

AESTHETIC VARIATIONS AND DEFECTS

Homogeneous pink granite varieties are quarried in many countries. The most well-known varieties are from Spain and Italy, although other varieties from China have recently been placed on the market.

PRODUCER COUNTRIES

In view of the number of varieties available and the large quantities available, supply is usually very good. The market is often able to provide large quantities of large blocks.

AVAILABILITY

Homogeneous pink granite varieties are suitable for all the normal uses of dimension stone in both interiors and exteriors. Owing to the fact that they are readily available and they have a soft color, they are particularly suited to large facings, floorings and pavings. Furthermore, in view of their relatively low cost, these materials are widely used in the private residential building sector too. They are generally polished, although excellent results can also be achieved with flaming too.

USES

PINK GRANITE

Ghiandone Limbara, Ghiandone Rosato, Rosa Baveno, Rosa Beta, Rosa Kali, Rosa Porriño, Rosa Nule.

MAIN COMMERCIAL VARIETIES

ITALIAN STANDARD			
compression breaking load	1.719	kg/cm²
compression breaking load after freezing	1.653	kg/cm²
imbibition coefficient (by weight)	0.31	%
ultimate tensile strength	115	kg/cm²
impact test	61	cm
thermal linear expansion coefficient	0.0072	mm/m°C
frictional wear test		mm
weight per unit of volume	2.583	kg/m³
elasticity module	498.900	kg/cm²
knoop microhardness	512	kg/mm²

PHYSICAL-MECHANICAL CHARACTERISTICS
(average reference values)

ASTM STANDARD			
absorption	(C97)	0.29	weight%
density	(C97)	2.619	kg/cu.m
compressive strength	(C170)	154	MPa
modulus of rupture	(C99)		MPa
flexural strength	(C880)	10.5	MPa
abrasion resistance	(C241)	51.4	hardness

PHYSICAL-MECHANICAL CHARACTERISTICS
(average reference values)

117

ORIENTED PINK GRANITE

MAIN AESTHETIC CHARACTERISTICS

Like the homogeneous and veined varieties of the same color, oriented pink granite varieties generally have a fairly wide color range which goes from light pink to deep pink with various intermediate shades. Unlike the other two groups, though, the pink color often dominates the other components of the rock, be they white or grey-black. On the whole, this gives the material a more even color. The materials are normally fine- or medium-grained, and the orientation is accentuated by the dark minerals present in thin, broken layers. Some varieties are coarse-grained, in which case they form subovoidal crystals some centimeters across (*ghiande*) parallel to the rift of the rock. There may be so many *ghiande* that they touch one another, or they may be less concentrated or isolated on a dark groundmass.

AESTHETIC VARIATIONS AND DEFECTS

The main aesthetic variation is a variation in the deepness of the pink color, although this is fairly limited, especially in the fine-grained materials. A significant defect is the occurrence of white veins (*catene*) and/or black veins, since these affect the uniformity of the color and the oriented pattern.

PRODUCER COUNTRIES

Fine-grained oriented pink granite varieties are quarried in Norway and the United States, while coarse-grained varieties are quarried in India and South Africa.

AVAILABILITY

These materials are generally available in the quality and quantity required by the market, which is anyway fairly limited. There may be variations in the pink color as regards large orders in particular. The blocks are normally medium-sized.

USES

From a technical viewpoint, oriented pink granite varieties are suitable for all the normal uses of dimension stone in interiors and exteriors alike. In view of their aesthetic characteristics and availability, they are best used for quality furnishings and special solid pieces though. The surface is normally polished, although the coarse-grained varieties also look attractive when flamed.

MAIN COMMERCIAL VARIETIES

African Lilac, Pink Royal, Pink Salisbury.

PHYSICAL-MECHANICAL CHARACTERISTICS
(average reference values)

compression breaking load	1.811	kg/cm²	ITALIAN	
compression breaking load after freezing		kg/cm²	STANDARD	
imbibition coefficient (by weight)	0.28	%		
ultimate tensile strength	161	kg/cm²		
impact test	80	cm		
thermal linear expansion coefficient	0.0080	mm/m°C		
frictional wear test		mm		
weight per unit of volume	2.580	kg/m³		
elasticity module	370.000	kg/cm²		
knoop microhardness		kg/mm²		

PHYSICAL-MECHANICAL CHARACTERISTICS
(average reference values)

absorption	(C97)	weight%	ASTM	
density	(C97)	kg/cu.m	STANDARD	
compressive strength	(C170)	MPa		
modulus of rupture	(C99)	MPa		
flexural strength	(C880)	MPa		
abrasion resistance	(C241)	hardness		

VEINED PINK GRANITE

The crystalline groundmass of veined pink granite varieties has a distinct flowing appearance created by the uneven overlapping of alternate, undulating, broken pink and black-grey veins. The pink veins may vary from pale pink to deep pink (and sometimes orange), and there is often white dotting, which reduces the deepness of the overall pink color. Significant variations may also occur as regards the shape, thickness and concentration of the veins. In some cases the pink and grey-black veins are so closely amalgamated that the rock becomes grey-pink in color. The grain size is almost never constant and varies from medium to large as seen on a cut slab.

MAIN AESTHETIC CHARACTERISTICS

As is true of all veined granites, there may be significant variations in the aesthetic characteristics of the commercial varieties belonging to the group in question. The most frequent variations concern the shape and size of the black-grey veins. If there are many or they are large, they darken the color of the stone; if there are few or they are small, they reduce the flowing pattern of the stone, which is obviously one of its qualities. In both cases, the stone loses its "personality" and looks like a bad copy of the original or even a completely different material. Another possible defect is the presence of straight white veins (*catene*) at right angles to the main orientation of the stone. If these are frequent or large, they may affect the flowing nature of the pattern.

AESTHETIC VARIATIONS AND DEFECTS

Classical producer countries of veined red granite varieties are India and Brazil. Some varieties are also produced in small quantities in South Africa.

PRODUCER COUNTRIES

PINK GRANITE

Availability varies according to the different varieties. Supplies are constant, although not in large quantities. The natural variations in the aesthetic characteristics may well lead to significant variations in large orders. In this case, it is advisable to carry out strict quality-control procedures on the the raw material.

AVAILABILITY

Veined pink granite varieties usually have the right characteristics to be used in interiors and exteriors alike, for facings, floorings and pavings. However, owing to their aesthetic characteristics and availability, they are best used for luxurious interiors, in the form of medium- to large-sized slabs, or for special pieces such as table tops. The veined pattern of these materials especially lends itself to quarter-match and book-match work. In order to highlight the movement of the pattern, it is always preferable to polish the surface.

USES

Lambada, Lilla Gerais, Kinawa, Indian Juparanà, Rosa Raisa, Rosa Samambaia, Tiger Skin.

MAIN COMMERCIAL VARIETIES

ITALIAN STANDARD

compression breaking load	1.776	kg/cm²
compression breaking load after freezing	1.610	kg/cm²
imbibition coefficient (by weight)	0.23	%
ultimate tensile strength	152	kg/cm²
impact test		cm
thermal linear expansion coefficient	0.0073	mm/m°C
frictional wear test		mm
weight per unit of volume	2.621	kg/m³
elasticity module	510.000	kg/cm²
knoop microhardness		kg/mm²

PHYSICAL-MECHANICAL CHARACTERISTICS
(average reference values)

ASTM STANDARD

absorption	(C97)	weight%
density	(C97)	kg/cu.m
compressive strength	(C170)	MPa
modulus of rupture	(C99)	MPa
flexural strength	(C880)	MPa
abrasion resistance	(C241)	hardness

PHYSICAL-MECHANICAL CHARACTERISTICS
(average reference values)

HOMOGENEOUS POLYCHROMATIC GRANITE

MAIN AESTHETIC CHARACTERISTICS

The most frequent aesthetic types have a homogeneous crystalline groundmass composed of predominantly reddish-brown, sky blue and black crystals. The deepness of the former two colors and their respective quantities vary from one variety to the next. The materials are medium- to fine-grained.

AESTHETIC VARIATIONS AND DEFECTS

The most common aesthetic variation is a variation in the deepness of the dominant colors. The occurrence of veins of different colors (*catene*) and black spots are invariably considered defects.

PRODUCER COUNTRIES

The most well-known varieties of homogeneous reddish-brown and sky blue granite varieties are extracted in the United States and Sweden.

AVAILABILITY

There are few areas where these materials are quarried. Nevertheless, the few commercial varieties commonly found on the international market are generally available in fairly good quantities, although often in small and medium blocks.

USES

The physical-mechanical properties of homogeneous reddish-brown and sky blue granite varieties are such that they can be used for floorings, pavings and facings in interiors and exteriors alike. Selection should take into account, though, the fact that in some materials the sky blue color is not very clear at a distance of a few meters. It is therefore advisable to use these materials for interior furnishings (including special solid pieces) in order to highlight the materials' peculiar aesthetic characteristics. The finished products are generally polished; flaming is possible but may reduce the material's aesthetic value.

POLYCHR. GRANITE

MAIN COMMERCIAL VARIETIES

Dakota Mahogany, Royal Mahogany.

PHYSICAL-MECHANICAL CHARACTERISTICS
(average reference values)

compression breaking load	1.894	kg/cm^2	ITALIAN
compression breaking load after freezing	1.742	kg/cm^2	STANDARD
imbibition coefficient (by weight)	0.38	%	
ultimate tensile strength	168	kg/cm^2	
impact test	48	cm	
thermal linear expansion coefficient	0.0083	mm/m°C	
frictional wear test		mm	
weight per unit of volume	2.839	kg/m^3	
elasticity module	571.705	kg/cm^2	
knoop microhardness		kg/mm^2	

PHYSICAL-MECHANICAL CHARACTERISTICS
(average reference values)

absorption	(C97)	0.16	weight%	ASTM
density	(C97)	2.660	kg/cu.m	STANDARD
compressive strength	(C170)	180	MPa	
modulus of rupture	(C99)		MPa	
flexural strength	(C880)	11.0	MPa	
abrasion resistance	(C241)		hardness	

ORIENTED POLYCHROMATIC GRANITE

The most frequent aesthetic types have a crystalline groundmass, the crystals of which are brown verging on red, ovoidal and a few centimeters across (*ghiande*) along with smaller, sky blue crystals. There are also small black minerals but these occur in smaller quantities. The brown crystals are isoriented and give the rock a definite rift.

MAIN AESTHETIC CHARACTERISTICS

The most common aesthetic variation is a variation in the deepness of the dominant colors. The occurrence of veins of different colors (*catene*) and black spots are invariably considered defects.

AESTHETIC VARIATIONS AND DEFECTS

The most well-known varieties of oriented reddish-brown and sky blue granite are extracted in India.

PRODUCER COUNTRIES

There are few areas where these materials are quarried. The few commercial varieties commonly found on the international market are generally available in limited quantities of medium-sized blocks.

AVAILABILITY

The physical-mechanical properties of oriented reddish-brown and sky blue granite varieties are such that they can be used for floorings, facings and pavings in interiors and exteriors alike. Selection should take into account, though, the fact that in some materials the sky blue color is not very clear at a distance of a few meters. It is therefore advisable to use these materials for interior furnishings (including special solid pieces) in order to highlight the materials' peculiar aesthetic characteristics. The finished products are generally polished; flaming is possible but may reduce the material's aesthetic value.

USES

Saphire Brown.

MAIN COMMERCIAL VARIETIES

POLYCHR. GRANITE

ITALIAN STANDARD			
compression breaking load	2.364	kg/cm^2
compression breaking load after freezing	2.228	kg/cm^2
imbibition coefficient (by weight)	0.18	%
ultimate tensile strength	312	kg/cm^2
impact test		cm
thermal linear expansion coefficient		mm/m°C
frictional wear test		mm
weight per unit of volume	2.680	kg/m^3
elasticity module		kg/cm^2
knoop microhardness		kg/mm^2

PHYSICAL-MECHANICAL CHARACTERISTICS
(average reference values)

ASTM STANDARD		
absorption	(C97)	weight%
density	(C97)	kg/cu.m
compressive strength	(C170)	MPa
modulus of rupture	(C99)	MPa
flexural strength	(C880)	MPa
abrasion resistance	(C241)	hardness

PHYSICAL-MECHANICAL CHARACTERISTICS
(average reference values)

VEINED POLYCHROMATIC GRANITE

MAIN AESTHETIC CHARACTERISTICS
The most frequent aesthetic types have a crystalline groundmass composed of green and reddish-colored crystals. The colored areas appear either in bands or lenticular bodies with faded edges where the two colors intermingle. The percentage of each color varies according to the different varieties, and there may be frequent color variations even on a cut slab, thereby creating bright-colored spots erratically distributed over the softer-colored mass. There are also small, irregular-shaped, black veins parallel to the rock's rift. The grain is generally medium.

AESTHETIC VARIATIONS AND DEFECTS
The most common aesthetic variation is a variation in the percentage of the two colors. This may be so prominent that the same variety sometimes has green as the dominant color and sometimes red. In some cases the colors look faded as if they were veiled, which reduces their brightness. A fairly common defect is the occurrence of *oil stains* (*macchie d'unto*), which may be large.

PRODUCER COUNTRIES
Veined green and reddish-colored granite varieties are only extracted in Brazil.

AVAILABILITY
There are quite a few areas where these materials are quarried. However, since the materials vary considerably, problems may arise with large orders as regards the constancy of the specific aesthetic characteristics and/or supply times.

USES
From a technical viewpoint, veined brown and reddish-colored granite varieties are suitable for floorings, paving and facings in interiors and exteriors alike. In view of their aesthetic characteristics and availability, their use is recommended above all for interior furnishings, even large areas. However, in such cases they should not be used where color characteristics are required to be constant. Careful quality-control procedures are recommended in any case. These materials are also appropriate for special solid pieces. The finished products are normally polished.

MAIN COMMERCIAL VARIETIES
Gran Violet, Saint Tropez, Tropical Guarani.

POLYCHR. GRANITE

PHYSICAL-MECHANICAL CHARACTERISTICS
(average reference values)

compression breaking load	1.920	kg/cm²	ITALIAN
compression breaking load after freezing	1.810	kg/cm²	STANDARD
imbibition coefficient (by weight)	0.15	%	
ultimate tensile strength		kg/cm²	
impact test		cm	
thermal linear expansion coefficient		mm/m°C	
frictional wear test		mm	
weight per unit of volume	2.720	kg/cm³	
elasticity module		kg/cm²	
knoop microhardness		kg/mm²	

PHYSICAL-MECHANICAL CHARACTERISTICS
(average reference values)

absorption	(C97)	weight%	ASTM
density	(C97)	kg/cu.m	STANDARD
compressive strength	(C170)	MPa	
modulus of rupture	(C99)	MPa	
flexural strength	(C880)	MPa	
abrasion resistance	(C241)	hardness	

HOMOGENEOUS VIOLET GRANITE

Homogeneous violet-colored granite varieties have a uniform groundmass composed of minerals which are mostly pink-violet in color and, to a lesser extent, grey and black. The grains are medium-sized. Scattered over the crystalline groundmass are small red-violet-colored crystals, either as isolated crystals or in irregular-shaped aggregates which enhance the material's appearance.

MAIN AESTHETIC CHARACTERISTICS

The main aesthetic variation is a variation in the color of the pink-violet-colored crystals. Black spots (*toppe*) and white veins (*catene*) may also occur.

AESTHETIC VARIATIONS AND DEFECTS

The most common homogeneous violet granite varieties are quarried in Saudi Arabia.

PRODUCER COUNTRIES

The quantities available are limited due to the fact that there is only one commercial variety normally found on the international market. The blocks are large.

AVAILABILITY

Homogeneous violet granite varieties have the right technical characteristics for all normal uses in the building industry, in interiors and exteriors alike. However, owing to their availability and, above all, color characteristics, they are best used where their peculiar color characteristics can be appreciated, since these are not seen from a distance. For the same reason it is preferable to polish the surface of these materials.

USES

Violetta.

MAIN COMMERCIAL VARIETIES

VIOLET GRANITE

PHYSICAL-MECHANICAL CHARACTERISTICS
(average reference values)

ITALIAN STANDARD			
compression breaking load	1.900	kg/cm²
compression breaking load after freezing	1.830	kg/cm²
imbibition coefficient (by weight)		%
ultimate tensile strength	190	kg/cm²
impact test		cm
thermal linear expansion coefficient		mm/m°C
frictional wear test		mm
weight per unit of volume	2.700	kg/m³
elasticity module	580.000	kg/cm²
knoop microhardness		kg/mm²

PHYSICAL-MECHANICAL CHARACTERISTICS
(average reference values)

ASTM STANDARD			
absorption	(C97)	0.13	weight%
density	(C97)	2.640	kg/cu.m
compressive strength	(C170)	207	MPa
modulus of rupture	(C99)		MPa
flexural strength	(C880)	16.5	MPa
abrasion resistance	(C241)		hardness

123

VEINED VIOLET GRANITE

MAIN AESTHETIC CHARACTERISTICS
Veined violet granite varieties are composed of a chaotic mass of black minerals, often in thin, winding veins, and light-colored minerals, in particular light grey and violet. The latter are unevenly distributed among the black minerals and form frequent small, shapeless bodies in between the black veins. In some varieties the crystals are also pink, verging on orange. Because of the high percentage of black minerals, these materials are rather dark and look darker and darker the greater the distance of the observer. They are medium to fine-grained.

AESTHETIC VARIATIONS AND DEFECTS
Unlike the majority of veined granite varieties, the aesthetic characteristics of these materials do not normally vary significantly. A common defect is the occurrence of tears (*strappi*) and some varieties often have black spots (*toppe*).

PRODUCER COUNTRIES
The most well-known commercial varieties of violet-colored granite available on the international market are quarried in India.

AVAILABILITY
These materials are generally fairly readily available both in terms of quantity and quality. The blocks are large.

USES
Veined violet granite varieties are suitable for all the normal uses in interiors and exteriors alike. They are frequently used for floorings, pavings and facings, for which large-sized tiles or slabs are preferable since they enhance the materials' aesthetic characteristics. A polished surface is recommended for the same reason.

MAIN COMMERCIAL VARIETIES
Paradiso, Paradiso Bash.

VIOLET GRANITE

PHYSICAL-MECHANICAL CHARACTERISTICS
(average reference values)

			ITALIAN STANDARD
compression breaking load	1.899	kg/cm^2	
compression breaking load after freezing	1.745	kg/cm^2	
imbibition coefficient (by weight)		%	
ultimate tensile strength		kg/cm^2	
impact test		cm	
thermal linear expansion coefficient	0.0063	mm/m°C	
frictional wear test		mm	
weight per unit of volume	2.641	kg/m^3	
elasticity module	532.000	kg/cm^2	
knoop microhardness		kg/mm^2	

PHYSICAL-MECHANICAL CHARACTERISTICS
(average reference values)

			ASTM STANDARD
absorption	(C97)	weight%	
density	(C97)	kg/cu.m	
compressive strength	(C170)	MPa	
modulus of rupture	(C99)	MPa	
flexural strength	(C880)	MPa	
abrasion resistance	(C241)	hardness	

124

HOMOGENEOUS SKY BLUE GRANITE

The best quality material has a medium to fine-grained, crystalline groundmass composed of blue, white and black crystals. The black crystals may be concentrated in small irregular spots haphazardly distributed over the groundmass. In some varieties, there are greenish-colored crystals too.

MAIN AESTHETIC CHARACTERISTICS

Frequent aesthetic variations are variations in the concentration of the blue and white crystals which alter the general color of the materials. Furthermore, these materials often tend to have many dark and/or large spots which may lead to a significant reduction in their quality. Other defects include medium to large, whitish-colored spots and large, light or dark veins which adversely affect the uniformity of the color and pattern of the material.

AESTHETIC VARIATIONS AND DEFECTS

Common commercial varieties are quarried in Brazil and Zambia.

PRODUCER COUNTRIES

Availability of homogeneous sky blue granite varieties is limited due to the very few quarrying areas and the low productivity of these areas. The blocks are fairly small too and are often sold as shapeless blocks.

AVAILABILITY

From a technical viewpoint, sky blue granite varieties are suitable for all the normal uses of dimension stone with no particular limits. However, their color characteristics and above all their limited availability (which also makes them expensive materials) limit their use to small facings, floorings and pavings and more frequently to special solid pieces and in any case only top-quality projects. The surface is always polished.

USES

Azul Bahia, Blu King.

MAIN COMMERCIAL VARIETIES

SKY BLUE GRANITE

ITALIAN STANDARD			
compression breaking load	176.6	kg/cm²
compression breaking load after freezing		kg/cm²
imbibition coefficient (by weight)		%
ultimate tensile strength	16.5	kg/cm²
impact test	40	cm
thermal linear expansion coefficient	0.0012	mm/m°C
frictional wear test	0.75	mm
weight per unit of volume	2.553	kg/m³
elasticity module		kg/cm²
knoop microhardness		kg/mm²

PHYSICAL-MECHANICAL CHARACTERISTICS (average reference values)

ASTM STANDARD			
absorption	(C97)	weight%
density	(C97)	kg/cu.m
compressive strength	(C170)	MPa
modulus of rupture	(C99)	MPa
flexural strength	(C880)	MPa
abrasion resistance	(C241)	hardness

PHYSICAL-MECHANICAL CHARACTERISTICS (average reference values)

125

HOMOGENEOUS BLUE GRANITE

MAIN AESTHETIC CHARACTERISTICS

The most typical varieties are composed of a homogeneous blue and black groundmass. The blue crystals are up to a few centimeters across and are so numerous and so large compared to the black crystals that they take up almost the entire structure of the rock. The blue color of the individual crystals varies according to the angle of incidence of the light, thereby generating the iridescence and metal reflections typical of these materials. The color ranges from light blue to dark blue with numerous intermediate shades depending on the variety.

AESTHETIC VARIATIONS AND DEFECTS

The main aesthetic variations, albeit infrequent, are variations in the deepness of the color. Some varieties have a kind of opalescence which dims the brightness of the blue crystals.

PRODUCER COUNTRIES

The classical varieties of homogeneous blue granite all come from Norway, although they are also produced in Ukraine.

AVAILABILITY

Despite the limited number of quarrying areas and the low productivity of the quarries, homogeneous blue granite varieties are fairly easy to find on the market. The lighter-colored varieties are found in relatively larger quantities than the darker ones, for which availability problems may be incurred. The blocks are generally medium and large.

USES

From a technical viewpoint, homogeneous blue granite varieties are suitable for all the normal uses of dimension stone in interiors and exteriors. However, their color characteristics and availability make them expensive materials (they include some of the most expensive varieties of dimension stone) and this prevents their use on a large scale. Consequently, they are used mainly for facings and floorings in prestigious public buildings and special solid pieces in luxury furnishings. The darker varieties in particular are commonly used in funerary art too. The surface is polished.

MAIN COMMERCIAL VARIETIES

Artic Blu, Blue Pearl, Emerald Pearl, Labrador, Marina Pearl.

BLUE GRANITE

PHYSICAL-MECHANICAL CHARACTERISTICS
(average reference values)

			ITALIAN STANDARD
compression breaking load	2.250	kg/cm²	
compression breaking load after freezing	1.969	kg/cm²	
imbibition coefficient (by weight)		%	
ultimate tensile strength	201	kg/cm²	
impact test	46	cm	
thermal linear expansion coefficient	0.0085	mm/m°C	
frictional wear test		mm	
weight per unit of volume	2.740	kg/m³	
elasticity module	753.000	kg/cm²	
knoop microhardness		kg/mm²	

PHYSICAL-MECHANICAL CHARACTERISTICS
(average reference values)

				ASTM STANDARD
absorption	(C97)	0.19	weight%	
density	(C97)	2.678	kg/cu.m	
compressive strength	(C170)	123.9	MPa	
modulus of rupture	(C99)		MPa	
flexural strength	(C880)	10.3	MPa	
abrasion resistance	(C241)		hardness	

126

VEINED BLUE GRANITE

Veined blue granite have a medium- to fine-grained groundmass, which is usually a light bluish color, crossed by a close-knit pattern of irregular-shaped, erratic, dark blue veins. There are normally small red crystals in the groundmass too, which are more or less parallel to the veins. In some varieties the groundmass is dark blue, verging on black and may be crossed by infrequent, thin, pinkish-colored veins.

MAIN AESTHETIC CHARACTERISTICS

Veined blue granite varieties do not have significant variations as regards their aesthetic characteristics. These materialls are fairly *secchi* and hence tend to be fragile. They fairly frequently have tears *(strappi)* and less frequently oil stains.

AESTHETIC VARIATIONS AND DEFECTS

The main veined blue granite varieties available on the international market are quarried in India.

PRODUCER COUNTRIES

These materials are fairly readily available owing to the relatively high number of commercial varieties on the international market and the quantities produced. The light blue varieties are more frequently available in medium- and large-sized blocks, while the dark blue varieties are often in medium- and small-sized blocks.

AVAILABILITY

In view of their physical-mechanical characteristics, veined blue granite varieties are suitable for facings, floorings and pavings in interiors and exteriors alike. However, their color characteristics are such that they are mostly used for quality interiors and special solid pieces. The darker varieties are often used in funerary art too. Their pattern is enhanced when they are used in the form of large slabs. The surface is always polished.

USES

Himalayan Blu, Orissa Blu, Paradiso Blu, Samantha Blu, Vizag, Vizag Light.

MAIN COMMERCIAL VARIETIES

BLUE GRANITE

ITALIAN STANDARD			
compression breaking load	1.933	kg/cm^2
compression breaking load after freezing	1.590	kg/cm^2
imbibition coefficient (by weight)	0.22	%
ultimate tensile strength	111	kg/cm^2
impact test		cm
thermal linear expansion coefficient		mm/m°C
frictional wear test		mm
weight per unit of volume	2.623	kg/m^3
elasticity module	566.000	kg/cm^2
knoop microhardness		kg/mm^2

PHYSICAL-MECHANICAL CHARACTERISTICS
(average reference values)

ASTM STANDARD			
absorption	(C97)	weight%
density	(C97)	kg/cu.m
compressive strength	(C170)	MPa
modulus of rupture	(C99)	MPa
flexural strength	(C880)	MPa
abrasion resistance	(C241)	hardness

PHYSICAL-MECHANICAL CHARACTERISTICS
(average reference values)

127

HOMOGENEOUS GREEN GRANITE

MAIN AESTHETIC CHARACTERISTICS

The most well-known varieties have a crystalline groundmass which is either green, whitish or black. In aesthetic type (i) the green crystals are medium to large and dominate the other components of the rock in terms of color. The overall color is bottle green. Aesthetic type (ii) has medium-sized green crystals which, together with the other minerals, form a uniform crystalline mass, the overall color of which varies according to the different commercial varieties. The crystals in some varieties are slightly oriented, although this does not affect the overall uniformity of the pattern. In the third aesthetic type (iii) the green crystals are dominated by black crystals and fill the interstices left by the latter. In this case there are no white crystals and the materials are medium- to fine-grained and black-green in color.

AESTHETIC VARIATIONS AND DEFECTS

In aesthetic type (i) the distribution of the crystals of the three different colors may be fairly erratic. This causes irregular concentrations of dark and light colors, which are invariably considered aesthetic defects. One more significant defect in this type is the occurrence of oil stains and tears *(strappi),* which appear as small whitish-colored lines on the polished surface. The main aesthetic variation in type (ii) is the variation in the green color and as far as type (iii) is concerned, there may be an erratic distribution of the black and green crystals as in type (i).

PRODUCER COUNTRIES

Type (i) varieties are quarried in Finland; type (ii) varieties in India, Saudi Arabia and in Italy too; type (iii) are only extracted in India.

AVAILABILITY

Homogeneous green granite varieties are not very common. The more readily available materials are type (i) varieties. They are available on the market in fairly good quantities, although in some cases there may be limits to supplies, especially for large orders. The blocks are generally medium and large. Types (ii) and (iii), however, are limited in terms of quantity and are available in small- and medium-sized blocks.

USES

The homogeneous green granite varieties available on the international market generally have the right technical characteristics to be used both for facings and floorings in interiors and exteriors.
Owing to their limited availability, type (ii) and (iii) varieties are more suited to small projects and special solid pieces or anyway quality furnishings. The most appropriate surface treatment is polishing, although good mechanical results can be achieved with flaming on type (i) varieties, yet this greys the overall color.

MAIN COMMERCIAL VARIETIES

Aesthetic type (i): Baltic Green.
Aesthetic type (ii): Oriental Green, Verde Aosta, Verde Argento, Verde Mergozzo.
Aesthetic type (iii): Verde Fiorito.

PHYSICAL-MECHANICAL CHARACTERISTICS
(average reference values)

	(i)	(ii)	(iii)		
compression breaking load	1.770	2.525	2.200	kg/cm²	ITALIAN STANDARD
compression breaking load after freezing	1.750		1.970	kg/cm²	
imbibition coefficient (by weight)	0.15	0.26	0.20	%	
ultimate tensile strength	116	146	115	kg/cm²	
impact test	60	70		cm	
thermal linear expansion coefficient	0.0065			mm/m°C	
frictional wear test				mm	
weight per unit of volume	2.585	2.636	2.720	kg/m³	
elasticity module	530.000			kg/cm²	
knoop microhardness		400		kg/mm²	

PHYSICAL-MECHANICAL CHARACTERISTICS
(average reference values)

absorption	(C97)	weight%	ASTM STANDARD
density	(C97)	kg/cu.m	
compressive strength	(C170)	MPa	
modulus of rupture	(C99)	MPa	
flexural strength	(C880)	MPa	
abrasion resistance	(C241)	hardness	

GREEN GRANITE

ORIENTED GREEN GRANITE

There are basically three aesthetic types of oriented green granite on the international market. Like some homogeneous varieties, type (i) varieties have green, black and subordinate, whitish-colored crystals. The green crystals are large and dominate the other components of the rock in terms of color. The overall color is bottle green and the rock's rift is given by the orientation of the green crystals. The second aesthetic type (ii) varieties have a crystalline mass which ranges in color from deep green to dark green according to the different varieties. The green crystals are medium and coarse and are intermingled with smaller, black crystals. All the crystals have an orientation which gives the rock a definite polarity. Another feature of this type is a limited quantity of yellowish-colored speckles evenly distributed over the green crystalline mass. The third aesthetic type (iii) varieties have a medium- to fine-grained, light green groundmass which is fairly uniform, over which there are dark, shapeless masses (*fiocchi*) a few centimeters across and red-violet-colored crystals, either isolated or in groups. The dark masses and the red-violet-colored crystals produce a slightly oriented pattern overall.

In type (i) the distribution of the crystals of the three different colors may be fairly erratic, which causes irregular concentrations of dark and, less frequently, light colors which are invariably aesthetic defects. One significant defect in this type is the occurrence of *oil stains* (*macchie d'unto*). The main aesthetic variation in type (ii) is an increased concentration of the yellowish-colored speckles which alters the overall color characteristics. Some varieties may also have *oil stains*. As far as type (iii) is concerned, the main variation concerns the color of the groundmass which verges on shades of grey.

Type (i) varieties are quarried in South Africa and Brazil, while the majority of type (ii) and type (iii) varieties are extracted in Brazil.

Type (i) varieties are available in good quantities, despite the fact that they come from practically only one quarrying area. The blocks are medium to large. Type (ii) varieties are less readily available than type (i) and supply problems may arise for large orders. Strict quality-control is recommended for this type. Again the blocks are generally medium and large. There are no real problems as regards the supply of medium-sized quantities of type (iii) materials. The blocks are large.

GREEN
GRANITE

			(i)	(ii)	(iii)	
ASTM STANDARD	absorption	(C97)	0.20		0.21	weight%
	density	(C97)	2.713		2.620	kg/cu.m
	compressive strength	(C170)	219		164.5	MPa
	modulus of rupture	(C99)	11.7		19.3	MPa
	flexural strength	(C880)	13.2		13.9	MPa
	abrasion resistance	(C241)				hardness

129

Oriented green granite varieties generally have the right technical characteristics to be used both in interiors and exteriors.

In view of the fact that they are more readily available, type (i) varieties can be used in fairly large projects too, although strict quality-control procedures are recommended. Type (ii) and (iii) varieties are more suitable for special solid pieces in quality interiors. The most common surface finishing is polishing, although good results can be achieved with flaming on type (i) varieties, yet this greys the overall color.

MAIN COMMERCIAL VARIETIES

Aesthetic type (i): Verde Fontein, Verde Lavras, Verde Mare.
Aesthetic type (ii): Verde Esmeralda.
Aesthetic type (iii): Verde Eucalipto.

GREEN GRANITE

PHYSICAL-MECHANICAL CHARACTERISTICS
(average reference values)

	(i)	(ii)	(iii)		ITALIAN STANDARD
compression breaking load	1.920	1.850	2.240	kg/cm²	
compression breaking load after freezing	1.822			kg/cm²	
imbibition coefficient (by weight)	0.14		0.16	%	
ultimate tensile strength	200	205	160	kg/cm²	
impact test		40	52	cm	
thermal linear expansion coefficient		0.0035	0.0060	mm/m°C	
frictional wear test				mm	
weight per unit of volume	2.700	2.690	2.735	kg/m³	
elasticity module				kg/cm²	
knoop microhardness				kg/mm²	

VEINED GREEN GRANITE

There are at least two different aesthetic types of veined green granite. Type (i) varieties have a dark green crystalline groundmass generally composed of medium-sized crystals and crossed by winding, black veins a few centimeters thick which create a chaotic pattern. In some varieties, the color of some crystals in the groundmass verges on pink. Type (ii) varieties have a medium- to fine-grained crystalline mass with light green, continuous veins alternating with thinner, whitish-colored veins (close to one another) forming a flowing pattern which is clearly visible on a cut slab.

MAIN AESTHETIC CHARACTERISTICS

In type (i) there may be signficant variations in the pattern, although these are generally tolerated by the market. One more serious defect is the occurrence of oil stains *(macchie d'unto)* and in some cases tears *(strappi)* which show up as small, whitish-colored lines on the polished surface. The main variation in type (ii) materials is a variation in the green color of the veins which may verge on grey, thereby reducing the quality.

AESTHETIC VARIATIONS AND DEFECTS

Type (i) varieties are essentially quarried in Brazil, while type (ii) varieties are extracted in India.

PRODUCER COUNTRIES

Type (i) varieties are available in fairly good quantities and the blocks are large. Delays may be incurred as regards supply times, though, in the case of large quantities. Availability of type (ii) varieties is limited since there is currently only one commercial variety quarried. Nevertheless, the quantities quarried guarantee a certain continuity in the production of large blocks.

AVAILABILITY

Both types of veined green granite have the right physical-mechanical characteristics to be used both in interiors and exteriors. However, in order to enhance their aesthetic characteristics, they are best used in interiors for floorings and facings alike, if possible in the form of slabs or, alternatively, large tiles. In addition, these materials are particularly suitable for special solid pieces in quality furnishings and in some cases good results can be achieved with book-match and quarter-match patterns. The surface is polished.

USES

Aesthetic type (i): Verde Acquamarina, Verde Candeias, Verde San Francisco, Verde Maritaca.
Aesthetic type (ii): Verde Marina.

MAIN COMMERCIAL VARIETIES

ITALIAN STANDARD		(i)	(ii)	
compression breaking load		2.607	2.300	kg/cm^2
compression breaking load after freezing		1.973	1.970	kg/cm^2
imbibition coefficient (by weight)		0.23	0.25	%
ultimate tensile strength		134	115	kg/cm^2
impact test				cm
thermal linear expansion coefficient				mm/m°C
frictional wear test				mm
weight per unit of volume		2.751	2.730	kg/m^3
elasticity module				kg/cm^2
knoop microhardness				kg/mm^2

PHYSICAL-MECHANICAL CHARACTERISTICS
(average reference values)

GREEN GRANITE

ASTM STANDARD			(i)	(ii)	
absorption	(C97)		0.16		weight%
density	(C97)		2.635		kg/cu.m
compressive strength	(C170)		142		MPa
modulus of rupture	(C99)		13.8		MPa
flexural strength	(C880)				MPa
abrasion resistance	(C241)				hardness

PHYSICAL-MECHANICAL CHARACTERISTICS
(average reference values)

HOMOGENEOUS GREY GRANITE

MAIN AESTHETIC CHARACTERISTICS

Homogeneous grey granite have a homogeneous groundmass composed of grey, whitish and, to a lesser extent, black crystals (i). The grain may be fine, medium or coarse. In the latter case, there are *ghiandonato* varieties too. The overall color of the different varieties ranges from light grey to dark grey and is determined by the quantities of the three types of crystals. In some fine- and medium-grained varieties there are no grey crystals and the strong contrast between the white and black crystals creates the so-called *sale e pepe* effect. Materials are also available on the market with grey (in this case verging on a bluish color), white and black minerals which are concentrated in areas of various shapes and sizes and make the overall color of the material very uneven (ii).

AESTHETIC VARIATIONS AND DEFECTS

The possible aesthetic variations which are, however, fairly infrequent, are caused by concentrations of grey or white crystals. This makes the overall color uneven. More serious defects are white veins of various shapes and sizes (*catene*) and black veins and spots (*bisce* and *toppe*).

PRODUCER COUNTRIES

Homogeneous grey granite varieties are produced in many countries. The most well-known medium- and coarse-grained varieties on the international market are extracted in Italy and Spain, while the fine-grained ones are extracted in Brazil and Portugal. Some varieties are also quarried in China.

AVAILABILITY

These materials, especially the medium- and coarse-grained varieties, are some of the most common dimension stone varieties available, although the fine-grained varieties are relatively less common. They are usually readily available and are traded in large-sized blocks. However, it is not uncommon to find a certain percentage of material with aesthetic defects in lots for large orders.

USES

Homogeneous grey granite varieties are suitable for all the normal uses of dimension stone in both interiors and exteriors. Owing to the fact that they are readily available, they generally cost less than other-colored granites. Hence, they can be more widely used in various areas of the building industry. The surface of these materials can be polished, flamed (medium- and coarse-grained varieties) or even bush-hammered. In the latter case, the overall color appears a little lighter.

MAIN COMMERCIAL VARIETIES

Aesthetic type (i): Aveiro, Ghiandone Grigio, Grigio Perla, Grigio Malaga, Grigio Sardo, Grigio Sardo Champagne, Gris Perla, Padang Light, Padang Dark, Saint Louis. Aesthetic type (ii): Azul Aran.

PHYSICAL-MECHANICAL CHARACTERISTICS
(average reference values)

	(i)	(ii)		
compression breaking load	1.533	911	kg/cm²	ITALIAN STANDARD
compression breaking load after freezing	1.556		kg/cm²	
imbibition coefficient (by weight)	0.47	1.0	%	
ultimate tensile strength	150	101	kg/cm²	
impact test	69	135	cm	
thermal linear expansion coefficient	0.0080		mm/m°C	
frictional wear test		0.5	mm	
weight per unit of volume	2.623	2.550	kg/m³	
elasticity module	490.000		kg/cm²	
knoop microhardness			kg/mm²	

PHYSICAL-MECHANICAL CHARACTERISTICS
(average reference values)

		(i)	(ii)		
absorption	(C97)	0.30		weight%	ASTM STANDARD
density	(C97)	2.600		kg/cu.m	
compressive strength	(C170)	167		MPa	
modulus of rupture	(C99)			MPa	
flexural strength	(C880)	10.8		MPa	
abrasion resistance	(C241)	52.1		hardness	

ORIENTED GREY GRANITE

Oriented grey granite varieties have a homogeneous groundmass composed of grey, whitish and black crystals with a definite orientation. The grain may be fine, medium or coarse. The overall color of the different varieties ranges from light grey to dark grey and is determined by the quantities of the three types of crystals. In some fine- and medium-grained varieties the individual crystals do not have clear edges and this creates a general speckling effect. Some varieties have a *ghiandonato* pattern, whereby the whitish-colored crystals form sub-ovoidal *ghiande* a few centimeters across embedded in a grey-black groundmass.

MAIN AESTHETIC CHARACTERISTICS

The principal aesthetic variation is a variation in the overall grey color. In the *ghiandonato* varieties, the *ghiande* may be more or less concentrated, thereby altering the uniformity of the color and pattern of the rock. Straight, white veins (*catene*) are considered a defect too.

AESTHETIC VARIATIONS AND DEFECTS

Oriented grey granite materials are extracted in numerous countries, although the most well-known varieties on the international market are produced in Italy.

PRODUCER COUNTRIES

The availability of these materials varies according to the different varieties, although generally no real problems arise. In some cases large blocks are not available.

AVAILABILITY

Oriented grey granite varieties are suitable for facings, floorings and pavings in interiors and exteriors. Some varieties are used on local markets in solid pieces for door frames, window sills, shelves, etc. The surface may be polished or, as is not uncommon, honed or bush-hammered. If the material is used in solid pieces, a split face finish is possible too. Only in a few cases are good results achieved with flaming.

USES

Beola Bianca, Beola Ghiandonata, Beola Grigia, Serizzo Antigorio, Serizzo Formazza, Serizzo Ghiandone, Serizzo Scuro Valmasino.

MAIN COMMERCIAL VARIETIES

ITALIAN STANDARD			
compression breaking load	1.720	kg/cm^2	
compression breaking load after freezing	1.664	kg/cm^2	
imbibition coefficient (by weight)	0.32	%	
ultimate tensile strength	139	kg/cm^2	
impact test	86	cm	
thermal linear expansion coefficient	0.0050	mm/m°C	
frictional wear test		mm	
weight per unit of volume	2.661	kg/m^3	
elasticity module		kg/cm^2	
knoop microhardness	487	kg/mm^2	

PHYSICAL-MECHANICAL CHARACTERISTICS
(average reference values)

GREY GRANITE

ASTM STANDARD		
absorption	(C97)	weight%
density	(C97)	kg/cu.m
compressive strength	(C170)	MPa
modulus of rupture	(C99)	MPa
flexural strength	(C880)	MPa
abrasion resistance	(C241)	hardness

PHYSICAL-MECHANICAL CHARACTERISTICS
(average reference values)

BLACK GRANITE

MAIN AESTHETIC CHARACTERISTICS

There are two aesthetically different types available on the market. The most well-known type (i) is dark grey in color because of the close association of grey and black minerals. The overall color is fairly homogeneous and no significant variations can be seen on a cut slab. The grain is medium and again this is fairly constant. The second type (ii) has a black crystalline groundmass, over which numerous small bright crystals are evenly distributed.

AESTHETIC VARIATIONS AND DEFECTS

Type (i) varieties may vary signficantly in color from one block to the next, to the extent that they are divided into dark grey and light grey varieties. The former are considered to be better quality materials. The raw material on the international market does not seem to have any major defects. In aesthetic type (ii) varieties though, if the material is cut in the wrong direction, this adversely affects the main aesthetic characteristic which is the occurrence of bright crystalline elements.

PRODUCER COUNTRIES

The types of black granite currently available on the international market are produced in South Africa and India.

AVAILABILITY

Despite the fact that all the varieties on the market come from practically only one quarrying area, type (i) is generally readily available, although darker-colored varieties in large blocks may only be available in limited quantities. Type (ii), on the other hand, is only available in limited quantities.

USES

Type (i) black granites are suitable for all uses in both interiors and exteriors. Thanks to the uniformity of the color, excellent aesthetic results can be achieved with large facings on prestigious public buildings where these materials can be combined with light-colored materials. In such cases, though, strict quality-control procedures are required. These materials are also widely used in funerary art. The usual finished products are large slabs, tiles in various sizes and solid pieces. The most frequent type of surface treatment is polishing and interesting effects can be achieved by combining polishing with impact treatment. Type (ii) materials are suitable for the above uses too, although they are best used for special solid pieces in luxury interiors where it is possible to appreciate the delicate brightness of the crystals (visible on a polished surface).

MAIN COMMERCIAL VARIETIES

Aesthetic type (i): Nero Africa.
Aesthetic type (ii): Galaxy Black.

PHYSICAL-MECHANICAL CHARACTERISTICS
(average reference values)

	(i)	(ii)		
compression breaking load	2.823	2.370	kg/cm^2	ITALIAN STANDARD
compression breaking load after freezing	2.828	2.520	kg/cm^2	
imbibition coefficient (by weight)	0.06	0.02	%	
ultimate tensile strength	254	275	kg/cm^2	
impact test	70	75	cm	
thermal linear expansion coefficient	0.0060	0.0065	mm/m°C	
frictional wear test			mm	
weight per unit of volume	2.942	2.930	kg/m^3	
elasticity module			kg/cm^2	
knoop microhardness			kg/mm^2	

PHYSICAL-MECHANICAL CHARACTERISTICS
(average reference values)

		(i)	(ii)		
absorption	(C97)	0.09		weight%	ASTM STANDARD
density	(C97)	2.920		kg/cu.m	
compressive strength	(C170)	245		MPa	
modulus of rupture	(C99)	26		MPa	
flexural strength	(C880)			MPa	
abrasion resistance	(C241)			hardness	

ABSOLUTE BLACK GRANITE

This group includes the only granite varieties which are totally monochromatic like many marble and stone varieties. The best quality materials are those which have a fine-grained, deep black crystalline groundmass with no other features. The groundmass of the lower quality materials verges on a greyish color due to the presence of light grey minerals, but they are still fine-grained materials.

The only aesthetic variation tolerated is a lighter color, due either to an increase in the percentage content of the light grey minerals or, less frequently, to an increase in the grain size. In both cases, the value of the material is reduced. The occurrence of agglomerates (a few millimeters across) of bright crystals (*manine or stelline*) and white crystals which may be millimeters across are considered to be defects. Absolute black granites may also have what are known as oil stains.

Absolute black granite varieties are quarried in saleable quantities in Zimbabwe, South Africa and India.

Owing to the few quarrying areas and the very low productivity of such areas, the availability of these materials is limited. The best quality materials are only really available in small blocks (1-3 cu.m) and in small quantities. The lower-quality materials are available in relatively larger quantities of larger blocks.

The physical-mechanical characteristics of these materials are such that there are no limits to their possible uses. However, their use is restricted by their limited availability. The best quality materials are used above all for special solid pieces in luxury furnishings and funerary art. The lower quality materials may be more widely used for facings, floorings and pavings, perhaps combined with materials of other colors. The surface is always polished.

Absolute Black Belfast, Absolute Black India, Absolute Black Zimbabwe.

ITALIAN STANDARD				PHYSICAL-MECHANICAL CHARACTERISTICS (average reference values)
compression breaking load		3.011	kg/cm²	
compression breaking load after freezing		2.636	kg/cm²	
imbibition coefficient (by weight)		0.016	%	
ultimate tensile strength		280	kg/cm²	
impact test		69	cm	
thermal linear expansion coefficient			mm/m°C	
frictional wear test			mm	
weight per unit of volume		2.989	kg/m³	
elasticity module		105.000	kg/cm²	
knoop microhardness			kg/mm²	

ASTM STANDARD				PHYSICAL-MECHANICAL CHARACTERISTICS (average reference values)
absorption	(C97)	0.09	weight%	
density	(C97)	3.100	kg/cu.m	
compressive strength	(C170)	348.8	MPa	
modulus of rupture	(C99)		MPa	
flexural strength	(C880)	26.6	MPa	
abrasion resistance	(C241)		hardness	

BLACK
GRANITE

Quartzite

Quartzite varieties are available on the international market in the following colors:

PINK QUARTZITE

SKY BLUE QUARTZITE

Note: The values given for the physical-mechanical tests are only indicative, since they are taken from existing literature or material furnished by various stone producer/suppliers. Where values are not reported, information was not available or could not be confirmed. The author takes no responsibility for any mistakes or omissions regarding the values given.

PINK QUARTZITE

MAIN AESTHETIC CHARACTERISTICS	These materials have a basically homogeneous fine-grained, crystalline groundmass. The pink color varies from one variety to the next. The color is not very even, especially in the deeper pink varieties, and there are frequent mellow, light-colored veins which give the material a precise orientation (rift).
AESTHETIC VARIATIONS AND DEFECTS	The main aesthetic variations concern the deepness of the pink color. One significant defect is the occurrence of whitish-colored *catene* which affects the uniformity of the material.
PRODUCER COUNTRIES	All the varieties of pink quartzite regularly found on the international market are quarried in Brazil.
AVAILABILITY	Pink quartzite varieties are generally available in fairly good quantities of medium- and large-sized blocks.
USES	From a technical viewpoint, pink quartzite varieties are suitable for all the normal uses of dimension stone. However, their color characteristics generally limit their use to special projects. They are often used for special solid pieces such as table tops and bathroom facings. In such cases, it is advisable to perform strict quality-control procedures on the material.
MAIN COMMERCIAL VARIETIES	Quarzite Flamingo, Quarzite Rosa, Quarzite Rosa Chiaro, Quarzite Rosa Corallo.

PHYSICAL-MECHANICAL CHARACTERISTICS
(average reference values)

compression breaking load	1.900	kg/cm²	ITALIAN
compression breaking load after freezing	1.720	kg/cm²	STANDARD
imbibition coefficient (by weight)	0.43	%	
ultimate tensile strength	202	kg/cm²	
impact test	80	cm	
thermal linear expansion coefficient	0.0016	mm/m°C	
frictional wear test	0.47	mm	
weight per unit of volume	2.632	kg/m³	
elasticity module		kg/cm²	
knoop microhardness		kg/mm²	

PHYSICAL-MECHANICAL CHARACTERISTICS
(average reference values)

absorption	(C97)	weight%	ASTM
density	(C97)	kg/cu.m	STANDARD
compressive strength	(C170)	MPa	
modulus of rupture	(C99)	MPa	
flexural strength	(C880)	MPa	
abrasion resistance	(C241)	hardness	

SKY BLUE QUARTZITE

Sky Blue quartzite varieties have a fine-grained crystalline groundmass ranging in color from light blue to white with thin, broken, darker blue veins which generally have a definite orientation. The veins sometimes appear in bands a few dozen centimeters thick. The transition between the blue and white areas of the crystalline mass is gradual and delicate and the size of the areas varies depending on the quality of the material. The better quality materials have more blue areas.

MAIN AESTHETIC CHARACTERISTICS

The principal aesthetic variations concern the deepness and constancy of the blue color in the crystalline mass as well as the frequency of the deep blue veins. These variations are so frequent that it is difficult to establish precise quality standards and each block often has its own aesthetic qualities. As far as defects are concerned, blue quartzite varieties rather frequently have light greenish-colored areas which are considered unattractive and therefore lower the value of the material. Another fairly common defect is the occurrence of straight, yellowish-colored veins which often correspond to *peli furbi*. A decidedly more significant defect, though, is the occurrence of irregular-shaped, greyish areas and whitish-colored *catene*.

AESTHETIC VARIATIONS AND DEFECTS

All the sky blue quartzite varieties normally found on the international market are quarried in Brazil.

PRODUCER COUNTRIES

Although there are different varieties of blue quartzite, they are generally only found in small quantities and quarried in small-medium, often shapeless blocks.

AVAILABILITY

From a technical viewpoint, sky blue quartzite varieties are suitable for all the normal uses of dimension stone. However, their color characteristics and, above all, their limited availability and fairly high costs generally limit their use to special projects. These materials are normally used for luxury furnishings such as table tops, solid pieces and bathroom facings. In such cases, it is advisable to perform strict quality-control procedures on the material. They are also used for funerary art and decorations combined with other materials in facings, floorings and pavings.

USES

Azul Boquira, Azul Macaubas, Azul Imperial.

MAIN COMMERCIAL VARIETIES

ITALIAN STANDARD			
compression breaking load	2.130	kg/cm^2	
compression breaking load after freezing	2.090	kg/cm^2	
imbibition coefficient (by weight)	0.11	%	
ultimate tensile strength	203	kg/cm^2	
impact test	81	cm	
thermal linear expansion coefficient	0.0014	mm/m°C	
frictional wear test	0.54	mm	
weight per unit of volume	2.680	kg/m^3	
elasticity module		kg/cm^2	
knoop microhardness		kg/mm^2	

PHYSICAL-MECHANICAL CHARACTERISTICS
(average reference values)

ASTM STANDARD			
absorption	(C97)	weight%	
density	(C97)	kg/cu.m	
compressive strength	(C170)	MPa	
modulus of rupture	(C99)	MPa	
flexural strength	(C880)	MPa	
abrasion resistance	(C241)	hardness	

PHYSICAL-MECHANICAL CHARACTERISTICS
(average reference values)

139

Stone

There are relatively few commercial varieties on the international market belonging to the Stone group. These are materials which are mostly consumed in local markets and are not always readily available outside the country where they are quarried. This guide includes some of the most well-known varieties which are quarried in Italy but are known and often available outside Italy too. These are in the following colors:

YELLOW STONE

The most well-known varieties of yellow stone belong to the Sandstone group, although there are some varieties belonging to the Limestone and Trachyte groups (Lava Rocks).

RED STONE

The red Stone varieties most widely used in the building industry belong to the Porphyry group.

PINK STONE

Most pink Stone varieties belong to the Limestone group, although there are a few which belong to the Peperino group.

GREEN STONE

Green Stone materials are not very common. Existing materials mainly belong to the Schist Group.

GREY STONE

The majority of the most well-known commercial Stone varieties are grey in color. Most belong to the Sandstone and Schist groups, although some are Lava Rocks, Peperino and Conglomerates.

BLACK STONE

The most well-known varieties of black Stone belong to the Schist and Slate group.

Note: The values given for the physical-mechanical tests are only indicative, since they are taken from existing literature or material furnished by various stone producer/suppliers. Where values are not reported, information was not available or could not be confirmed. The author takes no responsibility for any mistakes or omissions regarding the values given.

YELLOW SANDSTONE

MAIN AESTHETIC CHARACTERISTICS
There are at least two aesthetic types of sandstone. The first type (i) is fine-grained and has a characteristic pattern composed of light yellow and brown bands of color, varying from a few millimeters to one centimeter thick. The bands are curvilinear and follow on from one another rather like waves on the seashore. The outer edge of each "wave" is dark brown. The second type (ii) is fine- to coarse-grained and has a basically homogeneous granular appearance. Its overall color is yellow.

AESTHETIC VARIATIONS AND DEFECTS
The main aesthetic variations in aesthetic type (i) concern the color and the pattern but, since these are the chief characteristics of the material, they are generally well tolerated. In aesthetic type (ii) a certain variation fairly frequently occurs in the yellow color.

PRODUCER COUNTRIES
Aesthetic type (i) materials are quarried in Italy, Germany and Australia. The most well-known aesthetic type (ii) materials are quarried in Italy and Australia.

AVAILABILITY
Aesthetic type (i) varieties are not very common and are generally available in limited quantities of medium-sized blocks. Aesthetic type (ii) varieties are not very common either, but the existing varieties are generally available in good quantities of small- to medium-sized blocks.

USES
Yellow sandstone of both aesthetic types can be used in interiors and exteriors alike. These materials are generally used for facings or special solid pieces (also in garden furniture). Aesthetic type (ii) varieties are often used in the form of small blocks to fulfil structural functions. The surface is generally honed.

MAIN COMMERCIAL VARIETIES
Aesthetic type (i): Pietra Dorata.
Aesthetic type (ii): Giallo Dorato, Santafiora.

PHYSICAL-MECHANICAL CHARACTERISTICS
(average reference values)

	(i)	(ii)		
compression breaking load	117		kg/cm^2	ITALIAN STANDARD
compression breaking load after freezing	87		kg/cm^2	
imbibition coefficient (by weight)	7.5		%	
ultimate tensile strength	27		kg/cm^2	
impact test	45		cm	
thermal linear expansion coefficient			mm/m°C	
frictional wear test			mm	
weight per unit of volume	1.995		kg/m^3	
elasticity module			kg/cm^2	
knoop microhardness			kg/mm^2	

PHYSICAL-MECHANICAL CHARACTERISTICS
(average reference values)

absorption	(C97)	weight%	ASTM STANDARD
density	(C97)	kg/cu.m	
compressive strength	(C170)	MPa	
modulus of rupture	(C99)	MPa	
flexural strength	(C880)	MPa	
abrasion resistance	(C241)	hardness	

RED PORPHYRY

These materials are composed of a fine-grained groundmass which is very compact and hard. They are dark red in color, verging on brown. Whitish-colored dots a few millimeters across are fairly evenly distributed over the groundmass.

RED STONE

MAIN AESTHETIC CHARACTERISTICS

The main aesthetic variation concerns the color which changes frequently. In some cases, the crystals which form the whitish-colored dots are not very hard and tend to crumble, thereby leaving small holes.

AESTHETIC VARIATIONS AND DEFECTS

The traditional producer country of red Porphyry is Italy.

PRODUCER COUNTRIES

Red Porphyry is available in good quantities. The raw material is mainly slabs varying from one centimeter to ten centimeters thick.

AVAILABILITY

Red Porphyry is typically used for road paving in the form of cubic stones, the sides of which are a few centimeters long, to create geometrical patterns. Raw slabs are often used for external paving, kerbs and other solid pieces.

USES

Porfido Rosso.

MAIN COMMERCIAL VARIETIES

ITALIAN STANDARD				**PHYSICAL-MECHANICAL CHARACTERISTICS** (average reference values)
	compression breaking load	2.850	kg/cm²	
	compression breaking load after freezing	2.837	kg/cm²	
	imbibition coefficient (by weight)	0.75	%	
	ultimate tensile strength	240	kg/cm²	
	impact test	60	cm	
	thermal linear expansion coefficient	0.0030	mm/m°C	
	frictional wear test		mm	
	weight per unit of volume	2.540	kg/m³	
	elasticity module		kg/cm²	
	knoop microhardness		kg/mm²	

ASTM STANDARD				**PHYSICAL-MECHANICAL CHARACTERISTICS** (average reference values)
	absorption	(C97)	weight%	
	density	(C97)	kg/cu.m	
	compressive strength	(C170)	MPa	
	modulus of rupture	(C99)	MPa	
	flexural strength	(C880)	MPa	
	abrasion resistance	(C241)	hardness	

143

PINK LIMESTONE

MAIN AESTHETIC CHARACTERISTICS
These materials are composed of a fine- to medium-coarse-grained groundmass according to the different varieties, often with fossil elements. The groundmass is usually soft pink in color, although in some cases it is deep pink. In some varieties there are holes a few millimeters across distributed over the groundmass.

AESTHETIC VARIATIONS AND DEFECTS
Significant color variations may occur in these materials. An increase in the number or size of the holes often constitutes a defect.

PRODUCER COUNTRIES
The most well-known varieties of pink Limestone are quarried in Italy.

AVAILABILITY
These materials are fairly common and are generally available in line with market requirements in terms of both quality and quantity.

USES
The pink Limestone varieties available on the market are normally suitable in interiors and exteriors for floorings and paving and, more frequently, for facings. They can sometimes be used as solid blocks to fulfil structural functions too.

MAIN COMMERCIAL VARIETIES
Pietra Persichina di Prun, Pietra di Finale, Pietra di Verezzi.

PHYSICAL-MECHANICAL CHARACTERISTICS
(average reference values)

			ITALIAN STANDARD
compression breaking load	803	kg/cm^2	
compression breaking load after freezing	748	kg/cm^2	
imbibition coefficient (by weight)	2.7	%	
ultimate tensile strength	60	kg/cm^2	
impact test	31	cm	
thermal linear expansion coefficient	0.0063	mm/m°C	
frictional wear test		mm	
weight per unit of volume	2.183	kg/m^3	
elasticity module	121.500	kg/cm^2	
knoop microhardness		kg/mm^2	

PHYSICAL-MECHANICAL CHARACTERISTICS
(average reference values)

			ASTM STANDARD
absorption	(C97)	weight%	
density	(C97)	kg/cu.m	
compressive strength	(C170)	MPa	
modulus of rupture	(C99)	MPa	
flexural strength	(C880)	MPa	
abrasion resistance	(C241)	hardness	

GREEN SCHIST

Green Schists have a fine-grained, homogeneous green groundmass, of varying shades according to the different varieties, but with no other prominent aesthetic characteristic. In some varieties, light-colored crystals occur which create delicate reflections. They are oriented materials with a prominent *fissilità* (parting) feature, that is, the tendency to cleave along the planes parallel to the direction of the rift.

The main aesthetic variations concern the color. Yellow-brownish-colored oxidization patinas frequently occur, although these do not generally reduce the quality of the material and often create a separate commercial variety.

Green schist varieties suitable for ornamental purposes are not very common. The most significant productions are from Spain and Italy.

Availability of these materials is limited above all because of the low number of quarrying areas. Nevertheless, the quantities produced of each individual variety are not extremely large but large enough to satisfy market requirements.

Green schist varieties are often used in external, country-style paving, small garden walls, pavings and other similar elements. The surface treatments used are honing, various types of impact treatment or a riven finish which enhances the materials' aesthetic characteristics.

Ardesia Verde, Pietra di Courtil.

ITALIAN STANDARD			
compression breaking load		kg/cm²
compression breaking load after freezing		kg/cm²
imbibition coefficient (by weight)	0.10	%
ultimate tensile strength	470	kg/cm²
impact test		cm
thermal linear expansion coefficient		mm/m°C
frictional wear test		mm
weight per unit of volume	2.800	kg/m³
elasticity module		kg/cm²
knoop microhardness		kg/mm²

ASTM STANDARD			
absorption	(C97)	weight%
density	(C97)	kg/cu.m
compressive strength	(C170)	MPa
modulus of rupture	(C99)	MPa
flexural strength	(C880)	MPa
abrasion resistance	(C241)	hardness

GREY SANDSTONE

MAIN AESTHETIC CHARACTERISTICS

These are fine-grained grey materials with a generally homogeneous granular appearance. The grey color varies considerably from one commercial variety to the next. Some varieties have occasional, misshapen, fine-grained dark grey or black spots which vary from a few centimeters to a few dozen centimeters across.

AESTHETIC VARIATIONS AND DEFECTS

The main aesthetic variation is the occurrence of lighter-colored rings or speckles which are generally well tolerated by the market. However, the occurrence of dark spots or a higher concentration of dark spots if they normally occur may constitute a significant color defect. Some varieties tend to cleave and lose their original physical-mechanical properties in a relatively short time.

PRODUCER COUNTRIES

The most well-known grey sandstone varieties are quarried in Italy.

AVAILABILITY

Grey sandstone varieties are fairly common, although they cannot always be used as dimension stone. The varieties existing on the market are generally available in good quantities of medium- and large-sized blocks.

USES

Grey sandstone can be used in interiors and exteriors alike, for facings, floorings and paving. However, the varieties which tend to cleave should not be used in exteriors or in floorings or paving. These materials are often used for special solid pieces (door frames, shelves, fireplaces, etc.), columns and small blocks to fulfil structural functions. The surface treatments generally used are honing and the various types of impact treatment, such as the scored finish typically used for old town centers. In some cases, excellent results can also be achieved with flaming. The harder varieties can be polished.

MAIN COMMERCIAL VARIETIES

Pietra di Bedonia, Pietra del Cardoso, Pietra di Matraia, Pietra Serena.

GREY STONE

PHYSICAL-MECHANICAL CHARACTERISTICS
(average reference values)

compression breaking load	1.214	kg/cm²	ITALIAN
compression breaking load after freezing	1.037	kg/cm²	STANDARD
imbibition coefficient (by weight)	1.2	%	
ultimate tensile strength		kg/cm²	
impact test		cm	
thermal linear expansion coefficient		mm/m°C	
frictional wear test	7.2	mm	
weight per unit of volume	2.616	kg/m³	
elasticity module		kg/cm²	
knoop microhardness		kg/mm²	

PHYSICAL-MECHANICAL CHARACTERISTICS
(average reference values)

absorption	(C97)	weight%	ASTM
density	(C97)	kg/cu.m	STANDARD
compressive strength	(C170)	MPa	
modulus of rupture	(C99)	MPa	
flexural strength	(C880)	MPa	
abrasion resistance	(C241)	hardness	

GREY SCHIST

There are two aesthetic types of grey schist. Type (i) materials are fine-grained and of an even grey color which varies according to the different varieties, although in general it verges on black. These materials have no other prominent aesthetic characteristics. In type (ii) varieties many whitish-colored layers and/or whitish-colored, elongated crystals a few centimeters across (*ghiande*) frequently occur in the grey groundmass. Some varieties can be polished. Both types have a well-defined rift which is only visible in terms of color in type (ii). Both types have a great tendency to cleave along the planes parallel to the rift (*fissilità*).

The main aesthetic variations in both aesthetic types concern the color. Yellow-brownish-colored patinas frequently occur, although these do not generally reduce the quality of the material and often create a separate commercial variety.

Grey schist varieties suitable for ornamental purposes are fairly common. Important productions are from Spain, India, Italy and many other countries.

These materials are normally readily available thanks to the high number of quarrying areas and the quantities produced of each individual variety. The quantities may not be extremely large but are large enough to satisfy market requirements.

Grey schist varieties are often used in the form of tiles for roofs, external, country-style paving, small garden walls, pavings and other similar elements. The surface treatments used are honing, various types of impact treatment or a riven finish which enhances the materials' aesthetic characteristics.

Aesthetic type (i): Valdeorras.
Aesthetic type (ii): Pietra di Luserna.

		(i)	(ii)	
ITALIAN STANDARD	compression breaking load		1.660	kg/cm²
	compression breaking load after freezing		1.630	kg/cm²
	imbibition coefficient (by weight)	0.28	0.30	%
	ultimate tensile strength	550	220	kg/cm²
	impact test		85	cm
	thermal linear expansion coefficient		0.0035	mm/m°C
	frictional wear test			mm
	weight per unit of volume	2.790	2.620	kg/m³
	elasticity module		650.000	kg/cm²
	knoop microhardness		490	kg/mm²

ASTM STANDARD	absorption	(C97)	weight%
	density	(C97)	kg/cu.m
	compressive strength	(C170)	MPa
	modulus of rupture	(C99)	MPa
	flexural strength	(C880)	MPa
	abrasion resistance	(C241)	hardness

147

GREY BASALT (LAVA ROCK)

MAIN AESTHETIC CHARACTERISTICS
These materials are composed of an iron grey groundmass with evenly distributed black and, to a lesser extent, white dots a few millimeters across. The groundmass normally has holes a few millimeters across, the concentration of which varies according to the different varieties.

AESTHETIC VARIATIONS AND DEFECTS
The main aesthetic variation concerns the color which may vary considerably. The holes may be larger or more numerous, in which case they become a structural defect.

PRODUCER COUNTRIES
The most well-known commercial varieties of grey basalt are quarried in Italy.

AVAILABILITY
There are relatively few grey basalt quarrying areas. However, the materials are generally available in line with market requirements in medium- and small-sized blocks.

USES
Grey basalt is often used for external paving, including high-traffic areas, kerbs, special solid pieces (garden fountains, etc.) and small blocks to fulfil structural functions. The surface treatments generally used are a sawn finish, honing or various types of impact treatment. Flaming is also possible.

MAIN COMMERCIAL VARIETIES
Pietra Basaltina, Pietra Lavica.

PHYSICAL-MECHANICAL CHARACTERISTICS
(average reference values)

				ITALIAN STANDARD
compression breaking load	1.011	kg/cm^2		
compression breaking load after freezing		kg/cm^2		
imbibition coefficient (by weight)	2.0	%		
ultimate tensile strength	124	kg/cm^2		
impact test	43	cm		
thermal linear expansion coefficient	0.0050	mm/m°C		
frictional wear test	4.3	mm		
weight per unit of volume	2.512	kg/m^3		
elasticity module		kg/cm^2		
knoop microhardness	216	kg/mm^2		

PHYSICAL-MECHANICAL CHARACTERISTICS
(average reference values)

				ASTM STANDARD
absorption	(C97)	weight%		
density	(C97)	kg/cu.m		
compressive strength	(C170)	MPa		
modulus of rupture	(C99)	MPa		
flexural strength	(C880)	MPa		
abrasion resistance	(C241)	hardness		

148

GREY PEPERINO

These materials are composed of a granular groundmass which is normally light grey with frequent dark dots a few millimeters across. Dark grey, subcircular elements varying from a few centimeters to a few dozen centimeters across also occur unevenly distributed over the groundmass.

There are frequent variations as regards the color and size of the subcircular elements.

The most well-known varieties of grey Peperino are quarried in Italy.

Grey Peperino is not very common. Nevertheless, the availability is fairly good, in line with market requirements.

Grey Peperino is often used for garden furniture such as tables, vases, walls, pavings, etc. and frequently for special solid pieces too.

Peperino Grigio.

ITALIAN STANDARD			
compression breaking load	450	kg/cm²
compression breaking load after freezing	260	kg/cm²
imbibition coefficient (by weight)	0.42	%
ultimate tensile strength	53	kg/cm²
impact test	40	cm
thermal linear expansion coefficient	0.0040	mm/m°C
frictional wear test		mm
weight per unit of volume	2.200	kg/m³
elasticity module	280.000	kg/cm²
knoop microhardness		kg/mm²

PHYSICAL-MECHANICAL CHARACTERISTICS
(average reference values)

ASTM STANDARD			
absorption	(C97)	weight%
density	(C97)	kg/cu.m
compressive strength	(C170)	MPa
modulus of rupture	(C99)	MPa
flexural strength	(C880)	MPa
abrasion resistance	(C241)	hardness

PHYSICAL-MECHANICAL CHARACTERISTICS
(average reference values)

149

BLACK SCHIST AND SLATE

MAIN AESTHETIC CHARACTERISTICS
These materials have a fine-grained, homogeneous, smoky black groundmass, of varying shades according to the different varieties, with no other prominent aesthetic characteristic. They also have a prominent *fissilità* (parting) feature, that is, the tendency to cleave along the planes parallel to the direction of the rift.

AESTHETIC VARIATIONS AND DEFECTS
The main aesthetic variation concerns the color and in some varieties the smoky black turns to dark grey quite quickly after its installation. In many cases, the occurrence of yellow-brownish-colored oxidization patinas does not reduce the quality of the material and often creates a separate commercial variety.

PRODUCER COUNTRIES
Black schist varieties used for ornamental purposes are fairly common. Important productions are from Spain and India. Italy is where the most important black slate in the world is produced.

AVAILABILITY
These materials are normally readily available thanks to the high number of quarrying areas and the quantities produced of each individual variety. The quantities may not be extremely large but are large enough to satisfy market requirements. Availability of slate is limited due to the low number of quarrying areas. It is produced in small- and medium-sized blocks.

USES
Black Slate and Schist materials are often used in the form of tiles (*abbadini*) for roofs. Slate is often used in interior design for tables, skirting boards and bathroom furnishings. It may also be used for low-traffic floorings. Thanks to the physical-mechanical properties of Slate, it is customarily used for billiard tables. The surface treatments used are a sawn or riven finish and honing. A polished surface may also be achieved using resin, but only on Slate. These materials are often used for ornaments too.

MAIN COMMERCIAL VARIETIES
Ardesia, La Cabrera.

BLACK STONE

PHYSICAL-MECHANICAL CHARACTERISTICS
(average reference values)

			ITALIAN STANDARD
compression breaking load	1.490	kg/cm²	
compression breaking load after freezing	1.330	kg/cm²	
imbibition coefficient (by weight)	0.32	%	
ultimate tensile strength	570	kg/cm²	
impact test	94	cm	
thermal linear expansion coefficient	0.0065	mm/m°C	
frictional wear test		mm	
weight per unit of volume	2.710	kg/m³	
elasticity module		kg/cm²	
knoop microhardness		kg/mm²	

PHYSICAL-MECHANICAL CHARACTERISTICS
(average reference values)

			ASTM STANDARD
absorption	(C97)	weight%	
density	(C97)	kg/cu.m	
compressive strength	(C170)	MPa	
modulus of rupture	(C99)	MPa	
flexural strength	(C880)	MPa	
abrasion resistance	(C241)	hardness	

150

Part Three

Glossary of Technical and Commercial Terms

Abbadino - a traditionally quadrangular-shaped element, the sides of which are approximately 56 cm, made in slate and used for roof tiles in Liguria, Italy. Other sizes are currently available too

Across-the-bed Cut - the sawing of a marble block perpendicular to the bedding plane or rift. Also: vein cut (US) in (1)

Allowance - customary deduction from the sizes of a block or slab made by the retailer (Corbella 1988) in (1)

Anchor - device to support and/or tie back stone units. Also: fixing (UK) in (1)

Axed Finish - having a rough and rugged surface achieved by using a punch or axe (1)

Basalt - fine-grained basic rock, composed essentially of plagioclase and pyroxene (1)

Bedding Plane - the direction of easiest splitting of stratified rocks. (1) Also *verso* (It)

Beveled edge - the surface resulting from cutting away the arris of a stone unit (1)

Biotite - black mineral of the mica group, a common element in granitic rocks

Bird's Beak - moulding with a round and convex profile resembling the beak of a bird. Also: half-bullnose and demi-bullnose (1)

Biscia - concentration of dark-colored minerals in light-colored granitic rocks forming a narrow, elongated band which adversely affects the uniformity of the rock's pattern; invariably a color defect

Book-match Pattern - specific type of symmetrical arrangement obtained by placing panels of the same block in a repetitive pattern (1)

Border - the usually narrow side portion of the face of a stone unit showing a different finishing from the rest of the face (1)

Boulder - in granitoid rocks, massive body remaining intact in the disintegrated outcropping portion of a deposit (1)

Bowing - buckling of exterior stone units due to shrinkage or shortening of the structure (1)

Bracciated - relating to rocks fractured and naturally cemented (1)

Breccia - rock consisting of sharp fragments bonded by a fine-grained matrix or cement (1)

Bullnose - moulding with a round profile (1)

Bush-hammered Finish - finish obtained by using a bush-hammer (1)

Bush-hammering - the dressing of a stone surface by using a bush-hammer or bush-hammering machine (1)

Calcite - mineral consisting of crystallized calcium carbonate (1)

Catena - vein filled with light-colored minerals (normally quartz and feldspar) occurring inside granitic rocks - a color and structural defect

Cement - precipitated mineral material bonding the fragments of a clastic sediment (1)

Chamfered Edge - almost imperceptible beveled edge (1)

Chamfering - the cutting of an angle to a bevel or chamfer (1)

Chlorite - term which identifies a group of minerals occurring in many dimension stones, giving a green color

Cladding - i) In British English, external vertical or near vertical non-loadbearing covering of stone units to a structure (BSI 8298); ii) in American English, any vertical non-loadbearing covering of stone units to a structure (1)

Clast - coarse fragment that is set in a finer-grained matrix or cement in clastic rocks (1)

Clastic - any consolidated or unconsolidated sediment formed from rock fragments. This type of sedimentary rock includes, besides sands and gravels, conglomerates, sandstone and shales (1)

Clay Hole (UK) - hole, from 5 mm to 25 mm across, filled with clay. Defect often found in marble, limestone and sandstone when slabbing large blocks (BSI 6100). Also: vug (US) in (1)

Cleavage - the structure possessed by some rocks, owing to which they split more readily in certain directions than in others (1)

Commercial Granite - term indicating all magmatic rocks and silicatic metamorphic rocks which can be polished well and used for ornamental purposes

Commercial Marble - term indicating metamorphic and sedimentary carbonatic rocks which can be polished and used for ornamental purposes. The term also includes some magmatic rocks such as ophiolites and ophicalcites. Commercial marble varieties are mainly composed of minerals varying in hardness from 3 to 4 on the Mohs scale

Coping - flat stone used as a cap on free-standing walls (MSSV) in (1)

Course - in excavation, geometrically defined rocky body along which the marble tends to have the same aesthetic characteristics

Course - in installation, a horizontal range of units the length of a wall (MIA 1987) in (1)

Crazy Paving - paving formed by pieces without definite shapes and dimensions. Also: randomly set paving (US)

Crystalline - referring to marble, commercial term indicating medium- and coarse-grained marble

Crystalline - relating to textures composed of crystals or fragments thereof (1)

Cubic Stock (US) - stone unit thicker than 50 mm (1)

Curtain wall - non-loadbearing panelled veneer spanning between columns (1)

Cut Sheet - fabrication drawing detailing piece mark, location and dimensions of each individual stone unit. Also: cut ticket and shop ticket (1)

Cut-To-Size Tile - non-standard tile made to specific size requirements

Defect - physical or chemical element occurring in natural stone which may alter the aesthetic characteristics recognized by the market or lower its physical-mechanical resistance much below the accepted values for similar materials, thereby affecting its use

Dentrite - aggregate of small crystals having a treelike structure inside some dimension stones. The dentrites in Solnophen Limestone are famous

Deposit - rocky body varying in shape and size of interest for mining purposes

Development - work done in preparing a deposit for the excavation of stone (1)

Dike - magmatic body, normally narrow and elongated,

which allows the magma deep down in the earth's crust to return to the surface

Dimensioned Piece - cut-to-size semi-finished stone such as slabs, strips, cubic stone units (1)

Dolly-Pointed Finish - semi-rough finish achieved by using a dolly point. Also: pointed finish (US) in (1)

Dolomia - sedimentary rock mostly composed of dolomite

Dolomite - magnesium carbonate mineral

Downfeed - rate of descent of a sawing device, expressed in cm/h or mm/h. Also: feed rate (1)

Drip - a recess cut into the underside of projecting stone to divert water and prevent it from running down the face of a wall or other surface of which it is a part (MIA 1987) in (1)

Durea - shapeless mass varying in size occurring inside a rock which is much harder than the rock itself. A durea is usually composed of quartz

Easy Way - direction of cleavage at right angle to and less pronounced than the rift. Also *secondo* (It)

Edge - the side which runs counter to the panel face and borders the surface area of the panel. In particular, the side of a stone unit whose dimensions are determined by the thickness and height of the panel. (UNI 8458) in (1)

End - the side which runs counter to the panel face and the panel edge, and whose dimensions are determined by its thickness and width. Also: head (US) in (1)

Excavation - work to produce blocks of raw material inside a quarry

Exposed Face - the finished side of a stone panel that will be seen in situ. Also: visible (1)

Fabrication - the process whereby face-finished dimensional stone is achieved (1)

Face - the frontal surface(s) of a stone panel (1)

Falda - referring to a block, thickness measured along the side at right angles to the *verso*

Feature Strip - decorative element of metal, stone, resins, etc., set in the joints of a patterned flooring. Also: insert strip (1)

Feldspar - mineral occurring in many granitic rocks which often determines the aesthetic characteristics of the same according to its quantity, shape and color

Finish - final surface applied to the face of dimensional stone during fabrication (MIA 1987). Also: texture (n), when achieved mechanically or thermally (1)

Flagstone - large flat piece of stone usually 2 to 8 cm in thickness (Ontario 1990) in (1)

Flamed Finish - rough texture achieved by flaming the surface of siliceous stones. Also: flame textured finish (UK), thermal finish (US) in (1)

Flaming - the obtaining of a rough finish by using a flame over the surface of stone. Also: flame texturing (UK), thermal treatment (US) and scorching (US) in (1)

Floor - covering of a surface subject to foot traffic (1)

Flooring Border - stone unit laid along the perimeter of a floor covering and bordering a flooring pattern. In exteriors, paving border (1)

Frescume - white or yellow lines or spots composed of various substances ... (omissis) ... which appear in highly-polished finished pieces, thereby damaging the aesthetic char-

acteristics ... (omissis) (2)

Garnet - term indicating a group of minerals typical of metamorphic rocks. Many commercial granite varieties have dark red garnet crystals which enhance their aesthetic characteristics

Gauging - the dressing of stone to a predetermined size (1)

Ghianda - large-sized crystals characteristic of the *ghiandonato* pattern

Ghiandonato - rock pattern characterized by the presence of large crystals (*ghiande*) embedded in a fine- or medium-grained groundmass

Gneiss - metamorphic rock with oriented pattern. Gneiss rocks belong to the Granite and Stone groups

Grain - i) direction of cleavage at right angle to and less pronounced than the rift. Also: easy way (US); ii) in slate quarrying, the direction of easiest splitting (1). In this sense, also *verso* (It)

Grain Size - term referring to the size of crystals forming a rock

Granite - intrusive magmatic rock formed from acid chemism magma

Granoblastic - having a texture in which the fragments are irregular and angular (1)

Groundmass - in sedimentary rocks, generally very fine-grained clastic material which occupies the gaps between the granules of a clastic sediment

Hard Way - plane at right angle to the rift and the grain, along which splitting is most difficult. Also *contro* (It)

Head - plane at right angles to the rift and the grain along which splitting is most difficult. Also: tough way (UK) and hard way (US) (1)

Hematite - iron oxide responsible for the red color in many dimension stones

Herringbone Pattern - herringbone arrangement of stone units on a surface (1)

Holocrystalline - completely made up of crystals or crystalline particles (1)

Honed Finish - having a dull polish or matt surface (BSI 8298) (1)

Honing - the smoothing of a stone surface with heads fitted with varying grit sizes (1)

Inlaid Floor - floor covering consisting of thin stone decorative units inserted in sinkings made in an underlying material (1)

Installation - the process of setting dimensional stone into place (MIA 1987) in (1). Also: erection (1)

Intrados - the interior surface of an arch (1)

Joint - fracture in the rocky mass which may be open or filled with different material from the mother rock (cement or groundmass)

Jointing Layout - the patterning of stone units and joints on a surface (1)

Kerbstone - random-length, solid piece of stone (UNI 8458) in (1)

Kerf - continuous groove cut into the side of a stone unit for the inserting of anchoring devices (1)

Labradorescence - iridescence typical of labradorite due to ferrous oxide and titanium inclusions or reflections inside the crystals

Labradorite - mineral belonging to the plagioclase group typical of magmatic rocks resulting from basic chemism and characterized by labradorescence. Labradorite is the chief mineral forming Blue Pearl type granite varieties

Limestone - sedimentary rock formed by the accumulation of organic remains and consisting mainly of calcium carbonate (1)

Limestone Onyx - carbonatic sedimentary rock formed by chemical precipitation in subaerial environment. See also: onyx

Limestone Tuff - clastic sedimentary rock composed mainly of carbonatic material. These rocks are soft and easy to cut and work but cannot be polished. They belong to the Stone group

Limonite - ferrous oxide responsible for the yellow color of many dimension stones

Liner - (i) reinforcement to naturally unsound types of stone, cross-pinned and glued to the stone unit. Also: stiffener (US); (ii) slab of structurally sound stone used as a backing material for patterned stone veneer. Liners are generally twice as thick as the material being used. Also: bond stone (1)

Lintel - loadbearing, horizontal member spanning above an opening (1)

Mafic - mineral composition showing the presence of dark-colored ferromagnesian minerals. Typical of igneous rocks formed by basic chemism

Magmatic - referring to rocks generated by the cooling of a magma. Also known as igneous

Marble - carbonatic metamorphic rock

Metamorphic - referring to rocks generated from changes in existing rocks due to variations in the original physical-chemical environment

Migmatite - silicatic metamorphic rock, the hardness of which is comparable to granite, but with a prominent oriented structure

Mock up - structural model of assembled stone units built for display and/or testing (1)

Natural Cleft Finish - finish for metamorphic rocks such as slate and quartzite, resulting from cleaving or separating stone along the bedding plane and showing the natural rock face. Also: rock faced finish (UK) and seam faced finish (US) (1)

Nodule - small lump of mineral or mineral aggregate with contrasting composition and greater hardness than surrounding rock (Ontario 1990) in (1)

Notch - V-shaped indentation made along the edge of a stone panel for the insertion of anchoring devices (1)

Offset Pattern - jointing layout where adjacent horizontal courses are laid offset one to another. Also: brick bond and broken bond (1)

Ogee - moulding with an S-shaped profile (1)

Ophicalcite - brecciated serpentine, often containing white calcite veins (1)

Ophiolite - term including basic magmatic and metamorphic rocks, many of which can be used for ornamental purposes. Also known as green rocks

Oriented Granite - term indicating commercial granite varieties, the minerals of which follow a definite orientation

Outcrop - the part of a rock formation that appears at the surface (1)

Out-of-square Cut - cut made in a stone panel not perpendicular to the face (1)

Parallel Scored Finish - surface with parallel uniform grooves. Also: machine tooled finish

Patterned Floor - floor covering achieved by arranging joints, stone materials and color and vein blending in the desired patterns (1)

Pelo - Hairline fracture - minute barely visible crack. Also: cutter (US) and chink (US) (1)

Pelo Chiuso - closed fracture visible as a chromatic discontinuity in the rocky mass

Pelo Cieco - **Vent** (UK) - naturally occurring hairline fracture found in stone when sawing a block (1)

Pelo Furbo - fracture which appears closed but opens when block is sawn, during processing or after installation of the finished product

Peperino - rock formed by the accumulation of debris of volcanic origin belonging to the Stone commercial group

Phenochryst - larger distinct crystal in a porphyritic texture. Also: inset (1)

Pitched Finish - rugged and convex finish obtained by using a pitching machine. Also: rockface finish (US) (1)

Plagioclase - group of minerals normally part of a very large number of granitic rocks

Plutonic - magmatic rock formed by consolidation of a magmatic body of a definite shape (pluto) at a considerable depth in the earth's crust

Polished Finish - having a surface with a high gloss (BSI 8298) (1)

Polishing - the dressing of stone to a glossy finish by using a polishing line (1)

Porphyritic - of texture consisting of larger crystals, called phenocrysts, which are spread through a more finely crystalline or glassy matrix or groundmass (1)

Porphyry - volcanic rock or a porphyritic texture regardless of its mineral composition (1)

Quarry - excavation where usable stone is extracted from the ground (1)

Quarry Bench - step-like portion of rock in a bench quarry (1)

Quarter-match Pattern - specific type of symmetrical arrangement achieved by placing panels of the same block in a repetitive pattern. Also: diamond match pattern (1)

Quartzite - metamorphic rock derived from a sandstone mainly composed of quartz

Quirk Miter - mitered edge for an external corner (1)

Rabbeted Joint - type of external corner. Also: rebated joint (UK) in (1)

Rabbeted Kerf - recessed kerf drilled in the edge of a stone panel for the insertion of anchoring devices. Also: rebated kerf (UK) in (1)

Raised Floor - flooring consisting of stone-faced panels placed on a grid and supported by pedestals (1)

Random Length Pattern - jointing layout achieved with pieces of varying height (1)

Random Piece - stone panel having constant width and varying height or converse (1)

Rift - in granite quarrying, the direction of easiest splitting (1). Also *verso* (It)

Riser - the upright member between two stair treads (1)

Rodding - the strengthening of structurally unsound marble by cementing rods into grooves or channels cut into the back of a marble unit (MIA 1987) in (1)

Rusticated Stone - stone unit with rustication

Rustication - decorative masonry achieved by recessing the edges of stones so that a channel is formed at each joint (1)

Saccharoidal - relating to rocks having a granular texture resembling crystalline sugar (1)

Sale e Pepe - pattern of granite varieties whose crystalline mass is composed mainly of fine-grained black and white minerals which resemble a mixture of salt and pepper grains

Sand Blasted Finish (US) - a matte textured finish with no gloss, accomplished by exposing the surface to a steady flow of sand under pressure (MIA 1987). Also: sanded finish (UK) in (1)

Sandstone - sedimentary rock composed mostly of mineral and rock fragments within the sand size range (2 to 0.06 mm) and having a minimum of 60% free silica, cemented or bonded to a greater or lesser degree by various materials including silica, iron oxides, carbonates or clay (ASTM C 119) in (1)

Saw Cut - straight cut to produce grooves, channels, seats for rods, etc. (Corbella 1988) in (1)

Sawn Finish - surface achieved by the gang sawing process (1)

Sawn Slab - slab whose face has not undergone any further treatment after sawing (1)

Schistose - of a rock having minerals arranged in nearly parallel layers (1)

Scoring - the making of uniform grooves on a stone surface by a tooth chisel (1)

Seasoning - process of storing stone after quarrying to reduce its moisture content and bring it to proper condition for use. Also: airing (1)

Secco - compact, fine-grained stone which is very fragile

Secondo - Grain - i) direction of cleavage at right angles to and less pronounced than the rift. Also: easy way (US); ii) in slate quarrying, the direction of easiest splitting (1)

Sedimentary - rocks formed by the accumulation of debris or chemical precipitation

Serpentine - metamorphic rock composed mainly of serpentine which gives the rock the typical dark green color

Shapeless - referring to blocks produced in a quarry of no definite shape or size

Side Slip Pattern - specific type of symmetrical arrangement obtained by placing panels of the same block side to side in a repetitive pattern (1)

Sill - a horizontal unit used at the base of an exterior opening in a structure (1)

Skirting - continuous strip of stone covering the joint between the wall and the adjoining flooring. Also: base (1)

Slab - a piece of stone cut from the quarry block prior to fabrication (MIA 1987) in (1)

Slabs - pieces of stone cut from the quarry block prior to fabrication (MIA 1987) in (1)

Slate - microcrystalline metamorphic rock most commonly derived from shale and composed mostly of micas, chlorite and quartz. The micaceous minerals have a subparallel orientation and thus impart strong cleavage to the rock which allows the latter to be split into thin but tough sheets (ASTM C 119) in (1)

Slit Face Ashlar - ashlar showing a split face finish (1)

Spandrel - part of the cladding spanning between two columns

Split face Finish (US) - rugged surface produced by splitting stone with a guillotine or chisel. Also: riven finish (UK) in (1)

Squared Block - referring to a block, cut into a regular parallelepiped of a specific size without structural defects

Squaring - the transformation of raw material into regular-shaped blocks either in the quarry or the sawmill

Stacked Bond - jointing layout characterized by unbroken vertical and horizontal joints running throughout the floor surface (1)

Standard-size Tile - machine-made tile with specified standard dimensions. Also: standard tile (1)

Stone - designation for rock that has been quarried and fabricated in a given shape and size for a specific function (1)

Stool - a flat unit of stone often referred to as an interior window sill (MIA 1987) in (1)

Strip - long and narrow piece of stone with the length coinciding with that of the block or slab. Strips are obtained either by means of a blockcutter or the lengthwise cut of a slab (1)

Stylolite - thin zigzagging veining subparallel to the *verso* of the rock occurring in some carbonatic sedimentary rocks. If occurring in large quantities, stylolites may determine the aesthetic characteristics of a dimension stone (e.g., Trani Filetto Rosso)

Subvolcanic - magmatic rock generated by the cooling of a magma located near the surface of the earth's crust, in bodies called *filoni* (dikes)

Syenite - intrusive magmatic rock composed mainly of feldspars, mafic minerals with either a limited amount of quartz or no quartz at all

Template - pattern, usually of thin board or wood, used as a guide for cutting a stone unit (1)

Terrazzo - flooring made by embedding small pieces of marble or granite in a mortar bed and, after hardening, grinding and polishing the surface (1)

Texture - the features of a rock depending on the size, shape, arrangement and distribution of the component minerals (1)

Tile - standard-sized stone unit thinner than 3/4 inch (20 mm) (1)

Tolerance - the range of variation allowed in maintaining a given dimension in cutting to size (1)

Toppa - color defect in granitic rocks caused by a xenolith

Trachyte - light-colored, very fine-grained volcanic rock, consisting chiefly of alkali feldspar and minor amounts of some mafic minerals (1)

Travertine - a porous or cellularly layered, partly crystalline calcity of chemical origin. Travertine is formed by precipitation from generally hot solutions of carbonated spring water, usually at the bottom of shallow pools (ASTM C 119) in (1)

Tread - the horizontal part of a step, subject to foot traffic (1)

Vein - i) a rock fissure filled with minerals deposited from solution by underground water; ii) narrow strip or streak of a different color found in some types of stone (1)

Veined - referring to a rock's pattern, characterized by veins

Veined Granite - term indicating commercial granite varieties with prominent veins or veining

Veining - see *Vein*

Volcanic Tuff - rocks formed by the sedimentary accumulation of volcanic material. These rocks are soft and easy to cut and work but cannot be polished. They belong to the Stone group

With-the-bed Cut - the sawing of a marble block parallel to the bedding plane or rift. Also: fleuri cut (US) (1)

Xenolith - crystalline agglomerate usually composed of mafic minerals occurring in granitic rocks formed by acid or intermediate chemism

Bibliographical References
(1) GIORNETTI M., *Glossario del settore lapideo,* Internazionale Marmi e Macchine, Carrara 1991
(2) PIERI M., *Marmologia, Dizionario di marmi e graniti italiani ed esteri*, Hoepli, Milano 1966
(3) AA.VV. *Dizionario di Scienze della Terra*, Rizzoli, Milano 1984

Part Four

Directory
of Natural Stone

BIANCO
CARRARA C

PRODUCER COUNTRY: Italy
AVAILABILITY: Good

FILE NUMBER: 0001

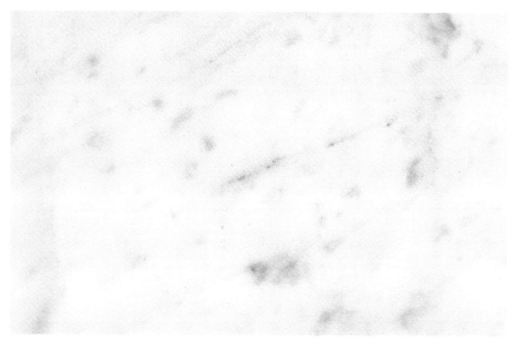

BIANCO
CARRARA C/D

PRODUCER COUNTRY: Italy
AVAILABILITY: Good

FILE NUMBER: 0002

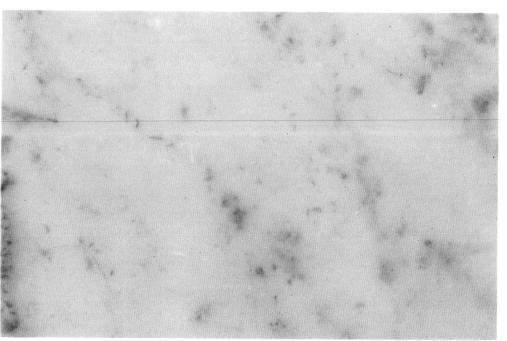

BIANCO
CARRARA D

PRODUCER COUNTRY: Italy
AVAILABILITY: Good

FILE NUMBER: 0003

BIANCO ARNI

PRODUCER COUNTRY: Italy
AVAILABILITY: Medium

FILE NUMBER: 0004

BIANCO ROYAL

PRODUCER COUNTRY: Turkey
AVAILABILITY: Good

FILE NUMBER: 0005

CALACATTA CARRARA

PRODUCER COUNTRY: Italy
AVAILABILITY: Medium

FILE NUMBER: 0006

CREVOLA
D'OSSOLA

PRODUCER COUNTRY: Italy
AVAILABILITY: Limited

FILE NUMBER: 0007

LASA
VENA ORO

PRODUCER COUNTRY: Italy
AVAILABILITY: Limited

FILE NUMBER: 0008

BIANCO
STATUARIO

PRODUCER COUNTRY: Italy
AVAILABILITY: Limited

FILE NUMBER: 0009
SUPPLIER: 23

BIANCO P

PRODUCER COUNTRY: Italy
AVAILABILITY: Limited

FILE NUMBER: 0010

BIANCO
LASA

PRODUCER COUNTRY: Italy
AVAILABILITY: Limited

FILE NUMBER: 0011

BIANCO
ACQUABIANCA

PRODUCER COUNTRY: Italy
AVAILABILITY: Medium

FILE NUMBER: 0012
SUPPLIER: 23

BIANCO
SIVEC

PRODUCER COUNTRY: Yugoslavia
AVAILABILITY: Medium

FILE NUMBER: 0013

BIANCO
THASSOS

PRODUCER COUNTRY: Greece
AVAILABILITY: Good

FILE NUMBER: 0014

WHITE
SAVANA

PRODUCER COUNTRY: Namibia
AVAILABILITY: Limited

FILE NUMBER: 0015

WHITE
GEORGIA

PRODUCER COUNTRY: USA
AVAILABILITY: Good

FILE NUMBER: 0016

WHITE
CHEROKEE

PRODUCER COUNTRY: USA
AVAILABILITY: Good

FILE NUMBER: 0017

PALISSANDRO
BLUETTE

PRODUCER COUNTRY: Italy
AVAILABILITY: Limited

FILE NUMBER: 0018

BIANCO NEVE
THASSOS

PRODUCER COUNTRY: Greece
AVAILABILITY: Medium

FILE NUMBER: 0019

PENTELIKON

PRODUCER COUNTRY: Greece
AVAILABILITY: Good

FILE NUMBER: 0020

CALACATTA
LUCCICOSO

PRODUCER COUNTRY: Italy
AVAILABILITY: Medium

FILE NUMBER: 0021

CALACATTA ORO

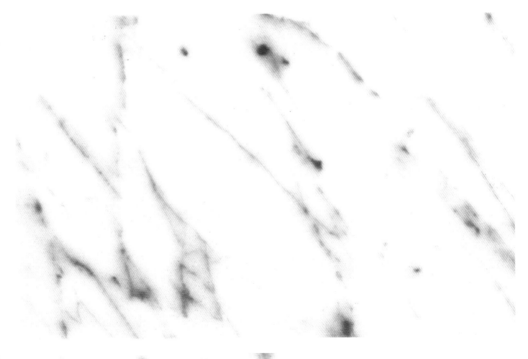

PRODUCER COUNTRY: Italy
AVAILABILITY: Limited

FILE NUMBER: 0022
SUPPLIER: 19, 23

BIANCO VENATO CARRARA

PRODUCER COUNTRY: Italy
AVAILABILITY: Good

FILE NUMBER: 0023

VENATINO GIOIA

PRODUCER COUNTRY: Italy
AVAILABILITY: Good

FILE NUMBER: 0024

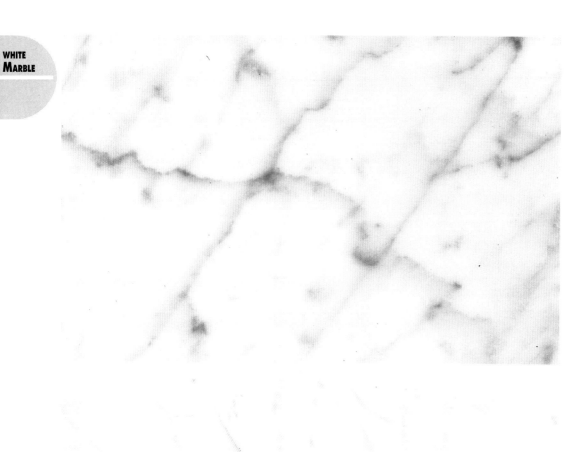

ULIANO VENATO

PRODUCER COUNTRY: Italy
AVAILABILITY: Medium

FILE NUMBER: 0025

BIANCO PENNSYLVANIA

PRODUCER COUNTRY: Italy
AVAILABILITY: Medium

FILE NUMBER: 0026
SUPPLIER: 10

STATUARIO VENATO

PRODUCER COUNTRY: Italy
AVAILABILITY: Medium

FILE NUMBER: 0027
SUPPLIER: 23

ZEBRINO

PRODUCER COUNTRY: Italy

AVAILABILITY: Limited

FILE NUMBER: 0028

WHITE MARBLE

CALACATTA ARNI

PRODUCER COUNTRY: Italy

AVAILABILITY: Limited

FILE NUMBER: 0029

CALACATTA CAMPOCECINA

PRODUCER COUNTRY: Italy

AVAILABILITY: Limited

FILE NUMBER: 0030

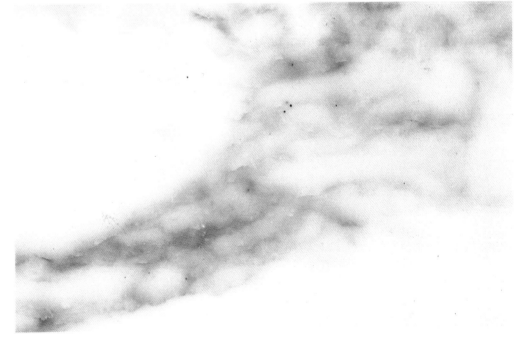

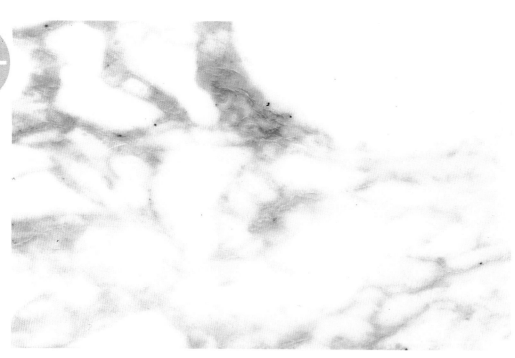

CALACATTA VAGLI

PRODUCER COUNTRY: Italy
AVAILABILITY: Limited

FILE NUMBER: 0031

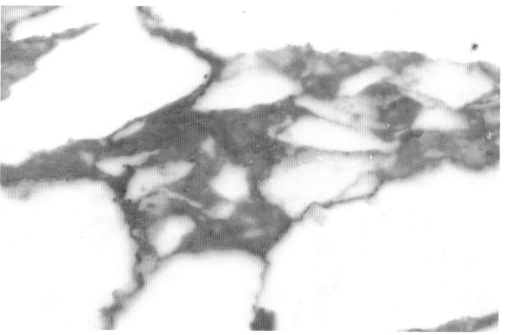

CALACATTA VAGLI EXTRA

PRODUCER COUNTRY: Italy
AVAILABILITY: Limited

FILE NUMBER: 0032

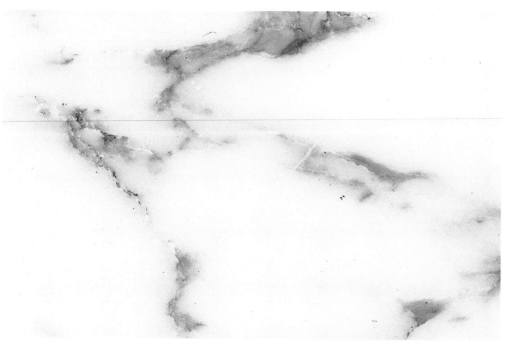

ARABESCATO CERVAIOLE

PRODUCER COUNTRY: Italy
AVAILABILITY: Medium

FILE NUMBER: 0033

ARABESCATO PIANA

PRODUCER COUNTRY: Italy
AVAILABILITY: Medium

FILE NUMBER: 0034
SUPPLIER: 22

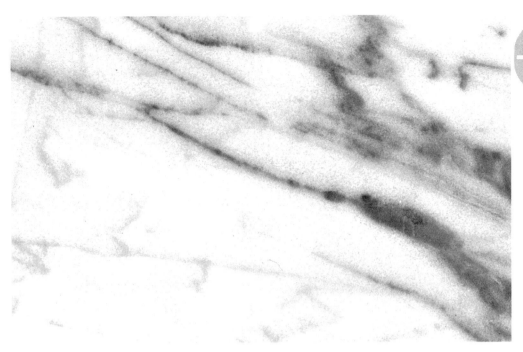

ARABESCATO CORCHIA CLASSICO

PRODUCER COUNTRY: Italy
AVAILABILITY: Medium

FILE NUMBER: 0035

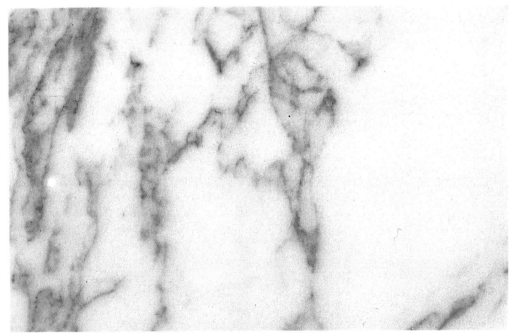

ARABESCATO FANIELLO

PRODUCER COUNTRY: Italy
AVAILABILITY: Medium

FILE NUMBER: 0036

173

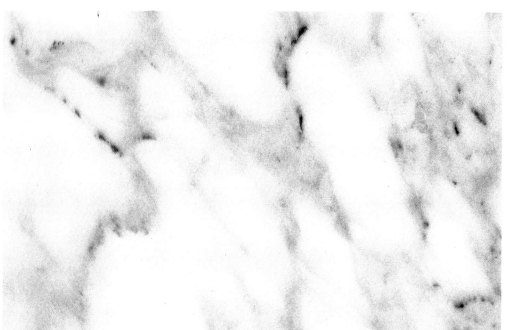

ARABESCATO
LA MOSSA

PRODUCER COUNTRY: Italy
AVAILABILITY: Limited

FILE NUMBER: 0037

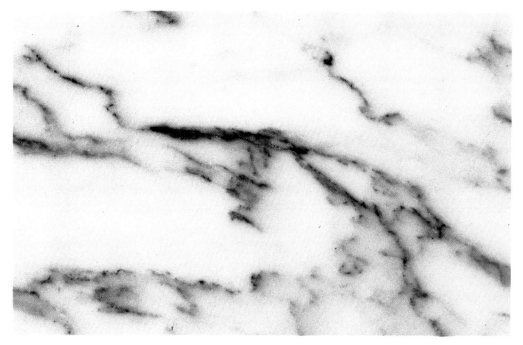

ARABESCATO
ARNI

PRODUCER COUNTRY: Italy
AVAILABILITY: Medium

FILE NUMBER: 0038

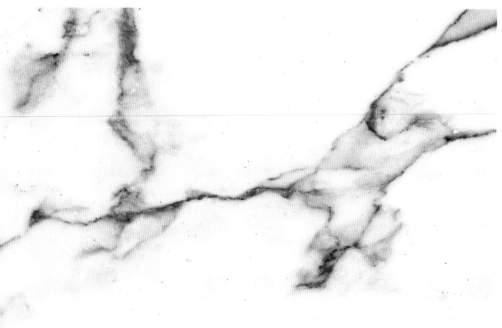

ARABESCATO
VAGLI

PRODUCER COUNTRY: Italy
AVAILABILITY: Limited

FILE NUMBER: 0039

BROUILLÉ

PRODUCER COUNTRY: Italy
AVAILABILITY: Limited

FILE NUMBER: 0040

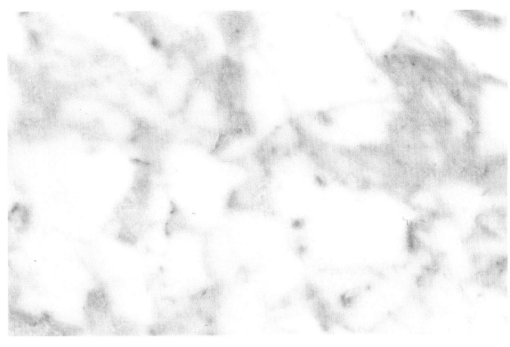

ARABESCATO SEA

PRODUCER COUNTRY: Italy
AVAILABILITY: Medium

FILE NUMBER: 0041

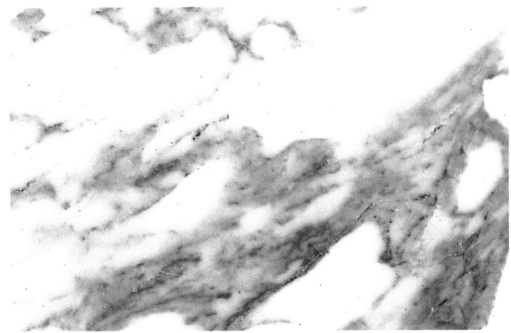

PERLINO BIANCO

PRODUCER COUNTRY: Italy
AVAILABILITY: Medium

FILE NUMBER: 0042
SUPPLIER: 16

BIANCONE

PRODUCER COUNTRY: Italy
AVAILABILITY: Medium

FILE NUMBER: 0043

CREMO
BELLO

PRODUCER COUNTRY: Turkey
AVAILABILITY: Good

FILE NUMBER: 0044
SUPPLIER: 9

TRAVERTINO
BIANCO

PRODUCER COUNTRY: Italy
AVAILABILITY: Limited

FILE NUMBER: 0045

WHITE ONYX

PRODUCER COUNTRY: Pakistan
AVAILABILITY: Limited

FILE NUMBER: 0046

WHITE
MARBLE

YELLOW
MARBLE

AFYON YELLOW

PRODUCER COUNTRY: Turkey
AVAILABILITY: Good

FILE NUMBER: 0047

GIALLO SIENA

PRODUCER COUNTRY: Italy
AVAILABILITY: Limited

FILE NUMBER: 0048

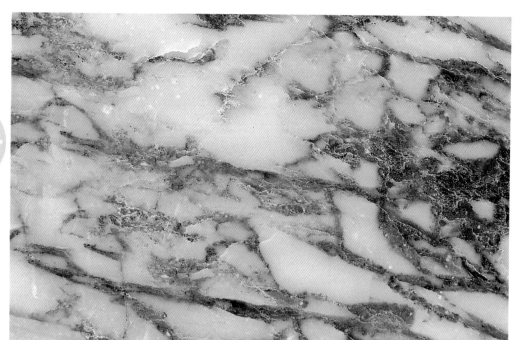

CALACATTA SIENA

PRODUCER COUNTRY: Italy

AVAILABILITY: Limited

FILE NUMBER: 0049

CREMA VALENCIA

PRODUCER COUNTRY: Spain

AVAILABILITY: Medium

FILE NUMBER: 0050

GIALLO REALE

PRODUCER COUNTRY: Italy

AVAILABILITY: Medium

FILE NUMBER: 0051

GIALLO
TAFOUK

PRODUCER COUNTRY: Israel
AVAILABILITY: Medium

FILE NUMBER: 0052
SUPPLIER: 1

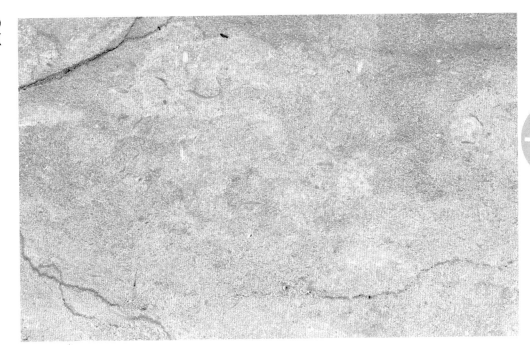

GOLDEN
TRAVERTINE

PRODUCER COUNTRY: Iran
AVAILABILITY: Limited

FILE NUMBER: 0053

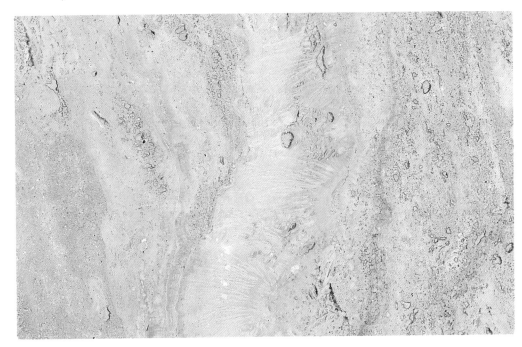

GOLDEN
TRAVERTINE
VEIN CUT

PRODUCER COUNTRY: Iran
AVAILABILITY: Limited

FILE NUMBER: 0054

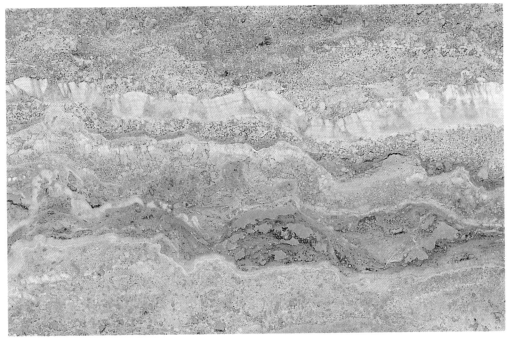

179

YELLOW
MARBLE

BEIGE
MARBLE

ALABASTRO EGIZIANO

PRODUCER COUNTRY: Egypt
AVAILABILITY: Limited

FILE NUMBER: 0055
SUPPLIER: 17

KARIBIB

PRODUCER COUNTRY: Namibia
AVAILABILITY: Limited

FILE NUMBER: 0056

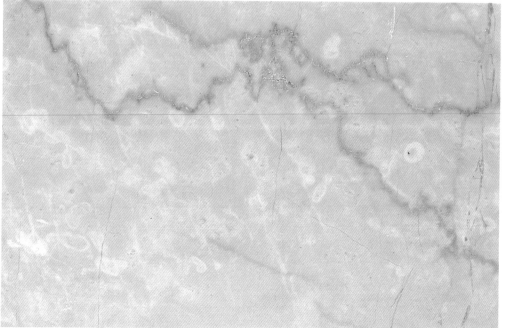

BOTTICINO CLASSICO

PRODUCER COUNTRY: Italy
AVAILABILITY: Medium

FILE NUMBER: 0057

BOTTICINO
SEMICLASSICO

PRODUCER COUNTRY: Italy
AVAILABILITY: Medium

FILE NUMBER: 0058

BEIGE
MARBLE

BOTTICINO
FIORITO

PRODUCER COUNTRY: Italy
AVAILABILITY: Medium

FILE NUMBER: 0059

BOTTICINO
ROYAL

PRODUCER COUNTRY: Italy
AVAILABILITY: Medium

FILE NUMBER: 0060

CREMA MARFIL

PRODUCER COUNTRY: Spain
AVAILABILITY: Good

FILE NUMBER: 0061

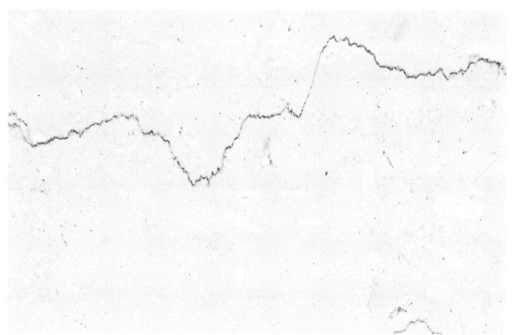

FILETTO ROSSO

PRODUCER COUNTRY: Italy
AVAILABILITY: Medium

FILE NUMBER: 0062
SUPPLIER: 14

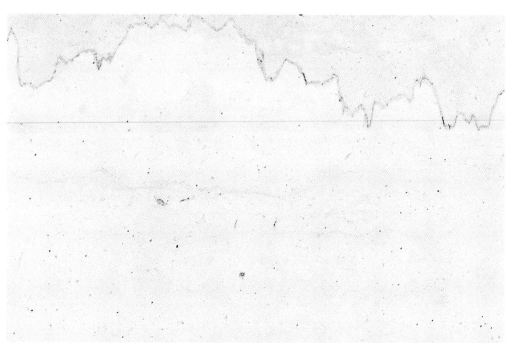

FILETTATO AMERICA

PRODUCER COUNTRY: Italy
AVAILABILITY: Medium

FILE NUMBER: 0063
SUPPLIER: 14

BEIGE
MARBLE

182

TRANI
CLASSICO

PRODUCER COUNTRY: Italy
AVAILABILITY: Good

FILE NUMBER: 0064
SUPPLIER: 14

BEIGE
MARBLE

TRANI
COCCIOLATO

PRODUCER COUNTRY: Italy
AVAILABILITY: Limited

FILE NUMBER: 0065

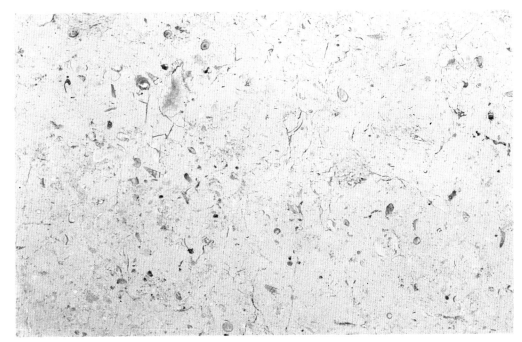

TRANI
FIORITO

PRODUCER COUNTRY: Italy
AVAILABILITY: Good

FILE NUMBER: 0066

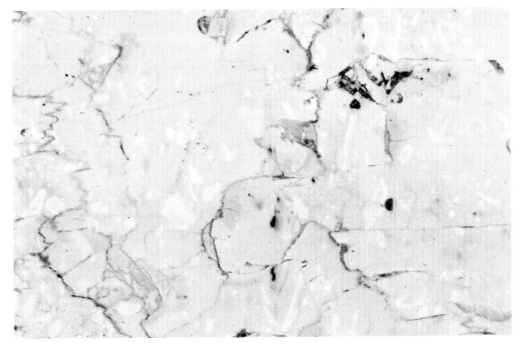

183

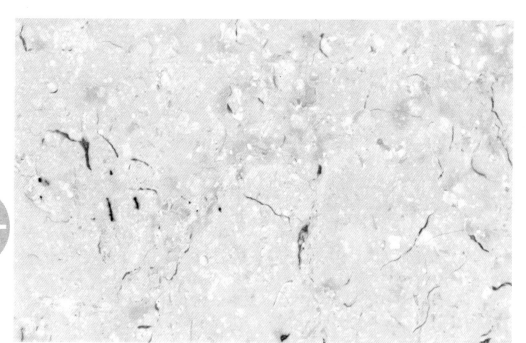

GALALA

PRODUCER COUNTRY: Egypt

AVAILABILITY: Good

FILE NUMBER: 0067

SUPPLIER: 17

SERPEGGIANTE ITALIA

PRODUCER COUNTRY: Italy

AVAILABILITY: Medium

FILE NUMBER: 0068

SUPPLIER: 14

VISONE

PRODUCER COUNTRY: Italy

AVAILABILITY: Medium

FILE NUMBER: 0069

SUPPLIER: 14

184

CREMA SICILIA

PRODUCER COUNTRY: Italy
AVAILABILITY: Good

FILE NUMBER: 0070
SUPPLIER: 12

BEIGE MARBLE

FIORITO DALIA

PRODUCER COUNTRY: Italy
AVAILABILITY: Medium

FILE NUMBER: 0071
SUPPLIER: 14

ROSA SAN MARCO

PRODUCER COUNTRY: Italy
AVAILABILITY: Medium

FILE NUMBER: 0072
SUPPLIER: 14

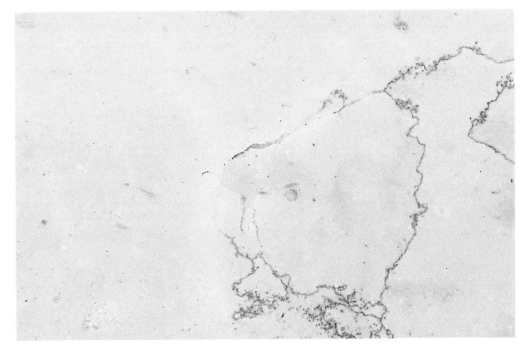

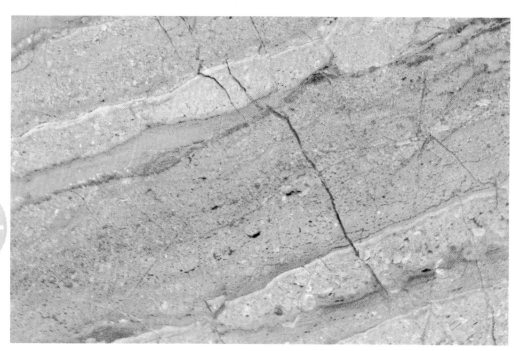

BRECCIA SARDA SCURA

PRODUCER COUNTRY: Italy
AVAILABILITY: Medium

FILE NUMBER: 0073

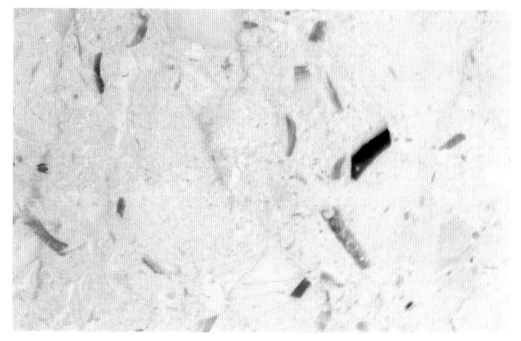

PERLATO SICILIA

PRODUCER COUNTRY: Italy
AVAILABILITY: Good

FILE NUMBER: 0074

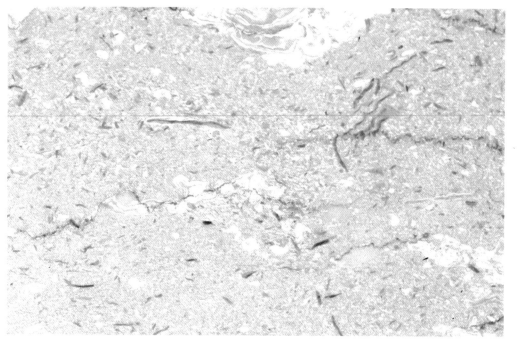

PERLATO ROYAL

PRODUCER COUNTRY: Italy
AVAILABILITY: Good

FILE NUMBER: 0075

PERLATO SVEVO

PRODUCER COUNTRY: Italy
AVAILABILITY: Medium

FILE NUMBER: 0076

BEIGE
MARBLE

PERLATINO

PRODUCER COUNTRY: Italy
AVAILABILITY: Medium

FILE NUMBER: 0077

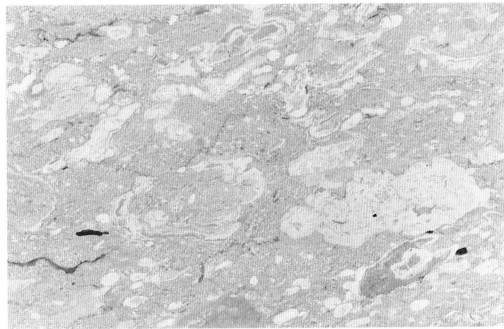

NOCCIOLATO CHIARO

PRODUCER COUNTRY: Italy
AVAILABILITY: Medium

FILE NUMBER: 0078

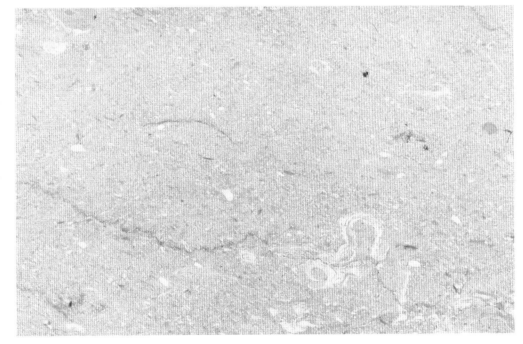

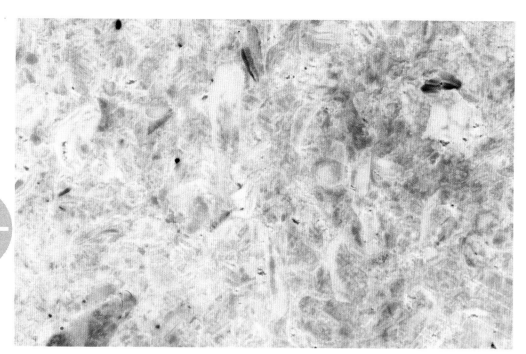

SPUMA
DI MARE

PRODUCER COUNTRY: Italy
AVAILABILITY: Limited

FILE NUMBER: 0079

AMBRATO

PRODUCER COUNTRY: Italy
AVAILABILITY: Medium

FILE NUMBER: 0080
SUPPLIER: 14

CREMO
SUPREMO

PRODUCER COUNTRY: Turkey
AVAILABILITY: Good

FILE NUMBER: 0081
SUPPLIER: 11

CREMA NUOVA

PRODUCER COUNTRY: Turkey
AVAILABILITY: Good

FILE NUMBER: 0082
SUPPLIER: 9

MEZZA PERLA

PRODUCER COUNTRY: Italy
AVAILABILITY: Good

FILE NUMBER: 0083

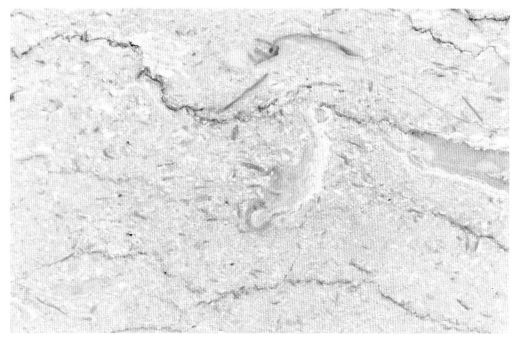

CHIAMPO PERLATO

PRODUCER COUNTRY: Italy
AVAILABILITY: Medium

FILE NUMBER: 0084

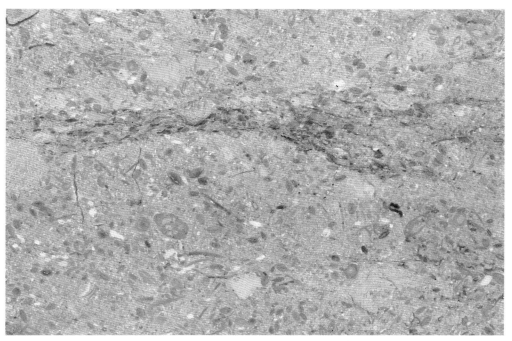

189

TRAVERTINO ROMANO CHIARO

PRODUCER COUNTRY: Italy
AVAILABILITY: Good

FILE NUMBER: 0085

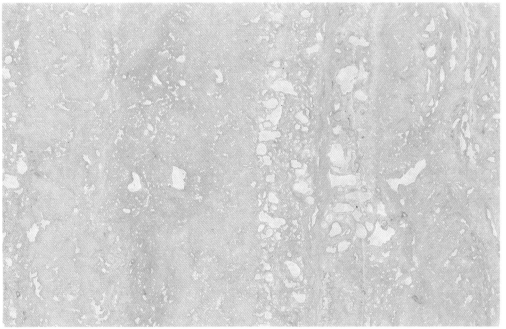

TRAVERTINO ROMANO CLASSICO

PRODUCER COUNTRY: Italy
AVAILABILITY: Good

FILE NUMBER: 0086

TRAVERTINO ROMANO CLASSICO IN FALDA

PRODUCER COUNTRY: Italy
AVAILABILITY: Good

FILE NUMBER: 0087

TRAVERTINO IBERICO

PRODUCER COUNTRY: Spain
AVAILABILITY: Good

FILE NUMBER: 0088

TRAVERTINO STRIATO

PRODUCER COUNTRY: Italy
AVAILABILITY: Good

FILE NUMBER: 0089

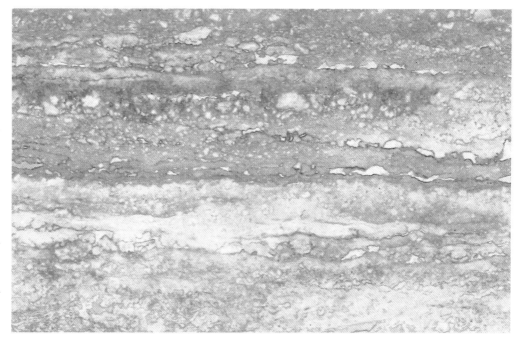

TRAVERTINO SCABAS

PRODUCER COUNTRY: Spain
AVAILABILITY: Medium

FILE NUMBER: 0090

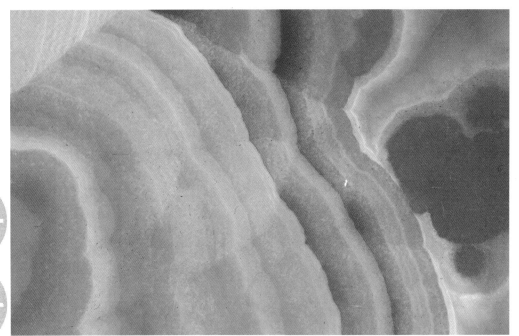

BROWN
ONYX

PRODUCER COUNTRY: Pakistan
AVAILABILITY: Limited

FILE NUMBER: 0091

BEIGE
MARBLE

BROWN
MARBLE

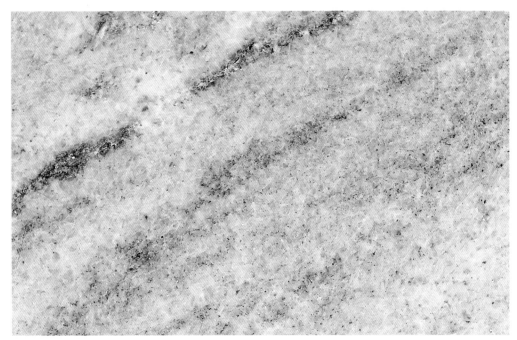

CHOCOLATE

PRODUCER COUNTRY: Brazil
AVAILABILITY: Limited

FILE NUMBER: 0092

PORFIRICO
RAMELLO
BRUNO

PRODUCER COUNTRY: Italy
AVAILABILITY: Limited

FILE NUMBER: 0093

MARRON
IMPERIAL

PRODUCER COUNTRY: Spain
AVAILABILITY: Limited

FILE NUMBER: 0094

BROWN
MARBLE

MARRON
EMPERADOR

PRODUCER COUNTRY: Spain
AVAILABILITY: Limited

FILE NUMBER: 0095

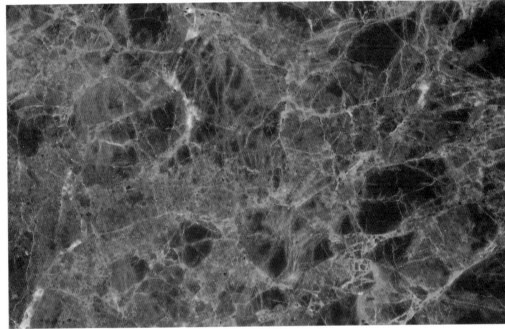

BRECCIA
PARADISO

PRODUCER COUNTRY: Italy
AVAILABILITY: Limited

FILE NUMBER: 0096

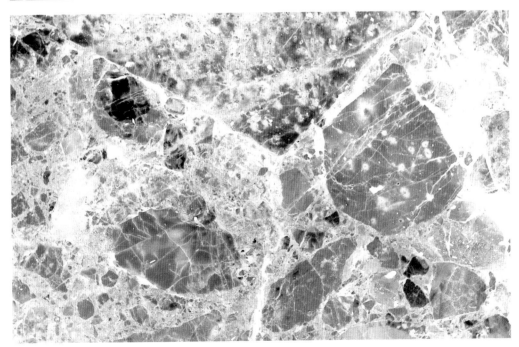

193

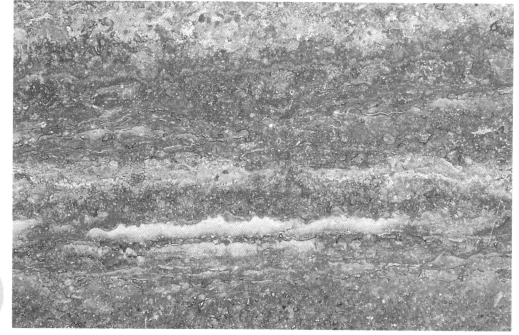

TRAVERTINO NOCE

Producer Country: Italy
Availability: Good

File number: 0097

BROWN
MARBLE

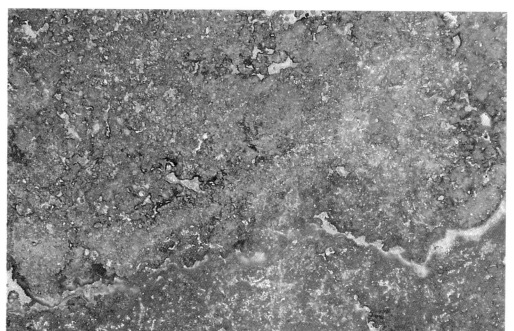

TRAVERTINO NOCE IN FALDA

Producer Country: Italy
Availability: Good

File number: 0098

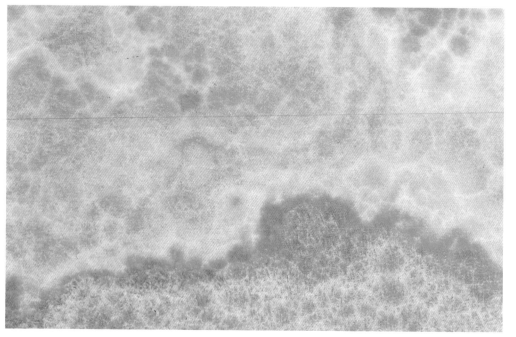

TANZANIA BROWN ONYX VEIN CUT

Producer Country: Tanzania
Availability: Limited

File number: 0099

TANZANIA
BROWN ONYX
VEIN CUT

PRODUCER COUNTRY: Tanzania
AVAILABILITY: Limited

FILE NUMBER: 0100

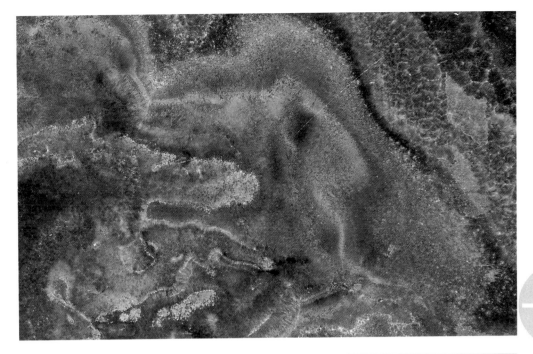

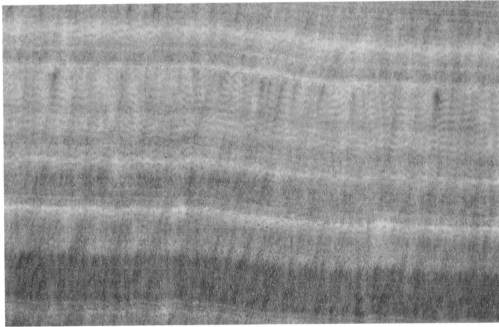

TANZANIA
BROWN ONYX

PRODUCER COUNTRY: Tanzania
AVAILABILITY: Limited

FILE NUMBER: 0101

BROWN MARBLE

RED MARBLE

ROSSO
LEPANTO

PRODUCER COUNTRY: Turkey
AVAILABILITY: Limited

FILE NUMBER: 0102

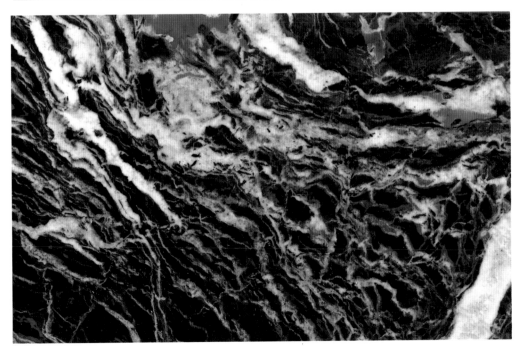

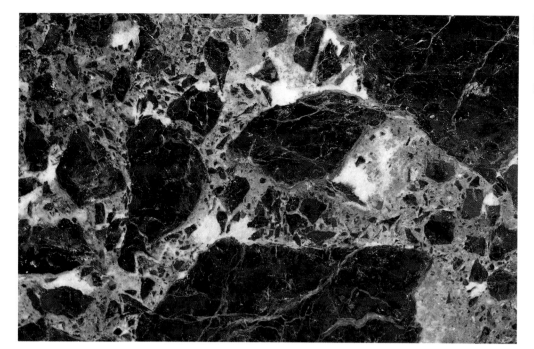

ROSSO ANTICO D'ITALIA

PRODUCER COUNTRY: Italy
AVAILABILITY: Limited

FILE NUMBER: 0103

RED MARBLE

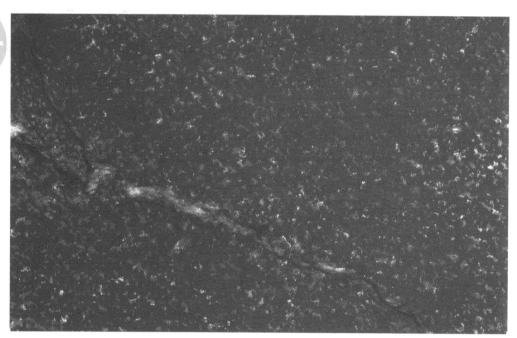

ROSSO LAGUNA

PRODUCER COUNTRY: Turkey
AVAILABILITY: Medium

FILE NUMBER: 0104

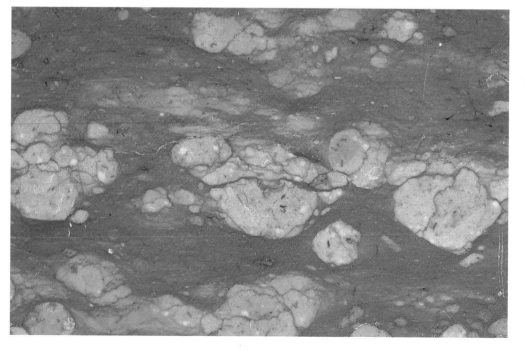

PORFIRICO RAMELLO ROSSO

PRODUCER COUNTRY: Italy
AVAILABILITY: Limited

FILE NUMBER: 0105

ROSSO
ASIAGO

PRODUCER COUNTRY: Italy

AVAILABILITY: Medium

FILE NUMBER: 0106

ROSSO
MANGIABOSCHI

PRODUCER COUNTRY: Italy

AVAILABILITY: Limited

FILE NUMBER: 0107

RED
MARBLE

ROSSO
VERONA

PRODUCER COUNTRY: Italy

AVAILABILITY: Medium

FILE NUMBER: 0108

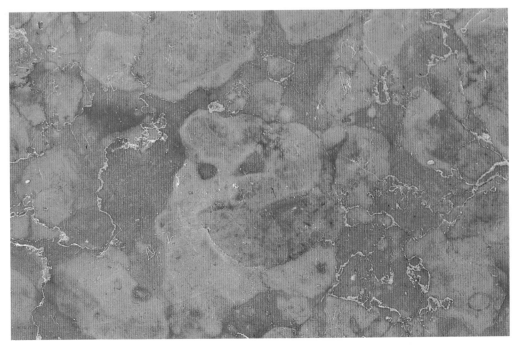

ROUGE GRIOTTE

PRODUCER COUNTRY: France
AVAILABILITY: Limited

FILE NUMBER: 0109

RED MARBLE

ROJO CORALITO

PRODUCER COUNTRY: Spain
AVAILABILITY: Medium

FILE NUMBER: 0110

ROSSO COLLEMANDINA

PRODUCER COUNTRY: Italy
AVAILABILITY: Limited

FILE NUMBER: 0111

ROUGE FRANCE
LANGUEDOC

PRODUCER COUNTRY: France
AVAILABILITY: Medium

FILE NUMBER: 0112
SUPPLIER: 2

ROUGE FRANCE
ISABELLE

PRODUCER COUNTRY: France
AVAILABILITY: Medium

FILE NUMBER: 0113
SUPPLIER: 2

RED
MARBLE

ROSSO
DI RUSSIA

PRODUCER COUNTRY: Georgia
AVAILABILITY: Medium

FILE NUMBER: 0114
SUPPLIER: 1

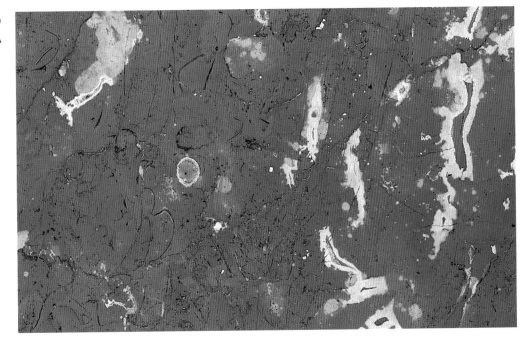

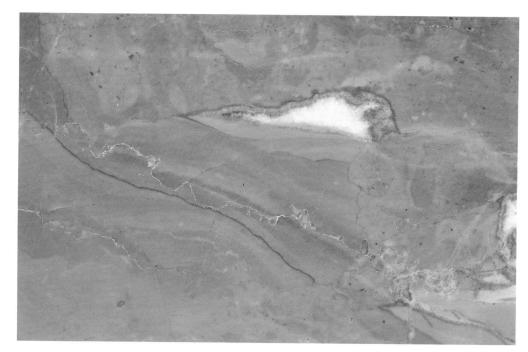

PORTASANTA

Producer Country: Italy
Availability: Limited

File number: 0115

RED MARBLE

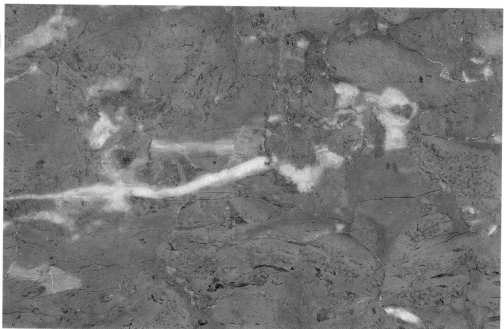

ROJO
ALICANTE

Producer Country: Spain
Availability: Medium

File number: 0116

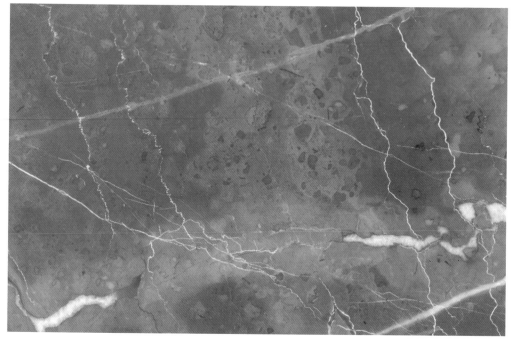

PELO
RED

Producer Country: Italy
Availability: Limited

File number: 0117

ROSSO SANT'AGATA

PRODUCER COUNTRY: Italy
AVAILABILITY: Limited

FILE NUMBER: 0118

ROJO DANIEL

PRODUCER COUNTRY: Spain
AVAILABILITY: Medium

FILE NUMBER: 0119

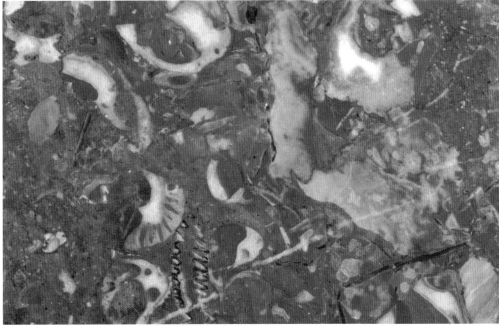

RED
MARBLE

ROSSO AGADIR

PRODUCER COUNTRY: Morocco
AVAILABILITY: Medium

FILE NUMBER: 0120
SUPPLIER: 17

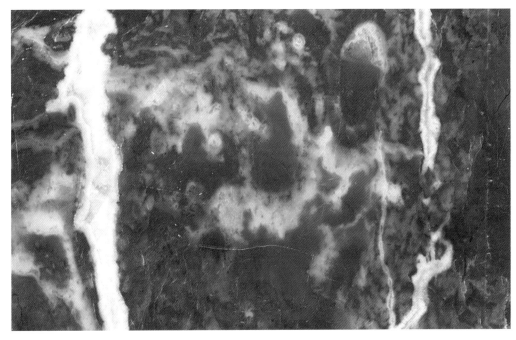

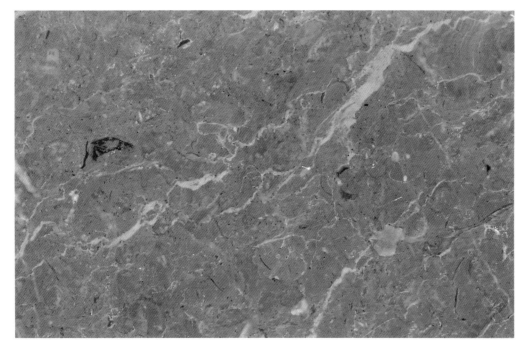

DUQUESA ROSADA

PRODUCER COUNTRY: Spain
AVAILABILITY: Limited

FILE NUMBER: 0121

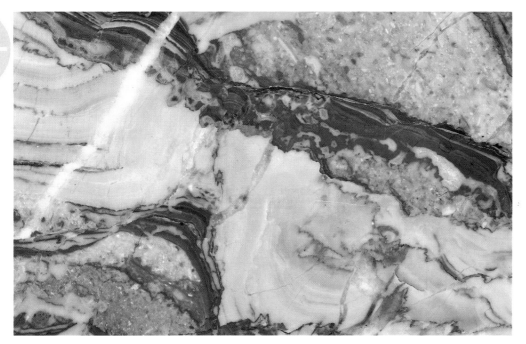

ARABESCATO OROBICO ROSSO

PRODUCER COUNTRY: Italy
AVAILABILITY: Limited

FILE NUMBER: 0122
SUPPLIER: 7

BRECCIA PERNICE

PRODUCER COUNTRY: Italy
AVAILABILITY: Limited

FILE NUMBER: 0123

ROSSO CARPAZI

PRODUCER COUNTRY: Albania
AVAILABILITY: Medium

FILE NUMBER: 0124
SUPPLIER: 10

TRAVERTINO ROSSO PERSIANO

PRODUCER COUNTRY: Iran
AVAILABILITY: Limited

FILE NUMBER: 0125

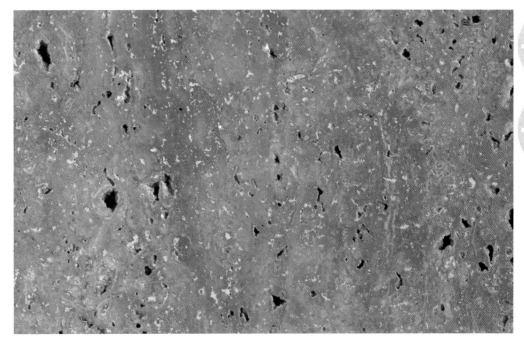

RED MARBLE

PINK MARBLE

ETOWAH

PRODUCER COUNTRY: USA
AVAILABILITY: Good

FILE NUMBER: 0126

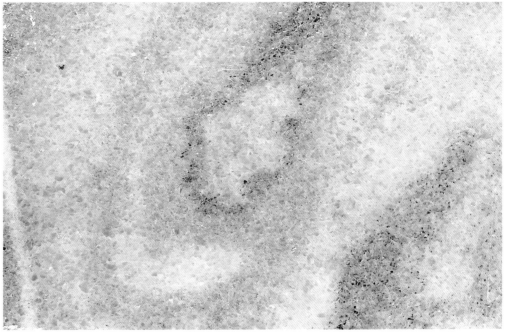

FIOR DI ROSA

PRODUCER COUNTRY: Italy
AVAILABILITY: Medium

FILE NUMBER: 0127
SUPPLIER: 14

ROSA WEST

PRODUCER COUNTRY: Namibia
AVAILABILITY: Good

FILE NUMBER: 0128
SUPPLIER: 14

PINK
MARBLE

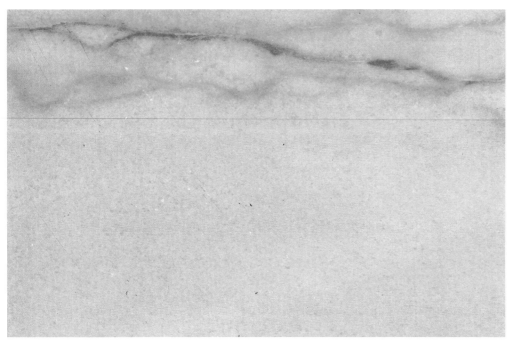

ROSA PORTOGALLO

PRODUCER COUNTRY: Portugal
AVAILABILITY: Good

FILE NUMBER: 0129

ROSA ESTREMOZ

PRODUCER COUNTRY: Portugal
AVAILABILITY: Good

FILE NUMBER: 0130

ROSA BELLISSIMO

PRODUCER COUNTRY: Turkey
AVAILABILITY: Good

FILE NUMBER: 0131
SUPPLIER: 9

PINK
MARBLE

NORWEGIAN ROSE

PRODUCER COUNTRY: Norway
AVAILABILITY: Medium

F'LE NUMBER: 0132

ROSA EGEO

<small>Producer Country:</small> Greece
<small>Availability:</small> Limited

<small>File number:</small> 0133

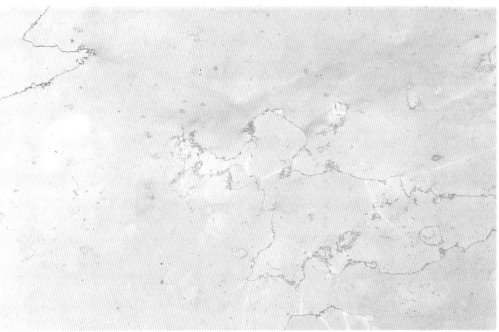

PINK
MARBLE

PERLINO ROSATO

<small>Producer Country:</small> Italy
<small>Availability:</small> Medium

<small>File number:</small> 0134
<small>Supplier:</small> 16

ROSA CENGI

<small>Producer Country:</small> Italy
<small>Availability:</small> Good

<small>File number:</small> 0138
<small>Supplier:</small> 16

206

ALPENINA

PRODUCER COUNTRY: Portugal
AVAILABILITY: Limited

FILE NUMBER: 0136

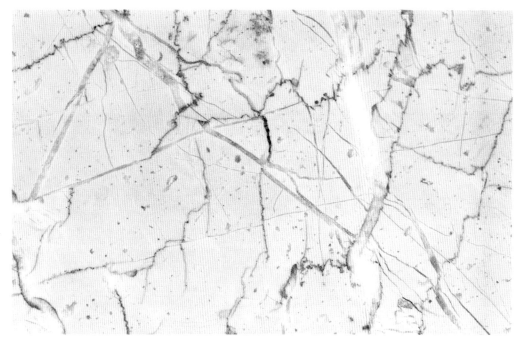

ROSALIA

PRODUCER COUNTRY: Turkey
AVAILABILITY: Good

FILE NUMBER: 0137
SUPPLIER: 9

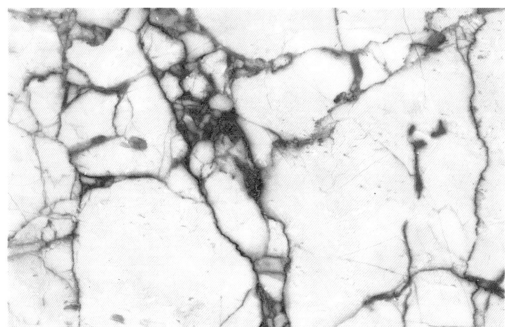

PINK
MARBLE

CHIAMPO ROSA

PRODUCER COUNTRY: Italy
AVAILABILITY: Medium

FILE NUMBER: 0135
SUPPLIER: 16

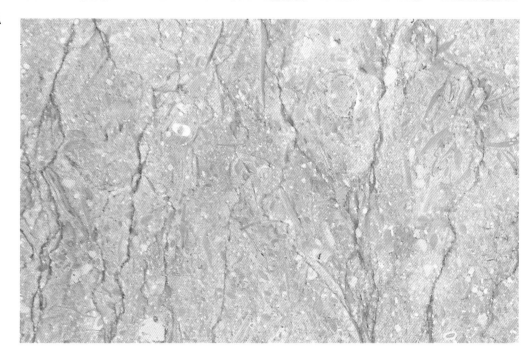

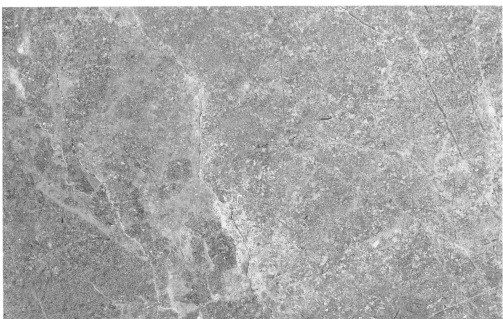

ROSA LEVANTE

PRODUCER COUNTRY: Spain
AVAILABILITY: Good

FILE NUMBER: 0139

PINK
MARBLE

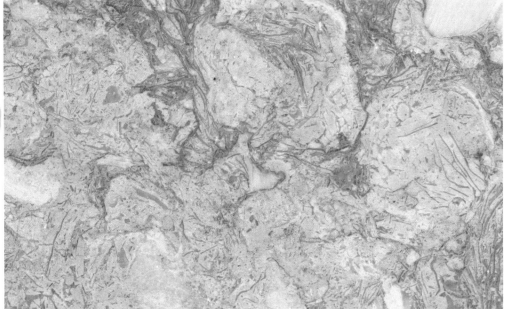

SAINT FLOURIAN

PRODUCER COUNTRY: Portugal
AVAILABILITY: Limited

FILE NUMBER: 0140

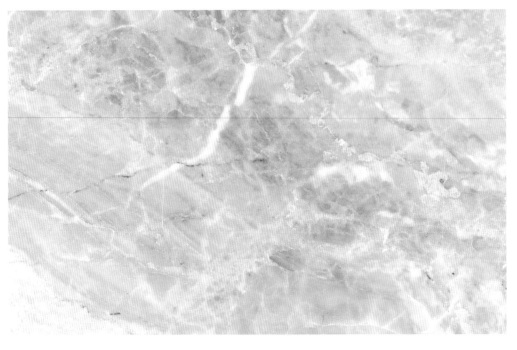

BRECCIA DAMASCATA

PRODUCER COUNTRY: Italy
AVAILABILITY: Limited

FILE NUMBER: 0141

BRECCIA
AURORA

PRODUCER COUNTRY: Italy
AVAILABILITY: Limited

FILE NUMBER: 0142

BRECCIA
ONICIATA

PRODUCER COUNTRY: Italy
AVAILABILITY: Limited

FILE NUMBER: 0143

PINK
MARBLE

ROSA
TEA

PRODUCER COUNTRY: Turkey
AVAILABILITY: Medium

FILE NUMBER: 0144

209

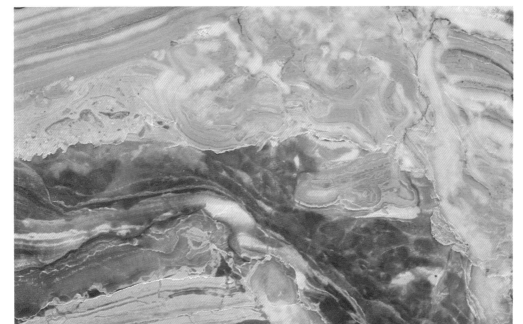

ARABESCATO OROBICO ROSA

Producer Country: Italy
Availability: Limited

File number: 0145
Supplier: 7

PINK
Marble

SKY BLUE
Marble

GREEN
Marble

AZUL CIELO

Producer Country: Argentina
Availability: Medium

File number: 0146
Supplier: 13

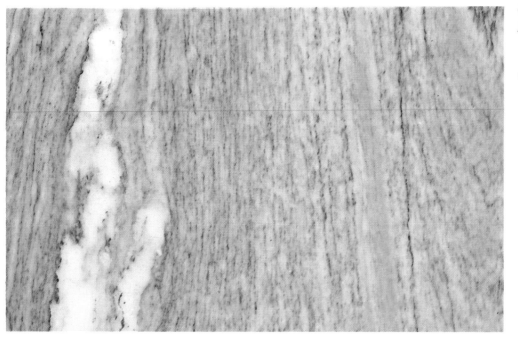

CIPOLLINO APUANO

Producer Country: Italy
Availability: Limited

File number: 0147

CREMO TIRRENO

PRODUCER COUNTRY: Italy
AVAILABILITY: Limited

FILE NUMBER: 0148

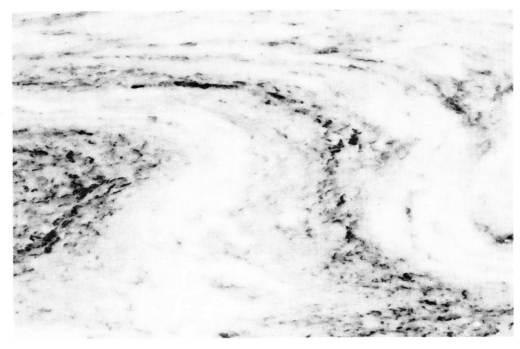

FANTASTICO

PRODUCER COUNTRY: Italy
AVAILABILITY: Limited

FILE NUMBER: 0149

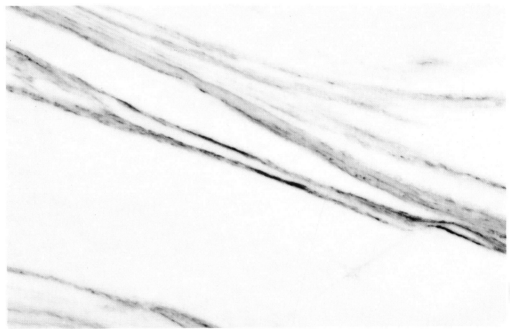

GREEN
MARBLE

VERDE ACCEGLIO

PRODUCER COUNTRY: Italy
AVAILABILITY: Medium

FILE NUMBER: 0150

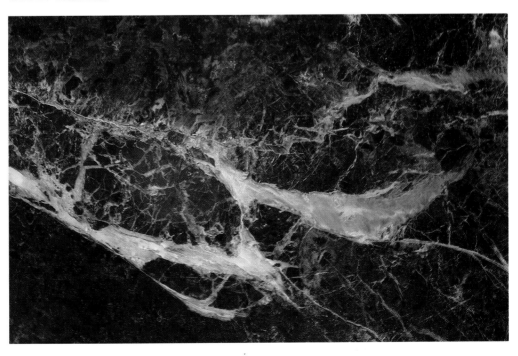

VERDE
ALPI

PRODUCER COUNTRY: Italy
AVAILABILITY: Medium

FILE NUMBER: 0151

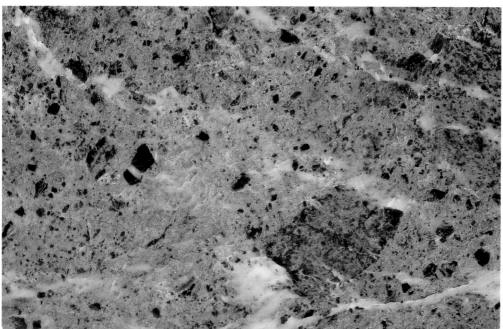

VERDE
AVER

PRODUCER COUNTRY: Italy
AVAILABILITY: Limited

FILE NUMBER: 0152

GREEN
MARBLE

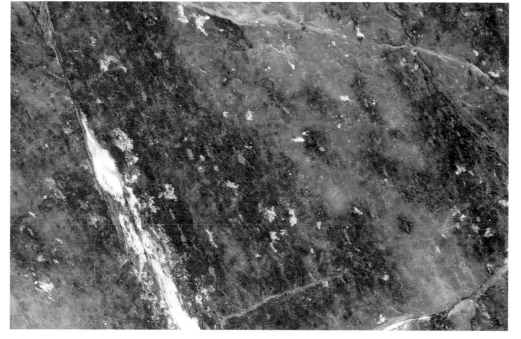

VERDE
GIADA

PRODUCER COUNTRY: Italy
AVAILABILITY: Limited

FILE NUMBER: 0153

212

VERDE
GRESSONEY

PRODUCER COUNTRY: Italy
AVAILABILITY: Limited

FILE NUMBER: 0154

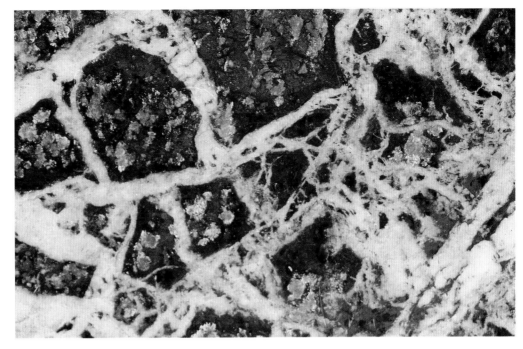

VERDE
GUATEMALA

PRODUCER COUNTRY: Guatemala
AVAILABILITY: Limited

FILE NUMBER: 0155

**GREEN
MARBLE**

VERDE
ISSOIRE

PRODUCER COUNTRY: Italy
AVAILABILITY: Limited

FILE NUMBER: 0156

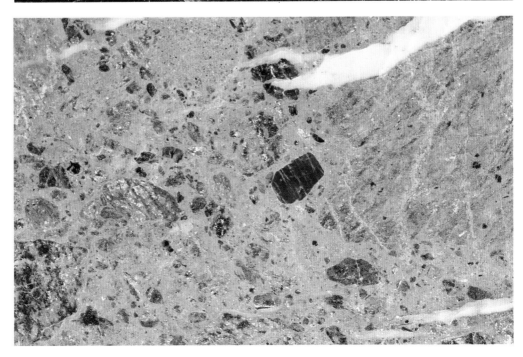

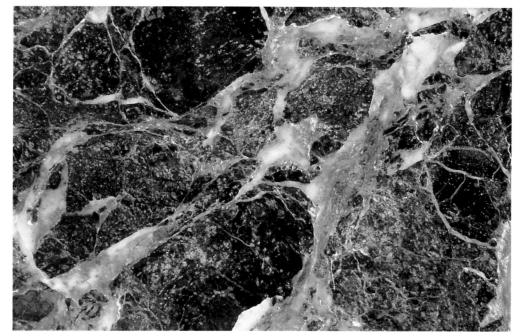

VERDE ISSOGNE

PRODUCER COUNTRY: Italy
AVAILABILITY: Medium

FILE NUMBER: 0157
SUPPLIER: 3

VERDE PATRIZIA

PRODUCER COUNTRY: Italy
AVAILABILITY: Limited

FILE NUMBER: 0158

GREEN
MARBLE

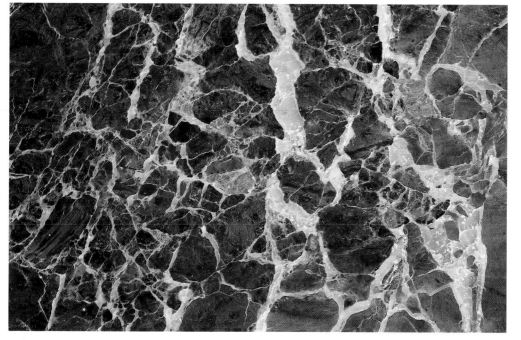

TINOS GREEN

PRODUCER COUNTRY: Greece
AVAILABILITY: Medium

FILE NUMBER: 0159

214

VERDE
S. DENIS

PRODUCER COUNTRY: Italy
AVAILABILITY: Medium

FILE NUMBER: 0160

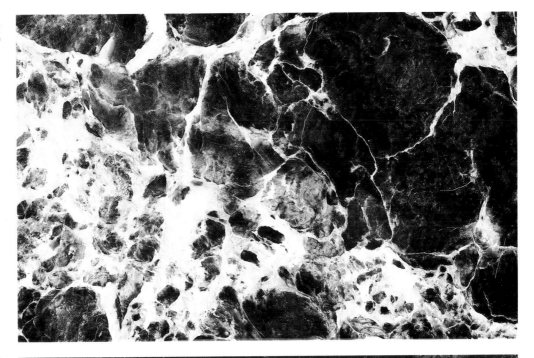

VERDE
RAMEGGIATO

PRODUCER COUNTRY: Italy
AVAILABILITY: Medium

FILE NUMBER: 0161
SUPPLIER: 1

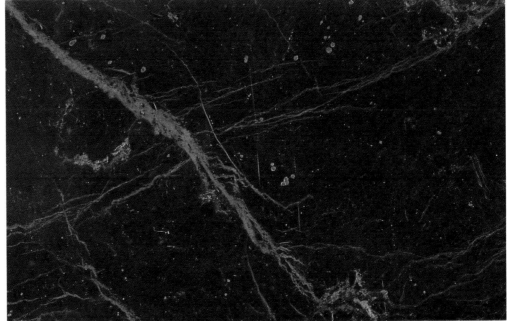

GREEN
MARBLE

VERMONT
GREEN

PRODUCER COUNTRY: USA
AVAILABILITY: Medium

FILE NUMBER: 0162

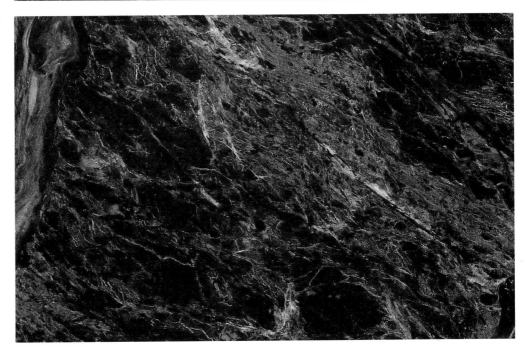

215

TAIWAN GREEN

PRODUCER COUNTRY: Taiwan
AVAILABILITY: Medium

FILE NUMBER: 0163

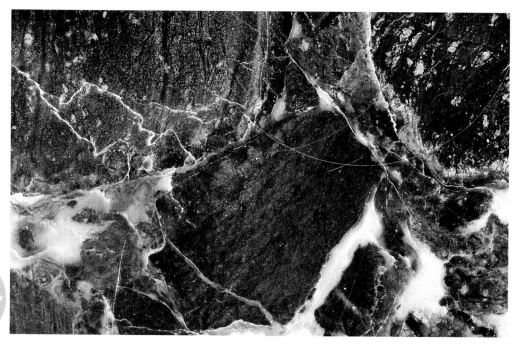

LARISSA GREEN

PRODUCER COUNTRY: Greece
AVAILABILITY: Limited

FILE NUMBER: 0164

GREEN
MARBLE

RAJASTAN GREEN

PRODUCER COUNTRY: India
AVAILABILITY: Good

FILE NUMBER: 0165
SUPPLIER: 20

SERPENTINO CLASSICO

PRODUCER COUNTRY: Italy
AVAILABILITY: Medium

FILE NUMBER: 0166

BRECCIA FAWAKIR

PRODUCER COUNTRY: Egypt
AVAILABILITY: Limited

FILE NUMBER: 0167
SUPPLIER: 17

GREEN MARBLE

GREEN ONYX

PRODUCER COUNTRY: Pakistan
AVAILABILITY: Limited

FILE NUMBER: 0168

BARDIGLIO
CARRARA

PRODUCER COUNTRY: Italy
AVAILABILITY: Medium

FILE NUMBER: 0169

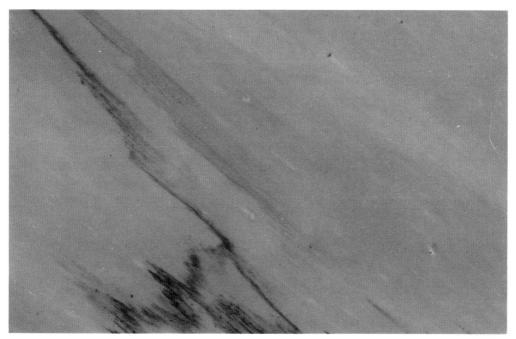

BARDIGLIO
IMPERIALE

PRODUCER COUNTRY: Italy
AVAILABILITY: Limited

FILE NUMBER: 0170

GREY
MARBLE

NUVOLATO
APUANO

PRODUCER COUNTRY: Italy
AVAILABILITY: Limited

FILE NUMBER: 0171

BARDIGLIO
FUMO DI LONDRA

PRODUCER COUNTRY: Italy
AVAILABILITY: Medium

FILE NUMBER: 0172
SUPPLIER: 10

BLU VENATO
D'ITALIA

PRODUCER COUNTRY: Italy
AVAILABILITY: Limited

FILE NUMBER: 0173

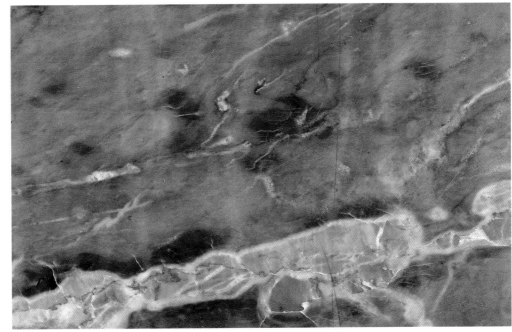

PEARL
GREY

PRODUCER COUNTRY: USA
AVAILABILITY: Good

FILE NUMBER: 0174

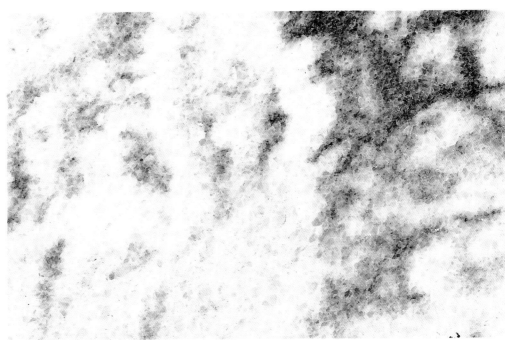

GREY
MARBLE

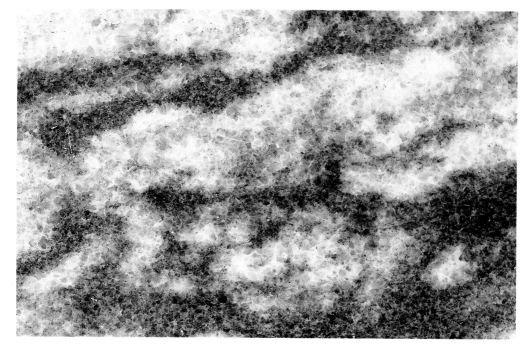

SOLAR GREY

PRODUCER COUNTRY: USA
AVAILABILITY: Good

FILE NUMBER: 0175

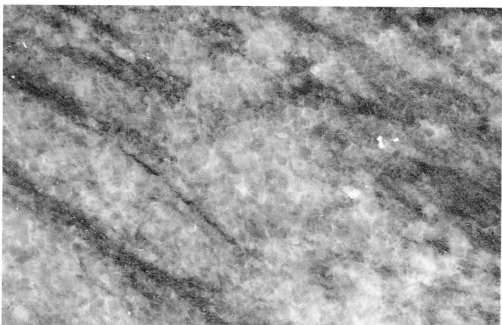

TRIGACHES

PRODUCER COUNTRY: Portugal
AVAILABILITY: Medium

FILE NUMBER: 0176

GREY
MARBLE

ANTIQUE SILVER

PRODUCER COUNTRY: USA
AVAILABILITY: Good

FILE NUMBER: 0177

220

SALOMÉ

PRODUCER COUNTRY: Turkey
AVAILABILITY: Medium

FILE NUMBER: 0178

SUPREN

PRODUCER COUNTRY: Turkey
AVAILABILITY: Limited

FILE NUMBER: 0179

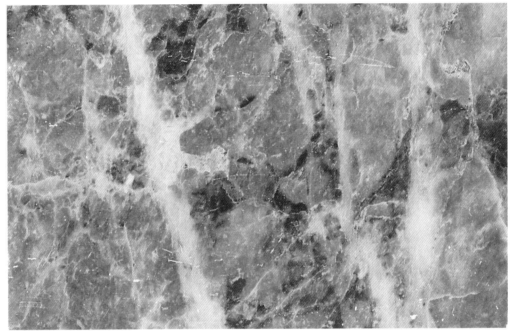

TEKMAR DOVE

PRODUCER COUNTRY: Turkey
AVAILABILITY: Good

FILE NUMBER: 0180
SUPPLIER: 9

GREY
MARBLE

FIOR DI PESCO CARNICO

PRODUCER COUNTRY: Italy
AVAILABILITY: Good

FILE NUMBER: 0181

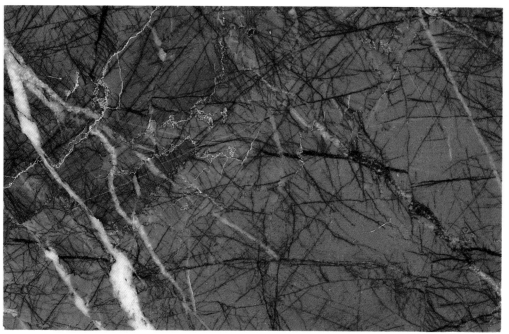

GRIGIO CARNICO

PRODUCER COUNTRY: Italy
AVAILABILITY: Medium

FILE NUMBER: 0182

GREY
MARBLE

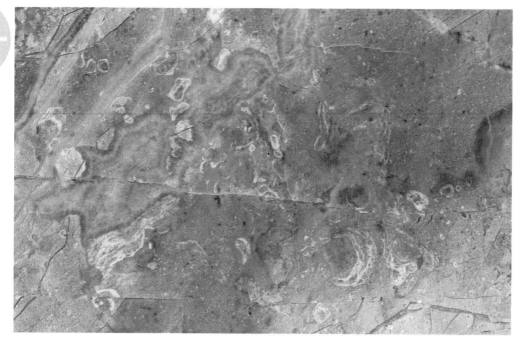

ARABESCATO OROBICO GRIGIO

PRODUCER COUNTRY: Italy
AVAILABILITY: Medium

FILE NUMBER: 0183

AURISINA FIORITA

Producer Country: Italy

Availability: Good

File number: 0184

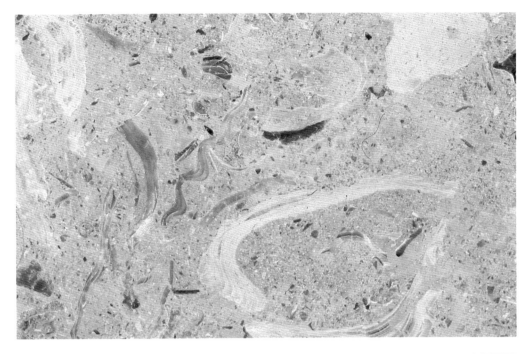

REPEN ZOLLA

Producer Country: Italy

Availability: Medium

File number: 0185

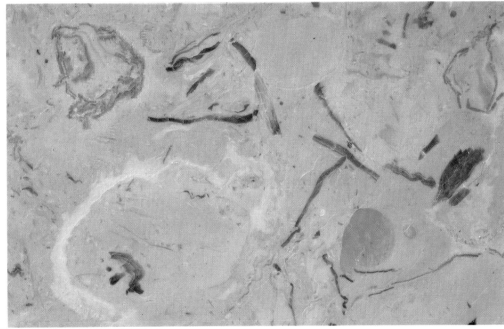

SILVER TRAVERTINO

Producer Country: Italy

Availability: Limited

File number: 0186

GREY MARBLE

223

NERO BELGIO

PRODUCER COUNTRY: Belgium
AVAILABILITY: Limited

FILE NUMBER: 0187

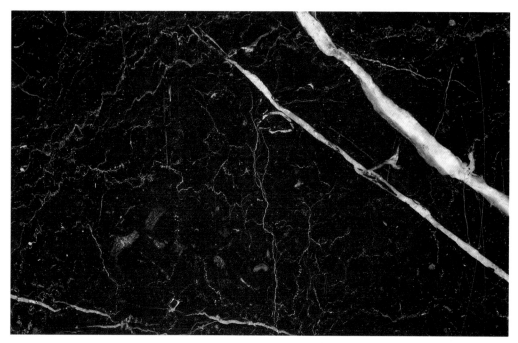

NERO MARQUINA

PRODUCER COUNTRY: Spain
AVAILABILITY: Good

FILE NUMBER: 0188

NOIR SAINT LAURENT

PRODUCER COUNTRY: France
AVAILABILITY: Limited

FILE NUMBER: 0189

BLACK
MARBLE

PORTORO

PRODUCER COUNTRY: Italy
AVAILABILITY: Limited

FILE NUMBER: 0190

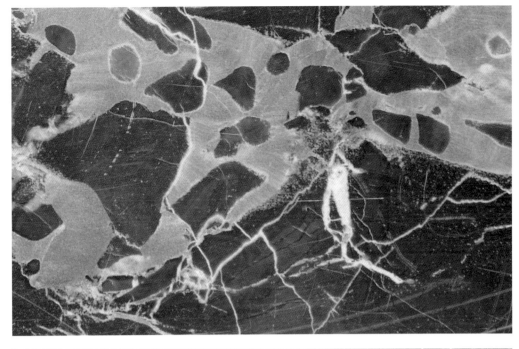

NERO
CRETA

PRODUCER COUNTRY: Greece
AVAILABILITY: Medium

FILE NUMBER: 0191

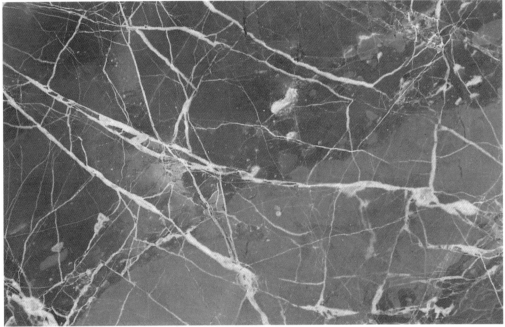

NEGRO
MEXICO

PRODUCER COUNTRY: Mexico
AVAILABILITY: Medium

FILE NUMBER: 0192

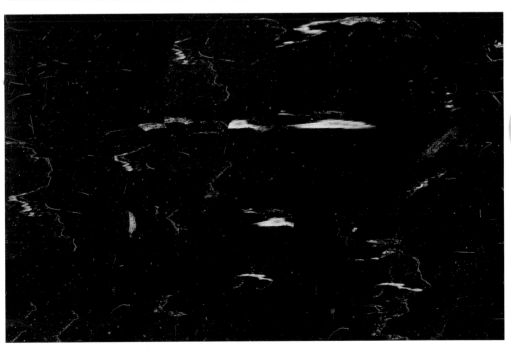

BLACK
MARBLE

225

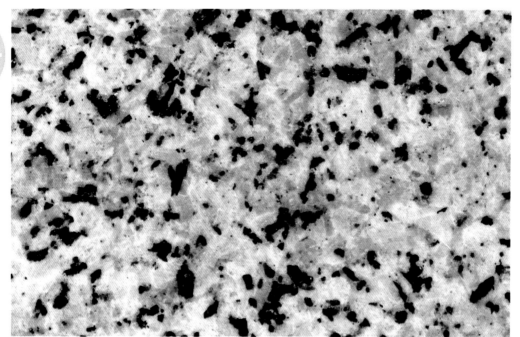

BLANCO
BERROCAL

PRODUCER COUNTRY: Spain
AVAILABILITY: Medium

FILE NUMBER: 0193

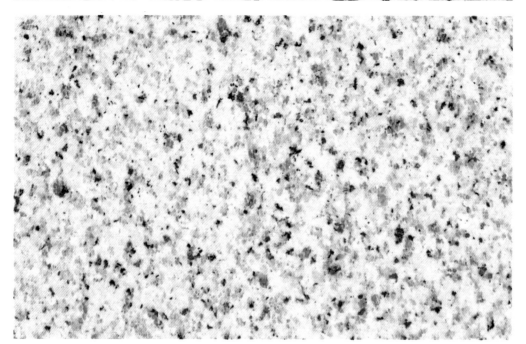

BLANCO
CRISTAL

PRODUCER COUNTRY: Spain
AVAILABILITY: Good

FILE NUMBER: 0194

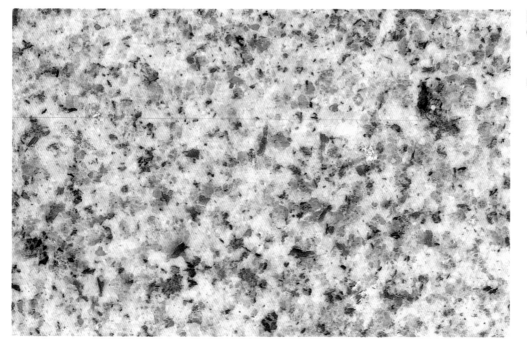

BLANCO
GALIZIA

PRODUCER COUNTRY: Spain
AVAILABILITY: Good

FILE NUMBER: 0195

BIANCO SARDO

PRODUCER COUNTRY: Italy
AVAILABILITY: Limited

FILE NUMBER: 0196

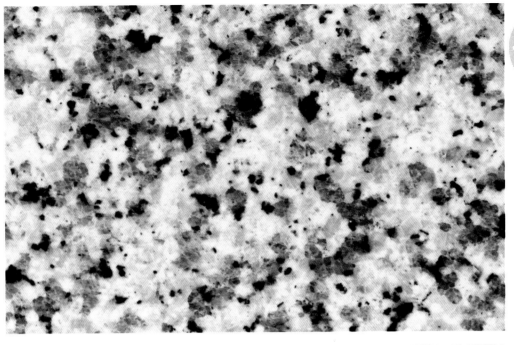

WHITE GRANITE

CAESAR WHITE

PRODUCER COUNTRY: USA
AVAILABILITY: Good

FILE NUMBER: 0197

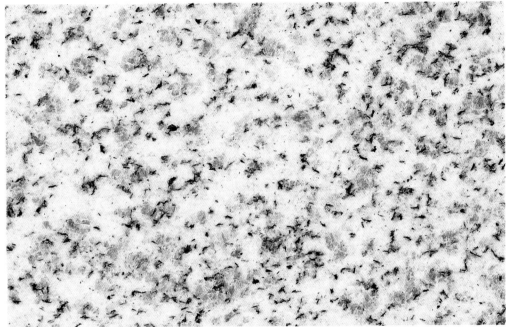

TOLGA WHITE

PRODUCER COUNTRY: Norway
AVAILABILITY: Medium

FILE NUMBER: 0198

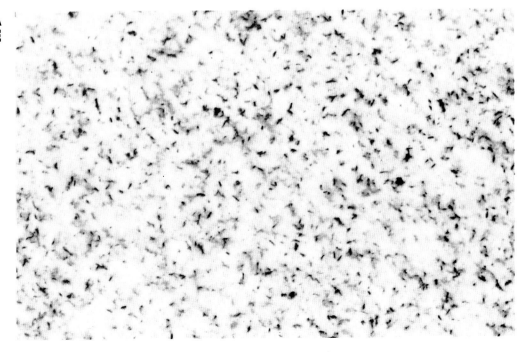

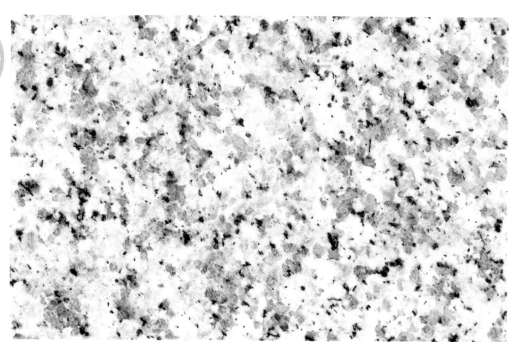

BIANCO BAVENO

PRODUCER COUNTRY: Italy
AVAILABILITY: Limited

FILE NUMBER: 0199
SUPPLIER: 4

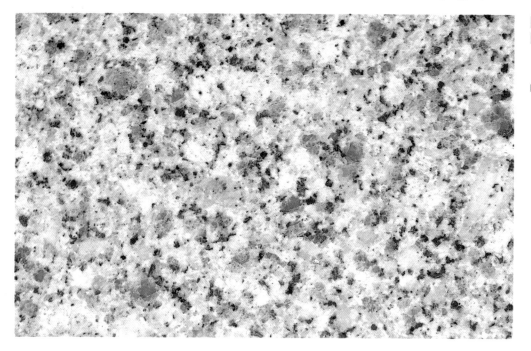

BLANCO REAL

PRODUCER COUNTRY: Spain
AVAILABILITY: Good

FILE NUMBER: 0200

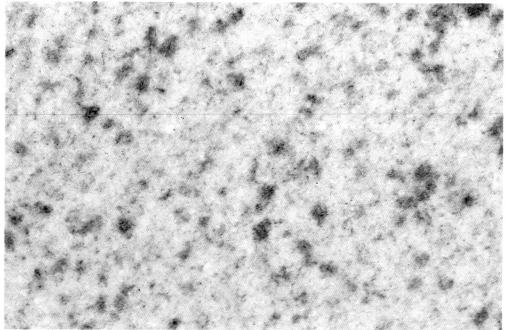

BETHEL WHITE

PRODUCER COUNTRY: Canada
AVAILABILITY: Good

FILE NUMBER: 0201

CARDINAL WHITE

PRODUCER COUNTRY: Brazil

AVAILABILITY: Limited

FILE NUMBER: 0202

IMPERIAL WHITE

PRODUCER COUNTRY: India

AVAILABILITY: Medium

FILE NUMBER: 0203

PANAFRAGOLA

PRODUCER COUNTRY: Brazil

AVAILABILITY: Medium

FILE NUMBER: 0204

**SAMBA
WHITE**

PRODUCER COUNTRY: Brazil
AVAILABILITY: Limited

FILE NUMBER: 0205

**SOLAR
WHITE**

PRODUCER COUNTRY: USA
AVAILABILITY: Good

FILE NUMBER: 0206

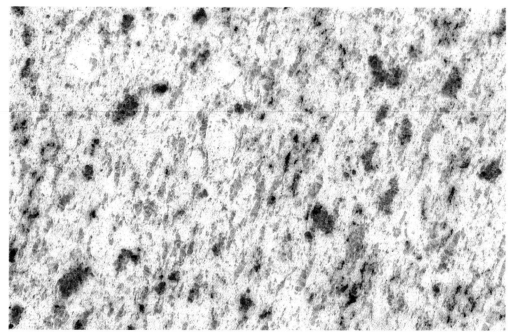

**GALAXY
WHITE**

PRODUCER COUNTRY: India
AVAILABILITY: Good

FILE NUMBER: 0207
SUPPLIER: 8

KASHMIR
WHITE

PRODUCER COUNTRY: India
AVAILABILITY: Good

FILE NUMBER: 0208

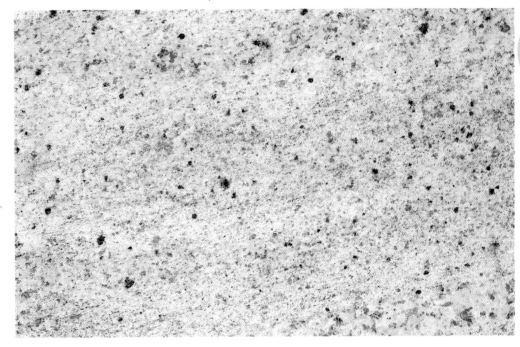

VISCOUNT
WHITE

PRODUCER COUNTRY: India
AVAILABILITY: Medium

FILE NUMBER: 0209

EIDELWEISS

PRODUCER COUNTRY: South Africa
AVAILABILITY: Medium

FILE NUMBER: 0210
SUPPLIER: 15

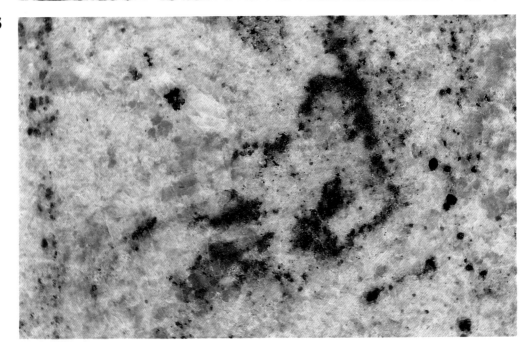

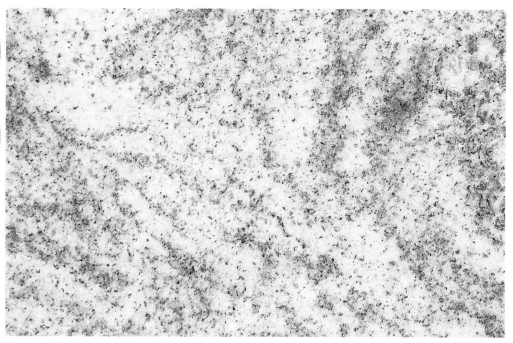

SILVER
CLOUD

PRODUCER COUNTRY: USA
AVAILABILITY: Good

FILE NUMBER: 0211

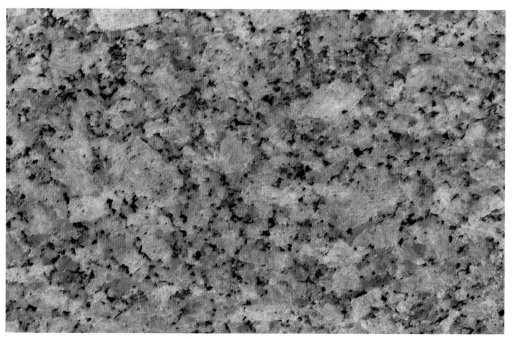

AMARELO
REAL

PRODUCER COUNTRY: Brazil
AVAILABILITY: Medium

FILE NUMBER: 0212

GIALLO
ANTICO

PRODUCER COUNTRY: Brazil
AVAILABILITY: Limited

FILE NUMBER: 0213

GIALLO VENEZIANO

PRODUCER COUNTRY: Brazil

AVAILABILITY: Medium

FILE NUMBER: 0214

SANTA CECILIA

PRODUCER COUNTRY: Brazil

AVAILABILITY: Medium

FILE NUMBER: 0215

GIALLO FIORITO

PRODUCER COUNTRY: Brazil

AVAILABILITY: Limited

FILE NUMBER: 0216

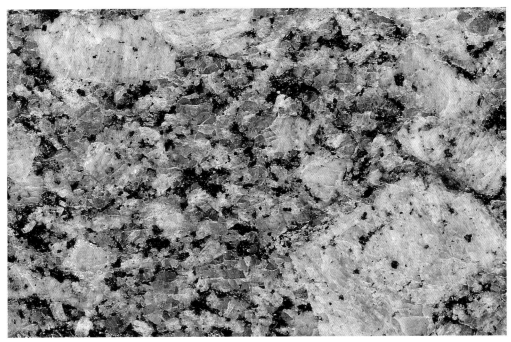

233

JUPARANÀ CLASSICO

PRODUCER COUNTRY: Brazil
AVAILABILITY: Limited

FILE NUMBER: 0217

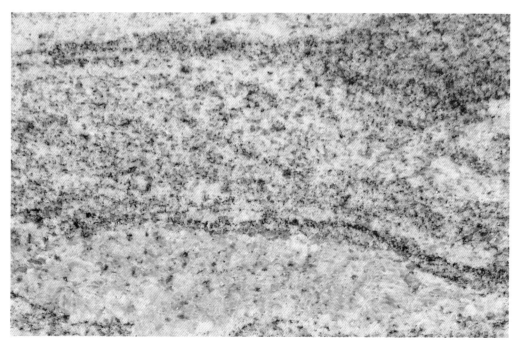

JUPARANÀ COLOMBO

PRODUCER COUNTRY: Sri Lanka
AVAILABILITY: Limited

FILE NUMBER: 0218

JUPARANÀ CHAMPAGNE

PRODUCER COUNTRY: Brazil
AVAILABILITY: Limited

FILE NUMBER: 0219

JUPARANÀ
DELICADO

PRODUCER COUNTRY: Brazil

AVAILABILITY: Limited

FILE NUMBER: 0220

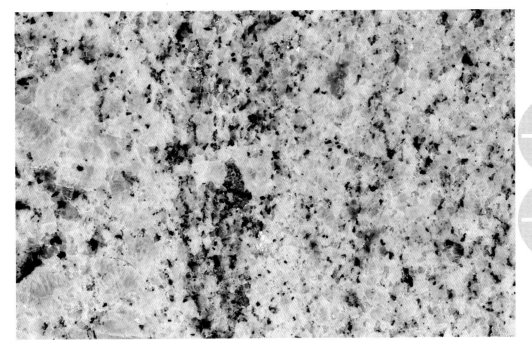

YELLOW
GRANITE

BROWN
GRANITE

SHIVAKASHI

PRODUCER COUNTRY: India

AVAILABILITY: Limited

FILE NUMBER: 0221

BALTIC
BROWN

PRODUCER COUNTRY: Finland

AVAILABILITY: Good

FILE NUMBER: 0222

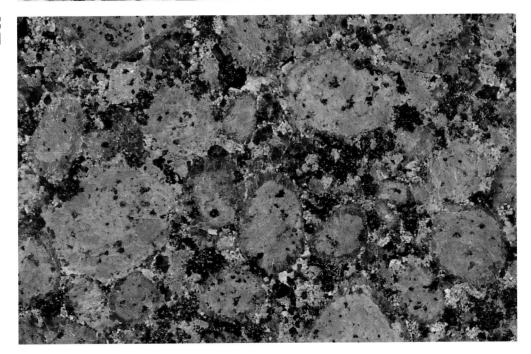

235

MONOLA BROWN

PRODUCER COUNTRY: Finland
AVAILABILITY: Medium

FILE NUMBER: 0223

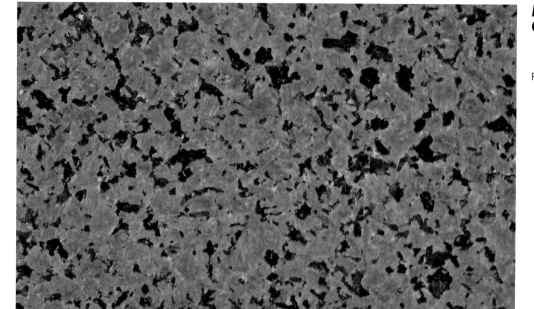

MARRON GUAIBA

PRODUCER COUNTRY: Brazil
AVAILABILITY: Limited

FILE NUMBER: 0224

CRYSTAL BROWN

PRODUCER COUNTRY: South Africa
AVAILABILITY: Medium

FILE NUMBER: 0225
SUPPLIER: 15

236

CALEDONIA

PRODUCER COUNTRY: Canada
AVAILABILITY: Medium

FILE NUMBER: 0226

BROWN
GRANITE

LABRADOR ANTIQUE

PRODUCER COUNTRY: Norway
AVAILABILITY: Medium

FILE NUMBER: 0227
SUPPLIER: 6

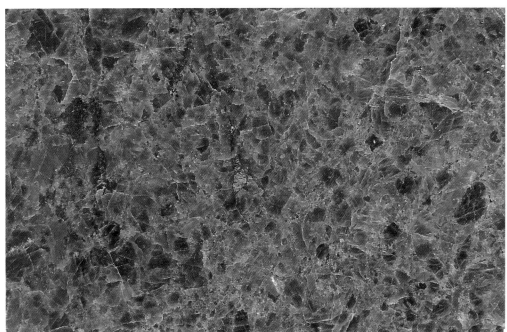

AUTUMN BROWN

PRODUCER COUNTRY: Canada
AVAILABILITY: Medium

FILE NUMBER: 0228

POLICHROME

PRODUCER COUNTRY: Canada
AVAILABILITY: Medium

FILE NUMBER: 0229

BROWN
GRANITE

RED
GRANITE

MARRON CAFÉ

PRODUCER COUNTRY: Brazil
AVAILABILITY: Limited

FILE NUMBER: 0230

AFRICAN RED

PRODUCER COUNTRY: South Africa
AVAILABILITY: Good

FILE NUMBER: 0231
SUPPLIER: 15

BALMORAL
RED FG

PRODUCER COUNTRY: Finland
AVAILABILITY: Medium

FILE NUMBER: 0232

BALMORAL
RED CG

PRODUCER COUNTRY: Finland
AVAILABILITY: Good

FILE NUMBER: 0233

CAPAÕ
BONITO

PRODUCER COUNTRY: Brazil
AVAILABILITY: Good

FILE NUMBER: 0234

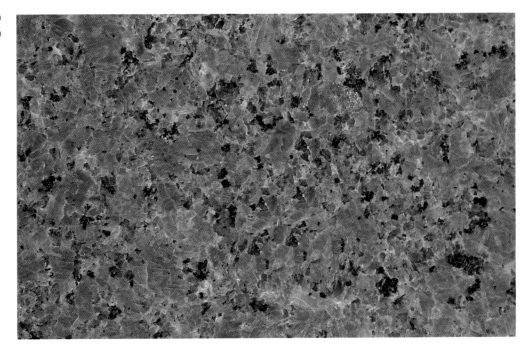

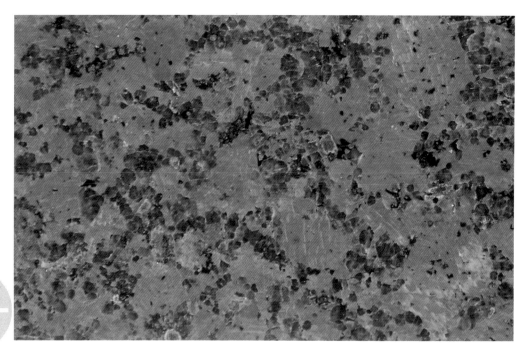

CARMEN RED

RED
GRANITE

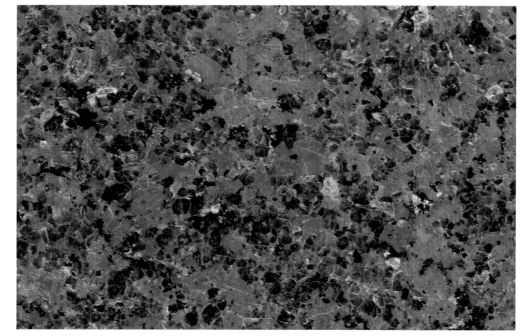

EAGLE RED

IMPERIAL RED

NEW IMPERIAL

PRODUCER COUNTRY: India
AVAILABILITY: Good

FILE NUMBER: 0238

NEW RUBIN

PRODUCER COUNTRY: India
AVAILABILITY: Limited

FILE NUMBER: 0239

ROSSO TOLEDO

PRODUCER COUNTRY: Ukraine
AVAILABILITY: Medium

FILE NUMBER: 0240

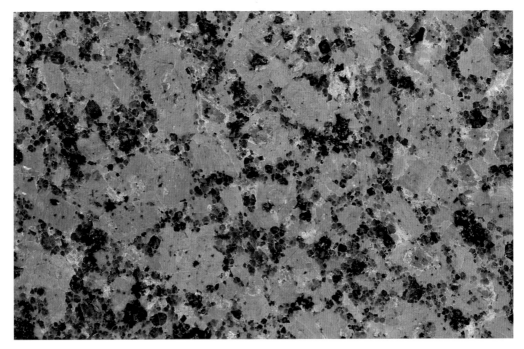

ROSSO
BRAGANZA

PRODUCER COUNTRY: BRAZIL
AVAILABILITY: LIMITED

FILE NUMBER: 0241

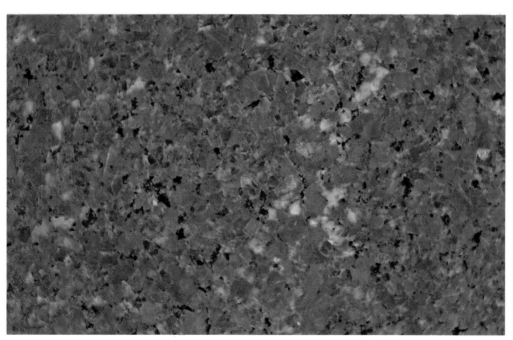

TRANAS
RED

PRODUCER COUNTRY: Sweden
AVAILABILITY: Limited

FILE NUMBER: 0242

ASWAN
RED

PRODUCER COUNTRY: Egypt
AVAILABILITY: Medium

FILE NUMBER: 0243

ROSSO
PERLA INDIA

PRODUCER COUNTRY: India
AVAILABILITY: Medium

FILE NUMBER: 0244

RED
GRANITE

ROSSO
SANTIAGO

PRODUCER COUNTRY: Ukraine
AVAILABILITY: Medium

FILE NUMBER: 0245

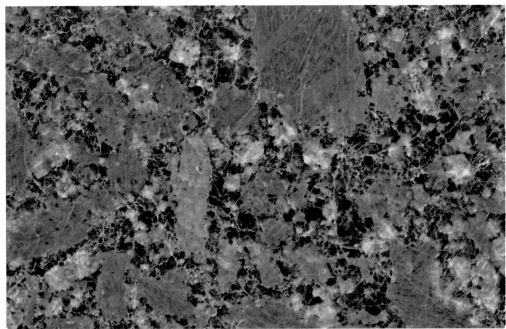

VANGA
RED

PRODUCER COUNTRY: Sweden
AVAILABILITY: Limited

FILE NUMBER: 0246

SIERRA CHICA

PRODUCER COUNTRY: Argentina
AVAILABILITY: Limited

FILE NUMBER: 0247

COBRA

PRODUCER COUNTRY: Brazil
AVAILABILITY: Limited

FILE NUMBER: 0248

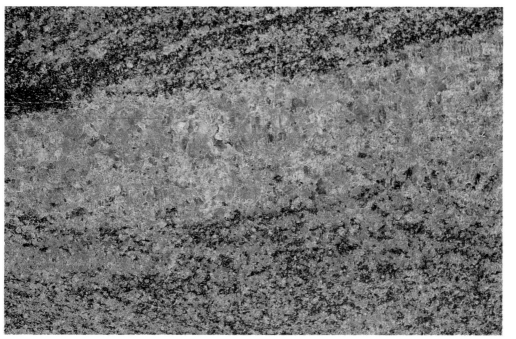

MULTICOLOR RED

PRODUCER COUNTRY: India
AVAILABILITY: Good

FILE NUMBER: 0249

JACARANDA

PRODUCER COUNTRY: Brazil
AVAILABILITY: Limited

FILE NUMBER: 0250

RED
GRANITE

RAINBOW

PRODUCER COUNTRY: India
AVAILABILITY: Medium

FILE NUMBER: 0251

TIGER
RED

PRODUCER COUNTRY: India
AVAILABILITY: Medium

FILE NUMBER: 0252

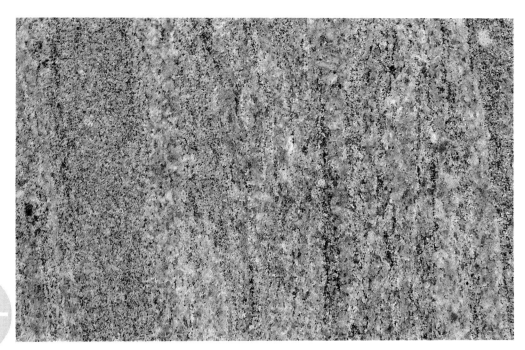

TUPIM

PRODUCER COUNTRY: Brazil
AVAILABILITY: Limited

FILE NUMBER: 0253

FUNIL

PRODUCER COUNTRY: Brazil
AVAILABILITY: Medium

FILE NUMBER: 0254

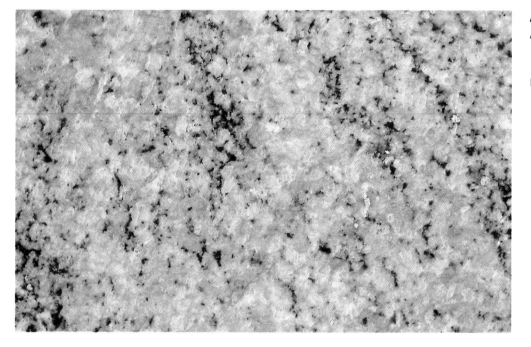

JUPARANÀ AFRICA

PRODUCER COUNTRY: South Africa
AVAILABILITY: Limited

FILE NUMBER: 0255

GHIANDONE LIMBARA

PRODUCER COUNTRY: Italy
AVAILABILITY: Good

FILE NUMBER: 0256

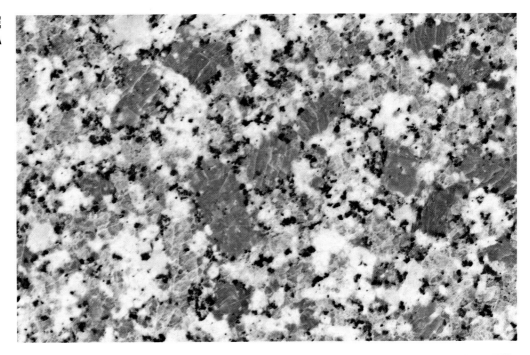

GHIANDONE ROSATO

PRODUCER COUNTRY: Italy
AVAILABILITY: Medium

FILE NUMBER: 0257

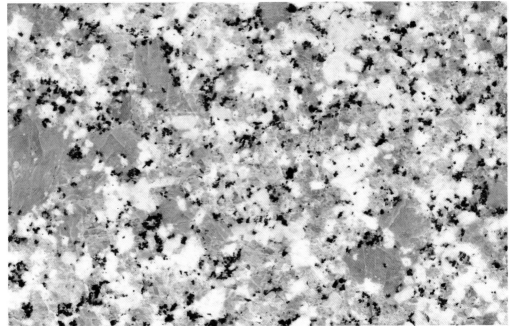

PINK GRANITE

ROSA PORRIÑO

PRODUCER COUNTRY: Spain
AVAILABILITY: Good

FILE NUMBER: 0258

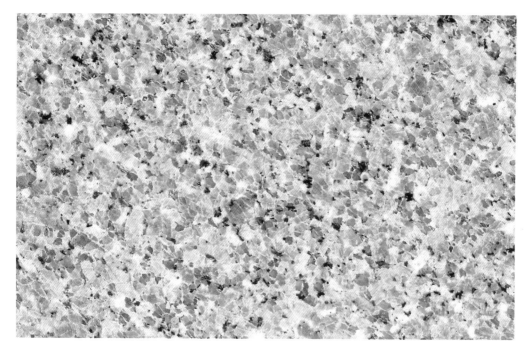

ROSA BAVENO

<small>Producer Country:</small> Italy
<small>Availability:</small> Limited

<small>File number:</small> 0259
<small>Supplier:</small> 4

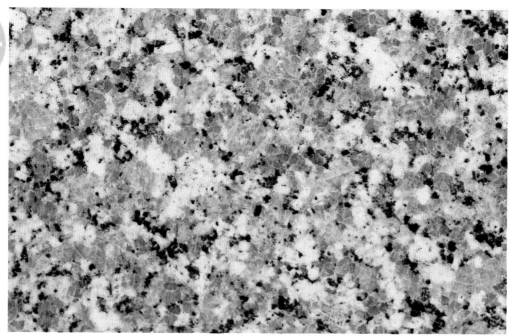

ROSA BETA

<small>Producer Country:</small> Italy
<small>Availability:</small> Medium

<small>File number:</small> 0260

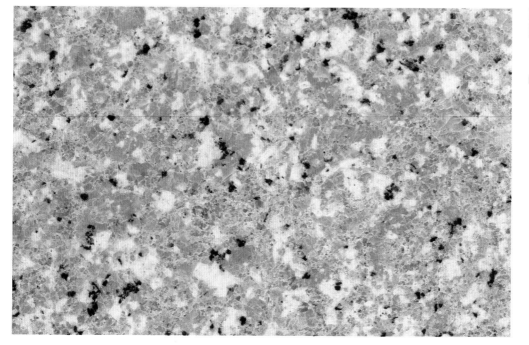

ROSA NULE

<small>Producer Country:</small> Italy
<small>Availability:</small> Medium

<small>File number:</small> 0261

248

ROSA
KALI

PRODUCER COUNTRY: Egypt
AVAILABILITY: Good

FILE NUMBER: 0262
SUPPLIER: 17

PINK
ROYAL

PINK
GRANITE

PRODUCER COUNTRY: Norway
AVAILABILITY: Limited

FILE NUMBER: 0263

PINK
SALISBURY

PRODUCER COUNTRY: USA
AVAILABILITY: Medium

FILE NUMBER: 0264

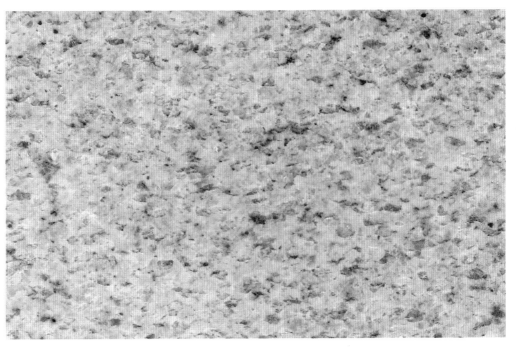

AFRICAN LILAC

PRODUCER COUNTRY: South Africa
AVAILABILITY: Medium

FILE NUMBER: 0265
SUPPLIER: 15

LAMBADA

PRODUCER COUNTRY: Brazil
AVAILABILITY: Medium

FILE NUMBER: 0266

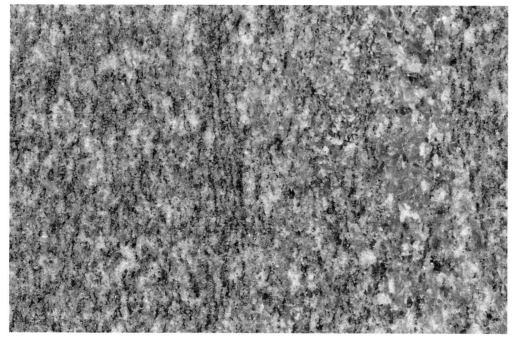

LILLA GERAIS

PRODUCER COUNTRY: Brazil
AVAILABILITY: Medium

FILE NUMBER: 0267

250

KINAWA

PRODUCER COUNTRY: Brazil

AVAILABILITY: Medium

FILE NUMBER: 0268

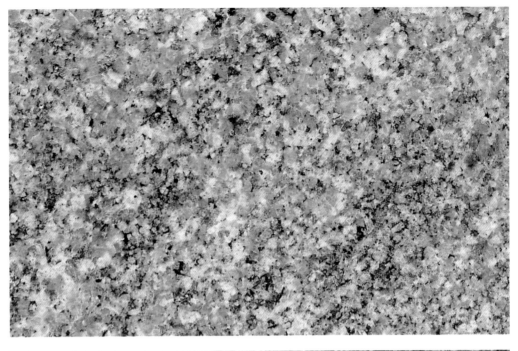

ROSA
SAMAMBAIA

PRODUCER COUNTRY: Brazil

AVAILABILITY: Limited

FILE NUMBER: 0269

PINK
GRANITE

TIGER
SKIN

PRODUCER COUNTRY: India

AVAILABILITY: Limited

FILE NUMBER: 0270

251

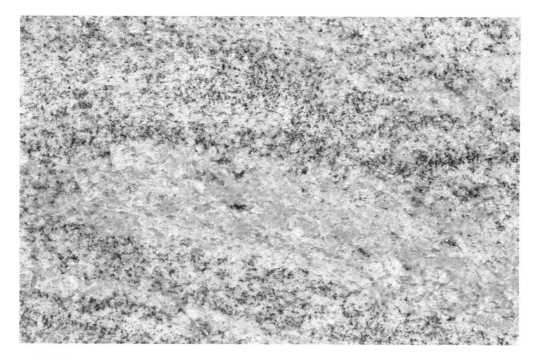

INDIAN
JUPARANÀ

<small>PRODUCER COUNTRY:</small> India
<small>AVAILABILITY:</small> Good

<small>FILE NUMBER:</small> 0271

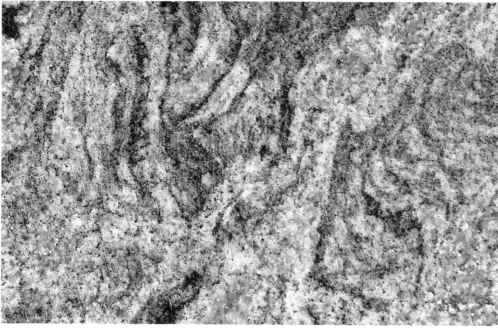

ROSA
RAISA

<small>PRODUCER COUNTRY:</small> Brazil
<small>AVAILABILITY:</small> Medium

<small>FILE NUMBER:</small> 0272

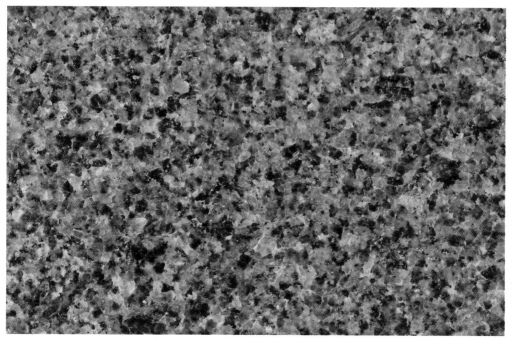

ROYAL
MAHOGANY

<small>PRODUCER COUNTRY:</small> Sweden
<small>AVAILABILITY:</small> Medium

<small>FILE NUMBER:</small> 0273

PINK GRANITE

POLYCHR. GRANITE

DAKOTA MAHOGANY

PRODUCER COUNTRY: USA
AVAILABILITY: Medium

FILE NUMBER: 0274

SAPHIRE BROWN

PRODUCER COUNTRY: India
AVAILABILITY: Medium

FILE NUMBER: 0275

POLYCHR. GRANITE

GRAN VIOLET

PRODUCER COUNTRY: Brazil
AVAILABILITY: Medium

FILE NUMBER: 0276

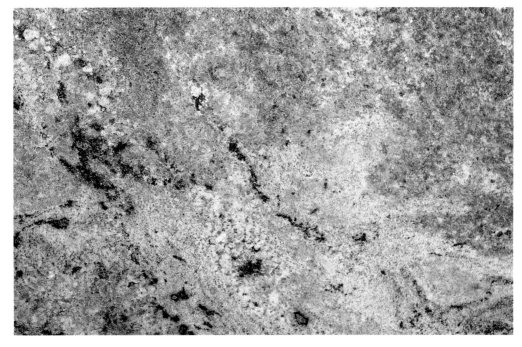

TROPICAL GUARANI

PRODUCER COUNTRY: Brazil
AVAILABILITY: Medium

FILE NUMBER: 0277

POLYCHR.
GRANITE

VIOLET
GRANITE

SAINT TROPEZ

PRODUCER COUNTRY: Brazil
AVAILABILITY: Medium

FILE NUMBER: 0278

VIOLETTA

PRODUCER COUNTRY: Saudi Arabia
AVAILABILITY: Medium

FILE NUMBER: 0279

PARADISO

PRODUCER COUNTRY: India
AVAILABILITY: Good

FILE NUMBER: 0280

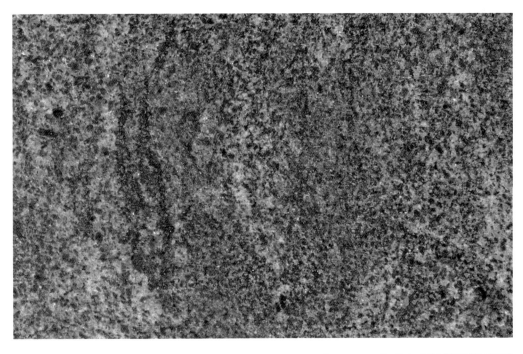

PARADISO BASH

PRODUCER COUNTRY: India
AVAILABILITY: Good

FILE NUMBER: 0281

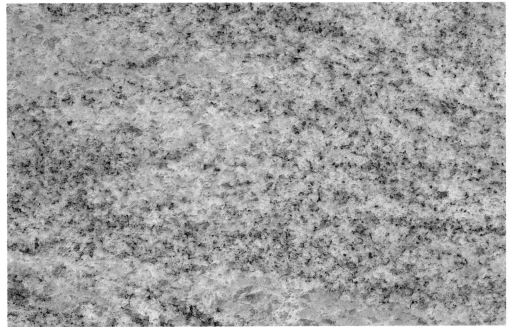

VIOLET GRANITE

SKY BLUE GRANITE

AZUL BAHIA

PRODUCER COUNTRY: Brazil
AVAILABILITY: Limited

FILE NUMBER: 0282

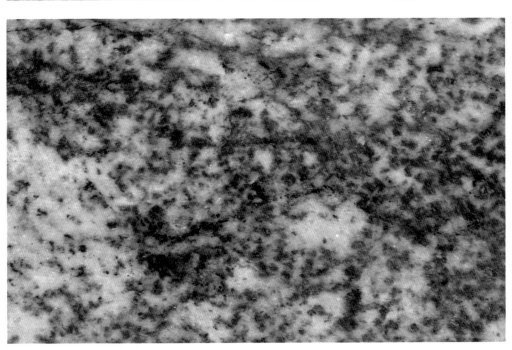

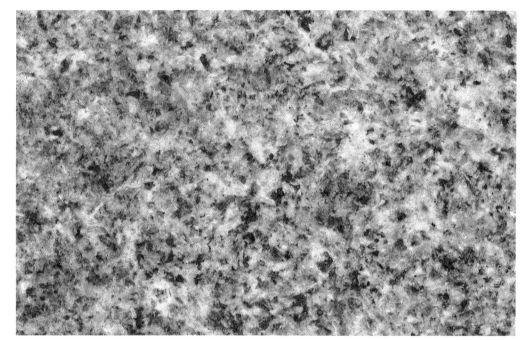

BLU KING

Producer Country: Zambia
Availability: Limited

File number: 0283
Supplier: 4

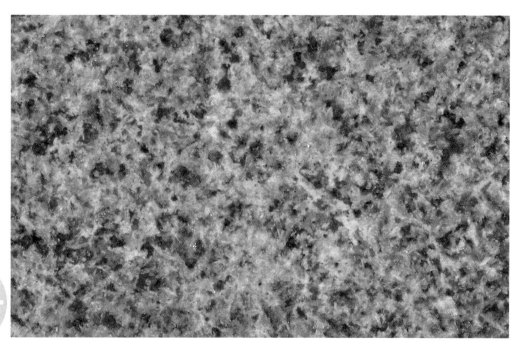

BLU KING

Producer Country: Zambia
Availability: Limited

File number: 0284
Supplier: 4

SKY BLUE
GRANITE

BLUE
GRANITE

ARTIC
BLU

Producer Country: Ukraine
Availability: Limited

File number: 0285

256

BLUE PEARL

PRODUCER COUNTRY: Norway
AVAILABILITY: Good

FILE NUMBER: 0286

EMERALD PEARL

PRODUCER COUNTRY: Norway
AVAILABILITY: Good

FILE NUMBER: 0287

LABRADOR

PRODUCER COUNTRY: Norway
AVAILABILITY: Good

FILE NUMBER: 0288

BLUE
GRANITE

MARINA
PEARL

PRODUCER COUNTRY: Norway
AVAILABILITY: Limited

FILE NUMBER: 0289

VIZAG

PRODUCER COUNTRY: India
AVAILABILITY: Good

FILE NUMBER: 0290

BLUE
GRANITE

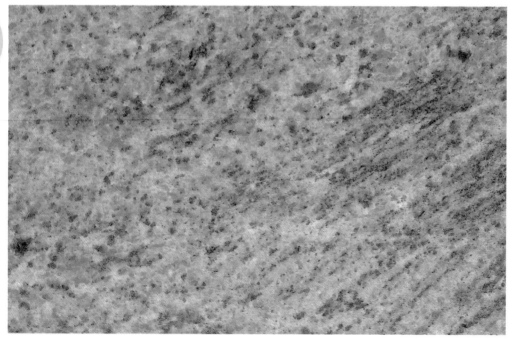

VIZAG
LIGHT

PRODUCER COUNTRY: India
AVAILABILITY: Good

FILE NUMBER: 0291

258

ORISSA BLU

PRODUCER COUNTRY: India
AVAILABILITY: Medium

FILE NUMBER: 0292

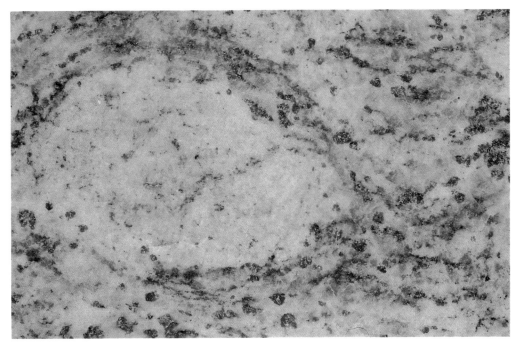

PARADISO BLU

PRODUCER COUNTRY: India
AVAILABILITY: Medium

FILE NUMBER: 0293

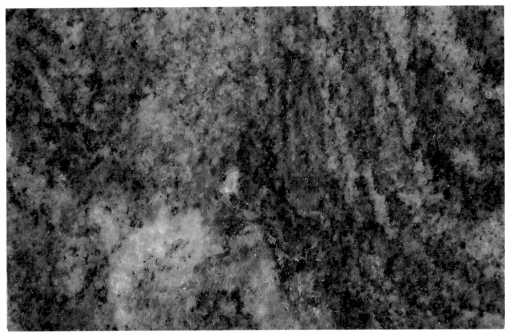

HIMALAYAN BLU

PRODUCER COUNTRY: India
AVAILABILITY: Medium

FILE NUMBER: 0294

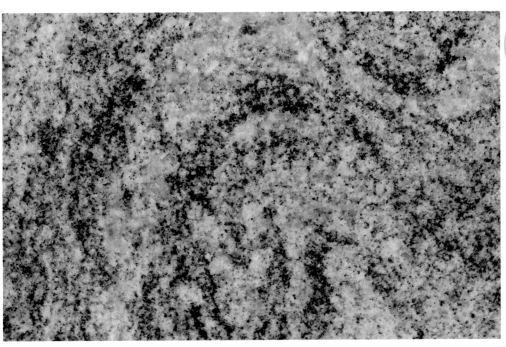

BLUE
GRANITE

BALTIC GREEN

PRODUCER COUNTRY: Finland
AVAILABILITY: Medium

FILE NUMBER: 0295

VERDE AOSTA

PRODUCER COUNTRY: Italy
AVAILABILITY: Limited

FILE NUMBER: 0296
SUPPLIER: 21

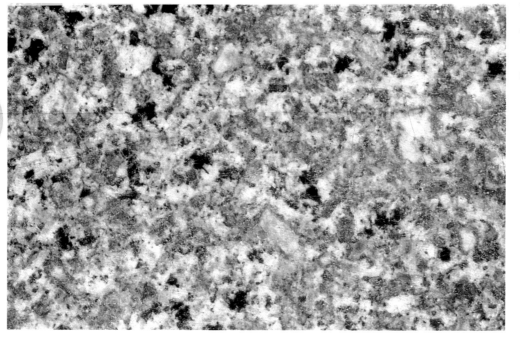

VERDE MERGOZZO

PRODUCER COUNTRY: Italy
AVAILABILITY: Limited

FILE NUMBER: 0297

GREEN
GRANITE

260

ORIENTAL GREEN

PRODUCER COUNTRY: Saudi Arabia
AVAILABILITY: Medium

FILE NUMBER: 0298

VERDE ARGENTO

PRODUCER COUNTRY: Italy
AVAILABILITY: Limited

FILE NUMBER: 0299

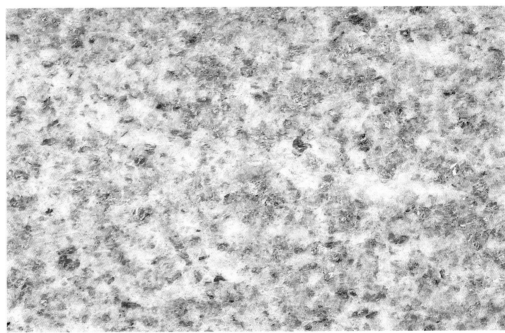

VERDE FIORITO

PRODUCER COUNTRY: India
AVAILABILITY: Limited

FILE NUMBER: 0300

GREEN
GRANITE

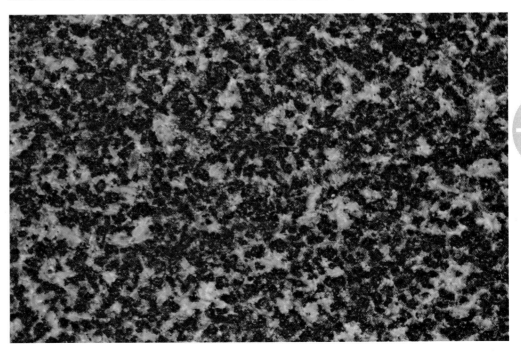

261

VERDE
LAVRAS

PRODUCER COUNTRY: Brazil
AVAILABILITY: Medium

FILE NUMBER: 0301

VERDE
MARE

PRODUCER COUNTRY: South Africa
AVAILABILITY: Good

FILE NUMBER: 0302
SUPPLIER: 15

FOUNTAINE
GREEN

PRODUCER COUNTRY: South Africa
AVAILABILITY: Good

FILE NUMBER: 0303

GREEN
GRANITE

VERDE ESMERALDA

PRODUCER COUNTRY: Brazil

AVAILABILITY: Limited

FILE NUMBER: 0304

VERDE EUCALIPTO

PRODUCER COUNTRY: Brazil

AVAILABILITY: Good

FILE NUMBER: 0305

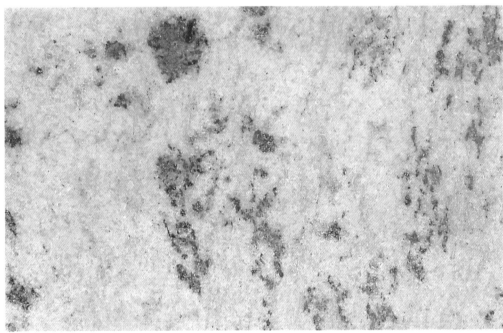

VERDE ACQUAMARINA

PRODUCER COUNTRY: Brazil

AVAILABILITY: Medium

FILE NUMBER: 0306

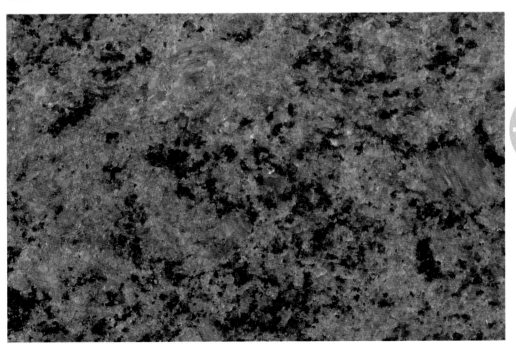

GREEN GRANITE

263

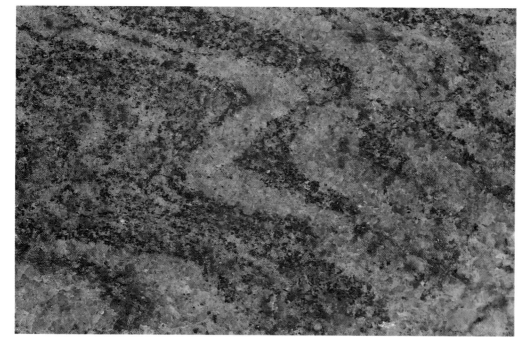

VERDE CANDEIAS

PRODUCER COUNTRY: BRAZIL
AVAILABILITY: MEDIUM

FILE NUMBER: 0307

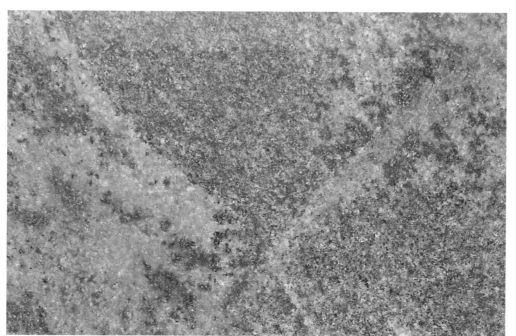

VERDE SAN FRANCISCO

PRODUCER COUNTRY: Brazil
AVAILABILITY: Medium

FILE NUMBER: 0308

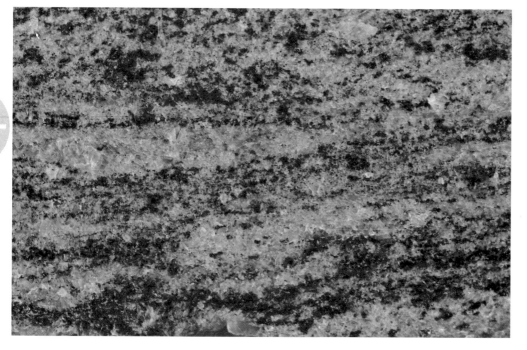

VERDE MARITACA

PRODUCER COUNTRY: Brazil
AVAILABILITY: Medium

FILE NUMBER: 0309

GREEN
GRANITE

264

VERDE
MARINA

PRODUCER COUNTRY: India
AVAILABILITY: Medium

FILE NUMBER: 0310

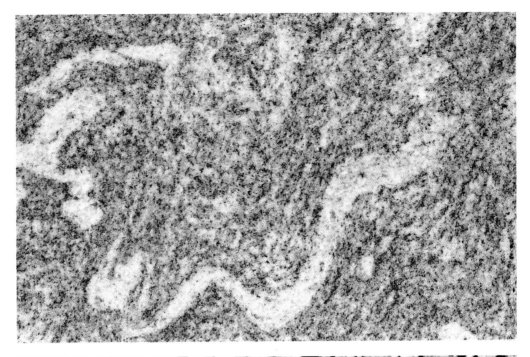

GRIGIO
MALAGA

PRODUCER COUNTRY: Italy
AVAILABILITY: Good

FILE NUMBER: 0311

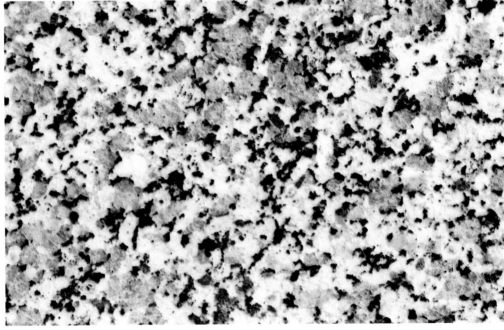

GRIGIO
PERLA

PRODUCER COUNTRY: Italy
AVAILABILITY: Good

FILE NUMBER: 0312

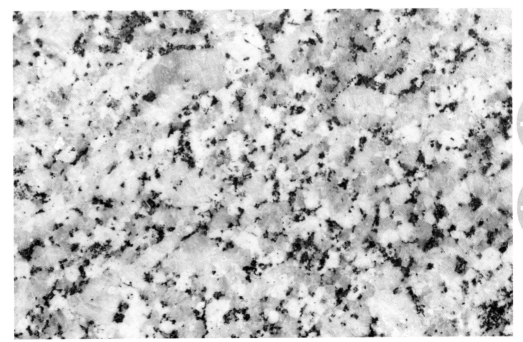

GREEN
GRANITE

GREY
GRANITE

265

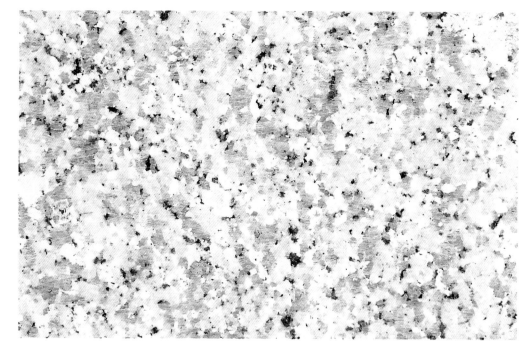

GRIGIO
SARDO

<small>PRODUCER COUNTRY:</small> Italy
<small>AVAILABILITY:</small> Good

<small>FILE NUMBER:</small> 0313

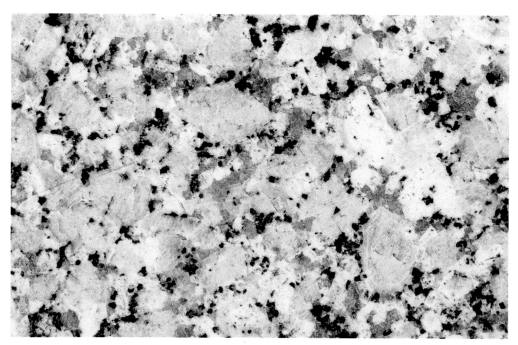

GRIS
PERLA

<small>PRODUCER COUNTRY:</small> Spain
<small>AVAILABILITY:</small> Medium

<small>FILE NUMBER:</small> 0314

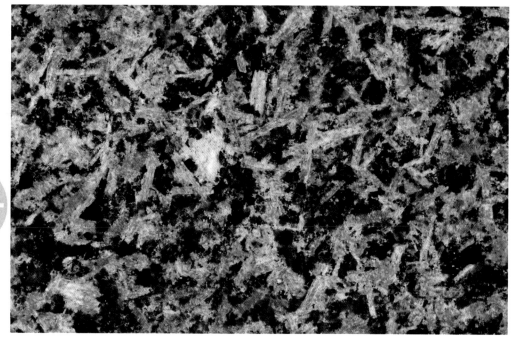

SAINT
LOUIS

<small>PRODUCER COUNTRY:</small> Portugal
<small>AVAILABILITY:</small> Limited

<small>FILE NUMBER:</small> 0315

GREY
GRANITE

266

AVEIRO

PRODUCER COUNTRY: Portugal
AVAILABILITY: Medium

FILE NUMBER: 0316

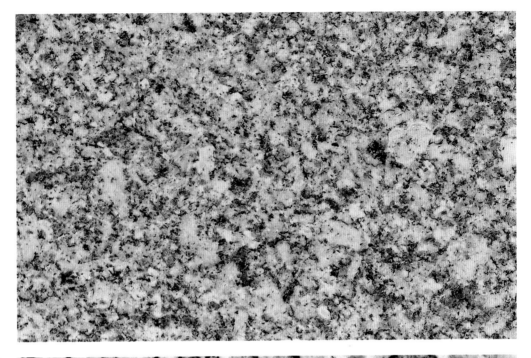

GRIGIO SARDO CHAMPAGNE

PRODUCER COUNTRY: Italy
AVAILABILITY: Limited

FILE NUMBER: 0317

GHIANDONE GRIGIO

PRODUCER COUNTRY: Italy
AVAILABILITY: Limited

FILE NUMBER: 0318

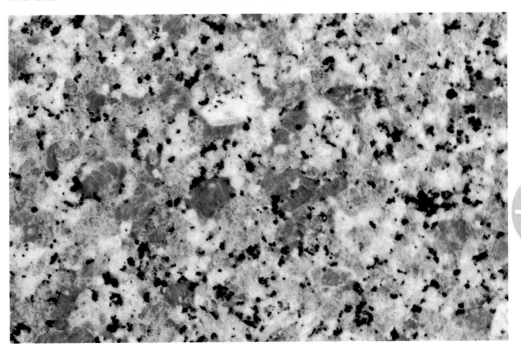

GREY
GRANITE

PADANG LIGHT

PRODUCER COUNTRY: China
AVAILABILITY: Medium

FILE NUMBER: 0319

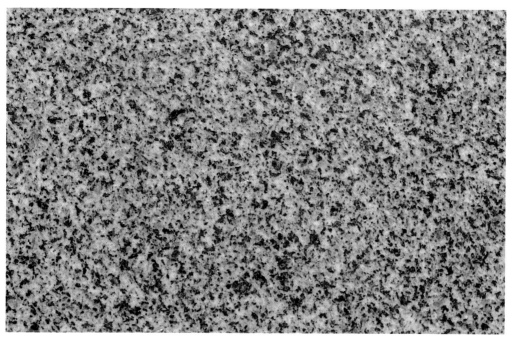

PADANG DARK

PRODUCER COUNTRY: China
AVAILABILITY: Medium

FILE NUMBER: 0320

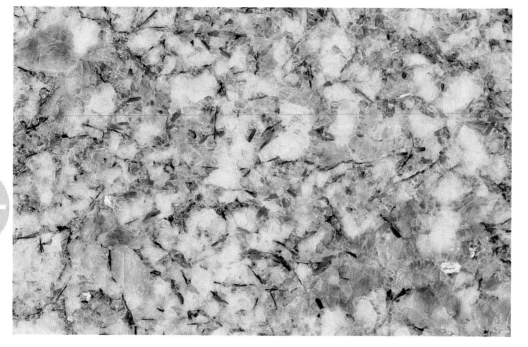

AZUL ARAN

PRODUCER COUNTRY: Spain
AVAILABILITY: Medium

FILE NUMBER: 0321

GREY
GRANITE

268

BEOLA
BIANCA

PRODUCER COUNTRY: Italy
AVAILABILITY: Medium

FILE NUMBER: 0322

BEOLA
GHIANDONATA

PRODUCER COUNTRY: Italy
AVAILABILITY: Medium

FILE NUMBER: 0323

BEOLA
GRIGIA

PRODUCER COUNTRY: Italy
AVAILABILITY: Medium

FILE NUMBER: 0324

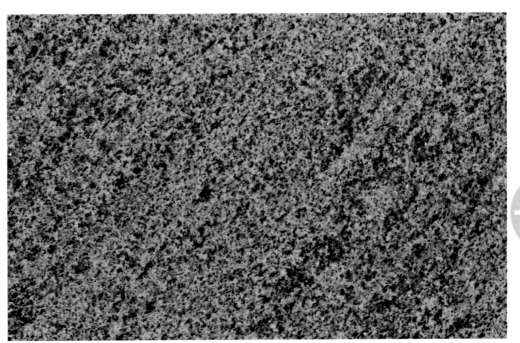

GREY
GRANITE

269

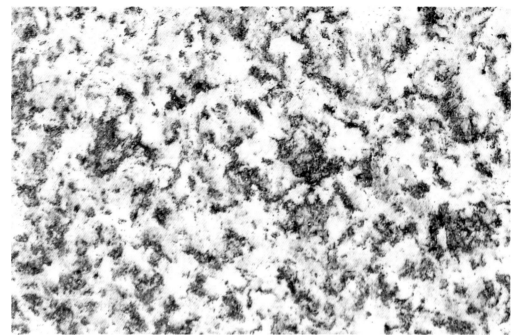

SERIZZO ANTIGORIO

Producer Country: Italy
Availability: Medium

File number: 0325

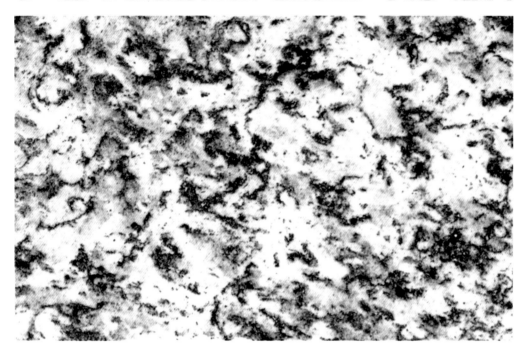

SERIZZO FORMAZZA

Producer Country: Italy
Availability: Medium

File number: 0326

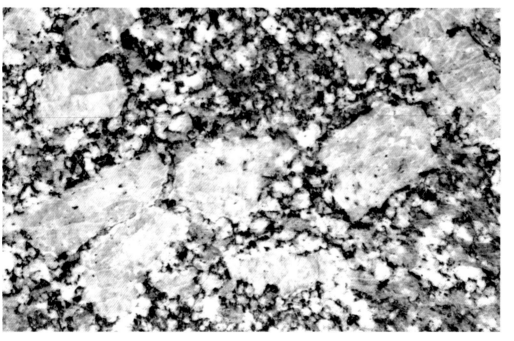

SERIZZO GHIANDONE

Producer Country: Italy
Availability: Medium

File number: 0327

GREY
GRANITE

270

SERIZZO SCURO
VALMASINO

PRODUCER COUNTRY: Italy
AVAILABILITY: Medium

FILE NUMBER: 0328

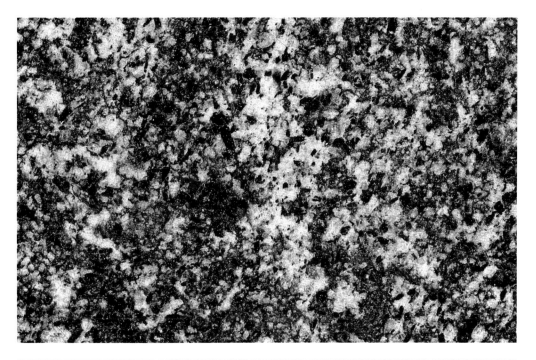

NERO
AFRICA

PRODUCER COUNTRY: South Africa
AVAILABILITY: Good

FILE NUMBER: 0329

GALAXY
BLACK

PRODUCER COUNTRY: India
AVAILABILITY: Medium

FILE NUMBER: 0330

GREY
GRANITE

BLACK
GRANITE

ABSOLUTE BLACK ZIMBABWE

PRODUCER COUNTRY: Zimbabwe
AVAILABILITY: Good

FILE NUMBER: 0331

ABSOLUTE BLACK INDIA

PRODUCER COUNTRY: India
AVAILABILITY: Limited

FILE NUMBER: 0332

ABSOLUTE BLACK BELFAST

PRODUCER COUNTRY: South Africa
AVAILABILITY: Limited

FILE NUMBER: 0333

BLACK
GRANITE

272

QUARZITE ROSA

PRODUCER COUNTRY: Brazil
AVAILABILITY: Good

FILE NUMBER: 0334

QUARZITE ROSA CHIARA

PRODUCER COUNTRY: Brazil
AVAILABILITY: Good

FILE NUMBER: 0335

QUARZITE FLAMINGO

PRODUCER COUNTRY: Brazil
AVAILABILITY: Medium

FILE NUMBER: 0336

273

PINK
QUARTZITE

SKY BLUE
QUARTZITE

QUARZITE ROSA CORALLO

PRODUCER COUNTRY: Brazil
AVAILABILITY: Good

FILE NUMBER: 0337

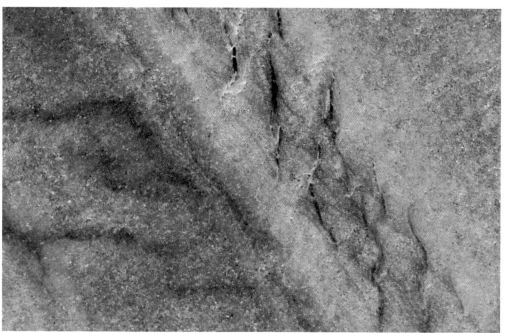

AZUL IMPERIAL

PRODUCER COUNTRY: Brazil
AVAILABILITY: Limited

FILE NUMBER: 0338
SUPPLIER: 18

AZUL MACAUBAS

PRODUCER COUNTRY: Brazil
AVAILABILITY: Limited

FILE NUMBER: 0339

PIETRA DORATA

PRODUCER COUNTRY: Italy

AVAILABILITY: Limited

FILE NUMBER: 0340

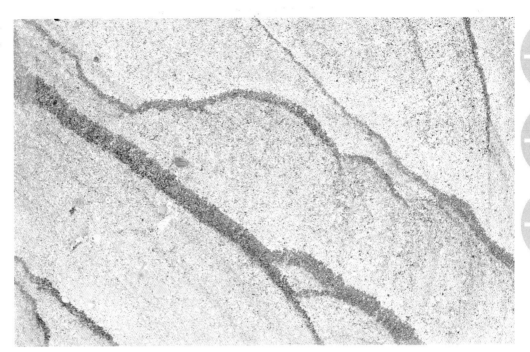

YELLOW STONE

RED STONE

PINK STONE

PORFIDO ROSSO

PRODUCER COUNTRY: Italy

AVAILABILITY: Good

FILE NUMBER: 0341

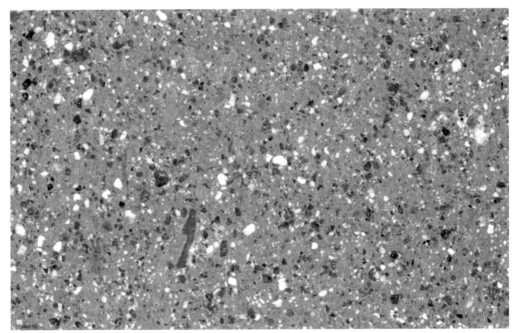

PIETRA PERSICHINA

PRODUCER COUNTRY: Italy

AVAILABILITY: Limited

FILE NUMBER: 0342

275

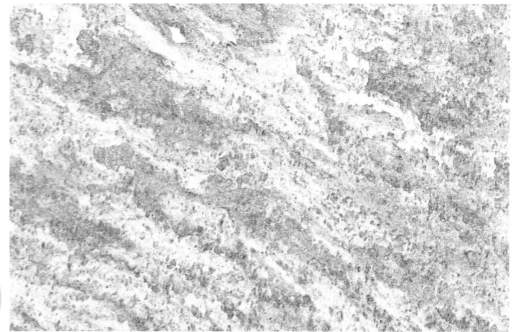

PIETRA DI COURTIL

PRODUCER COUNTRY: Italy
AVAILABILITY: Medium

FILE NUMBER: 0343
SUPPLIER: 21

GREEN
STONE

GREY
STONE

PIETRA DI BEDONIA

PRODUCER COUNTRY: Italy
AVAILABILITY: Limited

FILE NUMBER: 0344

PIETRA DEL CARDOSO

PRODUCER COUNTRY: Italy
AVAILABILITY: Limited

FILE NUMBER: 0345

PIETRA DI MATRAIA

PRODUCER COUNTRY: Italy
AVAILABILITY: Medium

FILE NUMBER: 0346
SUPPLIER: 5

PIETRA SERENA

PRODUCER COUNTRY: Italy
AVAILABILITY: Good

FILE NUMBER: 0347

PIETRA DI LUSERNA

PRODUCER COUNTRY: Italy
AVAILABILITY: Good

FILE NUMBER: 0348

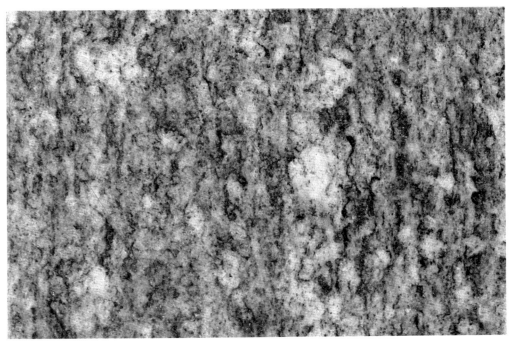

277

PIETRA BASALTINA

Producer Country: Italy
Availability: Medium

File number: 0349

PEPERINO GRIGIO

Producer Country: Italy
Availability: Medium

File number: 0350

ARDESIA

Producer Country: Italy
Availability: Good

File number: 0351

Stone Suppliers

1 - **CO.GE.MAR SRL**
Via Aurelia Ovest, 355/a - 54100 Massa - Italy
Tel. 0585 833390 Fax 0585 833331
E-mail cogemar@zia.ms.it

2 - **EVANGELISTI FRANCESCO**
Via Marina Vecchia, 462 - 54100 Massa - Italy
Tel. 0585 250478 Fax 0585 250478

3 - **FORTI ADOLFO SPA**
Via Carriona, 430/a - 54033 Carrara - Italy
Tel. 0585 857233 Fax 0585 52246
E-mail forti@zia.ms.it

4 - **GIACOMINI COMM. ALBERTO SPA**
Strada provinciale Valle Ossola 166, Km. 16 - 28020 Piedimulera - Italy
Tel. 0324 87382 Fax 0324 87384

5 - **MATRAIA SRL**
Via Traversa, 133 - 55013 Lammari - Italy
Tel. 0583 436066 Fax 0583 402217

6 - **MONDIAL MARMI SPA**
Via Fabrianese, 2/a - 006078 Ponte Valleceppi - Italy
Tel. 075 592181 Fax 075 5921830
E-mail mondialm@etr.it

7 - **SEMEA di GERVASONI & Co. SNC**
Via dei Fosà, 10 - 24014 Piazza Brembana - Italy
Tel. 0345 81085 Fax 0345 82200

8 - **STONIMPORT SRL**
Via Provinciale Massa-Avenza, 194/a - 54037 Marina di Massa - Italy
Tel. 0585 858231 Fax 0585 859635

9 - **TEKMAR MARBLE & GRANITE**
Bakanar Plaza eski Büyükdere Cad. No. 31 Kat. 13-14 Maslak Istambul - Turkey
Tel. (90) 212 2863200 Fax (90) 212 2863203
Internet address http://www.tekmarble.com.tr - E-mail tekmar@tekmarble.com.tr

10 - **UP & UP SRL**
Via Acquale, 3 - 54100 Massa - Italy
Tel. 0585 831132/832310/832367 Fax 0585 832038
E-mail up&up@zia.ms.it

11 - **INTERNATIONAL ITALMARMI DI NICASTRO & Co. SRL**
Viale Roma, 209 bis - 54100 Massa - Italy
Tel. 0585 254355 Fax 254307
E-mail intermar@tirreno.it

12 - **F.LLI CARUSO SPA**
S.S. 115 Km. 300,900 - 97019 Vittoria (Ragusa) - Italy
Tel. 0932 866778 Fax 0932 867255

13 - **CAMPA SRL**
Cno. Alta Gracia Km. 4 - 5017 Cordoba - Argentina
Tel. 051 941851 Fax 051 943430

14 - **MANZI MARMI SRL.**
Via Barletta, 71 - 70059 Trani - Italy
Tel. 0883 586818 / 586855 - Fax 0883 587704
E-mail: manzi.marmi@ulysse.it

15 - **KEELEY GRANITE (PTY) LIMITED**
4 Homestead Avenue Bryanston Sandton
P.O. Box 1050 Johannesburg 2000 - South Africa
Tel. (27 11) 4631910 Fax (27 119 706-7823
Internet address keeley.granite@digitec.co.za

16 - **MARMI FAEDO SPA**
Via Monte Cimone, 13 - 36073 Spagnago di Cornedo - Vicentino - Italy
Tel. 0445 953081 / 953034 - Fax - 0445 952889

17 - **MARMONIL SPA**
Viale Zaccagna, 43 - 54036 Marina di Carrara (MS) - Italy
Tel. 0585 631340/780304 Fax 0585 634770
E-mail marmonil@bicnet.it

18 - **ROSSITTIS GMBH NATURSTEIN-IMPORT**
Stehfenstraße 59-61 - 59439 Holzwickede - Germany
Tel. 02301 8505 - Fax 02301 8550
E-mail: throho@cww.de

19 - **ELLE MARMI SRL**
Via G. Galilei, 32 - 54033 Carrara - Italy
Tel. 0585 54963 Fax 0585 55006
E-mail ellemarmi@bicnet.it

20 - **TRIVEDI CRAFTS PVT LTD**
201, Paritosh, Usmanpura Riverside - Ahmedabad - 380013 India
Tel. 079 6568996/6423897 Fax 079 6569173
E-mail trivedik@ad1.vsnl.net.in

21 - **GUALTIERO VUILLERMIN SRL**
Via Circonvallazione 82 - 11029 Verres - Italy
Tel. 0125 929060 - Fax 0125 920428

22 - **MIRKO MENCONI MARMI SRL**
Via del Bravo, 18 - 54031 Avenza Carrara - Italy
Tel. 0585 8578848 / 857849 - Fax 0585 857847

23 - **GEMIGNANI & VANELLI MARMI SNC**
Via Aurelia, 40 - 54033 Carrara - Italy
Tel. 0585 856124 / 72222 - Fax 0585 73912

Bibliography

AA.VV., *Marmi italiani - Guida tecnica*, F.lli Vallardi, Milano, 1982

ASTM C97, *Standard Test Method for Absorption and Bulk Specific Gravity of Natural Building Stone,* American Society for Testing and Materials, Philadelphia, 1983

ASTM C99, *Standard Test Method for Modulus of Rupture of Natural Building Stone,* American Society for Testing and Materials, Philadelphia, 1952

ASTM C119, *Standard Definitions of Terms Relating to of Natural Building Stone,* American Society for Testing and Materials, Philadelphia, 1988

ASTM C170, *Standard Test Method for Compressive Strength of Natural Building Stone,* American Society for Testing and Materials, Philadelphia, 1950

ASTM C241, *Standard Test Method for Abrasion Resistance of Stone Subject to Foot Traffic,* American Society for Testing and Materials, Philadelphia, 1951

ASTM C503, *Standard Specification for Marble Dimension Stone (Exterior),* American Society for Testing and Materials, Philadelphia, 1989

ASTM C568, *Standard Specification for Limestone Dimension Stone.* American Society for Testing and Materials, Philadelphia, 1989

ASTM C615, *Standard Specification for Granite Dimension Stone.* American Society for Testing and Materials, Philadelphia, 1992

ASTM C616, *Standard Specification for Quartz-based Dimension Stone.* American Society for Testing and Materials, Philadelphia, 1995

ASTM C629, *Standard Specification for Slate Dimension Stone.* American Society for Testing and Materials, Philadelphia, 1989

ASTM C880, *Standard Test Method for Flexural Strength of Natural Building Stone,* American Society for Testing and Materials, Philadelphia, 1989

ASTM C1352, *Flexural Modulus of Elasticity of Dimension Stone,* American Society for Testing and Materials, Philadelphia

BLANCO G., *Pavimenti e rivestimenti lapidei*, La Nuova Italia Scientifica, Roma, 1991

BLANCO G., *Le pietre ornamentali in architettura*, La Nuova Italia Scientifica, Roma, 1993

BLASI P., BRADLEY F., PILI M., *Apuan Quarries, Survey, Analysis and Trend (1993),* Carrara, 1993

BOERI A., *Pietre naturali nelle costruzioni*, Hoepli, Milano, 1996

BRADLEY F., *Cenni sull'analisi geologica delle rocce ornamentali*, Technostone, Carrara, 1989

BRADLEY F., PILI M., *Quarries of Carrara, Survey, Analysis and Trend (1991-'92),* Carrara, 1993

BRADLEY, F., MUSETTI,C., *Attività e gestione tecnico-economica del'impresa di estrazione di materiale lapideo ornamentale*, ICE, Roma, 1995

BRADLEY, F., MUSETTI, C., PILI, M., *Quarries of Carrara, Situation and Trends - Report 1997*, Studio Marmo, Firenze

CALENZANI L., CORBELLA E., *Manuale dei marmi delle pietre, dei graniti*, F.lli Vallardi, Milano, 1989

CANAVESIO G., *Marmi, graniti, travertini e pietre. Indicazioni per la scelta in edilizia - Directory 1994-95,* Marmomacchine Club, Promorama Ed., Milano, 1994

CANAVESIO G., MILONE L., *I Rivestimenti Lapidei - Directory 1995-96,* Marmomacchine Club, Promorama Ed., Milano, 1996

CORBELLA E., ZINI R., *Manuale dei marmi, petre, graniti (Vol I - Guida Tecnica)*

GIORNETTI M.,*Glossario tecnico del settore lapideo*, Internazionale Marmi e Macchine, Carrara, 1991

GRASSI E., *SEI - Rivestimenti esterni*, Internazionale Marmi e Macchine, Carrara, 1993

MIA, *Dimensional Stone - Volume I*, Marble Institute of America, Farmington, 1990

MIA, *Dimensional Stone - Volume II*, Marble Institute of America, Farmington, 1993

MIGNANI A., QUADRELLI S., *SEI - Pavimenti e rivestimenti interni*, Internazionale Marmi e Macchine, Carrara, 1993

PIERI M., *Pigmentazione e tonalità cromatica nei marmi*, Hoepli, Milano, 1957

PIERI M., *Marmologia, Dizionario di marmi e graniti italiani e esteri*, Hoepli, Milano, 1966

UNI norma 8458, *Prodotti lapidei, terminologia e classificazione*, Ente Italiano di Unificazione, Milano, 1983

UNI norma EDL 173, *Pavimenti lapidei, terminologia e classificazione*, Ente Italiano di Unificazione, Milano, 1987

UNI norma EDL 199/1/2, *Descrizione petrografica dei materiali lapidei naturali*, Ente Italiano di Unificazione, Milano, 1988

UNI norma EDL 203, *Lapidei (grezzi e lavorati), Criteri per l'informazione tecnica*, Ente Italiano di Unificazione, Milano, 1988

WINKLER E.M., *Stone in architecture*, Springer-Verlag, Berlin, 1994

Index
of Natural Stone

Quartzite

Stone

About the CD-ROM

The accompanying CD-ROM contains screen resolution TIFF files for all of the samples in the book. With the appropriate graphics software, the CD images can be used by designers in developing concepts, preparing presentations for clients, and communicating visual information to others. Although the images are primarily intended for on-screen display, they can also be printed on either a black and white or color printer.

Further information about the image formats can be found on the readme.txt file on the CD.

Original images can be obtained from Studio Marmo, 6663 Sedgwick Place, Brooklyn NY 11220. E-mail: studiomarmo@firenze.net